MAINE-LY FUN!

Great Things to Do with Kids in Maine

MAINE-LY FUN!

Great Things
to Do
with Kids
in Maine

The Maine Children's
Cancer Program

Susan Whitehouse
Project Chairperson and Editor,
M.C.C.P. Board Member,
and Past President

DOWN EAST BOOKS

Copyright © 2003 by the Maine Children's
    Cancer Program. All rights reserved.
ISBN 0-89272-574-5
LCCN: 2002109174
Text design by Faith Hague
Cover Design by Chilton Creative
Printed at Versa Press, Inc., E. Peoria, Ill.
5   4   3   2   1

DOWN EAST BOOKS
A division of Down East Enterprise, Inc.,
publisher of *Down East*, the Magazine of Maine

Book orders: 1-800-685-7962
www.downeastbooks.com

*This book is dedicated to
all the children and their families
who have been treated at the Maine
Children's Cancer Program.
Their courage, strength, and spirit
are an inspiration to us all.*

All profits that the Maine Children's Cancer Program raises from the sale of this book will be used to support and advance the program.

THE MISSION OF THE MAINE CHILDREN'S CANCER PROGRAM

The purpose of the Maine Children's Cancer Program is to provide integrated, comprehensive, clinical research–based medical care and psychosocial and practical support services to infants, children, and adolescents with cancer from throughout the state of Maine. The Maine Children's Cancer Program strives not only to cure cancer in as many children as possible but also to support families throughout their experience of living with childhood cancer.

The Maine Children's Cancer Program, now in its seventeenth year, is based in a modern facility in Scarborough under the umbrella of the Maine Medical Center and the Barbara Bush Children's Hospital. The exemplary model of care, based in clinical science and provided along with strong psychosocial support by a team of dedicated, highly trained, and professional staff, ensures that the children of Maine get state-of-the-art cancer care.

For more information, or to send a contribution, contact the Maine Children's Cancer Program at:

100 U.S. Route 1
Unit 107
Scarborough, ME 04074
(207) 885-7565

*Thank you to all the contributors
who made this book possible.*

Project Chairperson
Susan Whitehouse

Project Sponsors
Susan and Ernie Whitehouse

Editorial Committee
Marian Albee
Joan Connick
Connie Robinson
Barbara Turitz

Special Thanks to
Jim Bouchard, Development
   Coordinator for Maine Children's
   Cancer Program
Susan Doliner, Associate Vice President
   for Development, Maine Medical
   Center
William Hubbell, Photographer
Dr. Craig Hurwitz, Medical Director
   for Maine Children's Cancer
   Program
Deirdre Lambert, Special Talent, Cover

2003 Maine Children's Cancer Program Board Members
Marian Albee
Andrew Brenner
Dan Crewe
John Devine
Rick Drouin
Gordon Erikson
Mark Franco
John Fridlington
Connie Goldberg
Robert Graves
Lee Jones
Larry Laderbush
Beth Madore
Julie Moss
Mary Noyes
Frederick Pape III
Jon Paradise
Tim Placey
Robert Porteous III
Jim Puckett
Don Richard
Connie Robinson
Chris Rogers
Barbara Turitz
Susan Whitehouse

Honorary Board Members
John Bay
William Dunnett
Roger Sicard

Special Assistance
Marian Albee, "The Performing Arts";
   "Fairs and Festivals"
Jim Bouchard, "Hiking"
John Fridlington, "Lighthouses"
Lee Jones, "Picking Fruit"
Beth Madore, "Historic Sites and Forts"
Julie Moss, "Trains, Planes, and Things
   that GO!"
Robert Porteous III, "Boating"
Connie Robinson, "Skiing"
Mike and Susan Swan, "Beaches"

Interns
Virginia Crocker, "Boating"
Ross Isacke, "Beaches"
Christine L. Pirani, "Lighthouses";
   "Museums"
Emily Young, "Islands"; "Parks"

Research Assistants
Jennifer Atkinson, "The Performing
   Arts"; "Hiking"; "Fun Places to Visit"
Nancy Green, "Historic Sites and Forts"
Summer Richards

Special Advisors
Carol Austin, "Things to Cook"
Borders Books and Music, Rita
   Swidrowski, Children's Bookseller,
   for detailed assistance with the
   "Books" chapter
Jennifer Conley
Sandi Dupré
Rebecca Fischman
Mike Slavin, "Web Sites"
Spencer Whitehouse

Graphics Assistance
Roni Barbera
Pam Fridlington

Rachel Guthrie
Jen Roe, Wild Olive Multimedia

Special Thanks to

Former First Lady Barbara Bush
Governor John Baldacci, First Lady
  Karen Baldacci, and Jack Baldacci
Former Governor Angus King and
  former First Lady Mary Herman
U.S. Senator Olympia Snowe and former
  Governor John McKernan
U.S. Senator Susan Collins
Congressman Tom Allen
Mrs. Caspar Weinberger
Julie Russem and Dr. Steve Blattner,
  Maine Children's Cancer Program
  Founders
Lisa and Leon Gorman
In memory and honor of Betty Noyce, by
  Pendred Noyce
Cindy Blodgett, former University of
  Maine basketball star
Rick Charette, children's entertainer
Jim King and Jon Stott, founders of
  Stonewall Kitchens
David Santoro, WGME-Channel 13
  Chief Meteorologist
Steven Romanoff, leader of Schooner Fare

Thank you to our many contributors for submitting great ideas for this book

Priscilla Alden
Nona Angela
The Animal Welfare Society, Inc.,
  West Kennebunk, Maine
Carol, Lin, Casey, and Monica Austin
The Baker-Miller Family
Joachim Barelmann, Executive Chef, MS
  Maasdam, Holland America Line
Arthur Bell and Robin Hodgkins
Denise Bell
Chris Beneman
Maureen Bennett
Boothbay Harbor Chamber of Commerce
Kitty Boyd
Marlies Boyd
Charlene Briggs
Kimberly Brown
Marcia Brown
Michael Brown

Heather Burke
Jake Burns
Lindsay Carter
Helen Cella
Peter Cheney
Bonnie Clark
Bert G. and Coral B. Clifford
  Charitable Foundation
Debbie Coito
Jennifer Conley and Family
Joan Connick
Christina Corbeau
Elizabeth D. Cotton
Mallory Cox
Kate Demont
Ellen Dondlinger
Mary, Anthony, Christina,
  and Michael Drace
Kathleen Driscoll
Sonja Ducharme
The Dupré Family
Charlie and Ann-Marie Eshbach
Martha Fenno
First Congregational Church,
  Scarborough
Joan Fischer
Annie and Jake Fischer
Leslie Fleming
Amy Ford
Janet Foster
Monique Gallant
Sarah Galletta
Judy George
The Goodrich Family
Jeff Gordon
Kristine Gorman
Melissa Gousse
Jane Greer
Connie Harrison
Judy Haynes
Randy Henry
Sandra Hesketh
Mary Ann Hodson
Mary Honan and the Honan Family
Ruby Houston
Mary Ellen Hurteau
Laurie Hyndman
Elinor Jones
Lee Jones

David Katino
Ginny Kern
Jan Lahaie
Betsy Lane
Sara Laprade
Twyla Leonard
Adriana M. Liberty
Ann Lebel Longley
Caterina MacLean
The Maine Potato Board
Betty Maltais
Cathy Manchester
Crystal Marshall
Denise Martin
Jean Ginn Marvin
Corinne McIntyre
Debbie Michaud
Joyce Milliken
Jane Moody
Jay Moody
Hannah Morehouse
Deanna Morissette
In memory of Graham Morissette
Julie Myers
Alexandra Nickless
Pam Nolan
Kimberly Oxford
Evelyn Paine
Joanne Paradis
Joyce Peterson
Taylor Pierpont
Thelma Piestrak
Joan Preston
Paula Prouty
Jared Rand
Vesta Vaughan Rand
Gail Rice
William Richardson
Mary Rickert
Marjorie J. Robbins
Nancy Russell
Annemarie Salzberg
Dave Scheffler
Beth Severance
Sally Shannon
Linda Shaw
Kathie Sheehan
Cindy Slaney
Jean Slayton

Jeff Slayton
Lisa Slayton
Doreen Smiley
Ann Smith
Nancy Smith
Joan Solari
Richard L. Stanley
Maribeth Stavrand
Cathy Steffke
Mary Stuart
Claire Studley
John Sullivan
Sweetser's Apple Barrel and Orchards
Beverly Tabet
Debbie Tewhey
In memory of Ednah Thomas
Christina Traister
Anna Verrill
Linda Wakefield
Pat Waldman
Ginny Walsh
Jo Ellen Weeks
Carol Ann White
Leslie Whitehouse
Margaret Whitehouse
Susan Whitehouse
Susie Woodworth
Nancy Yerrall

Sources Used

"25 Autumn Delights," *Down East,* October 1999.

Rindlaub, Curtis. *Maine Coast Guide for Small Boats.* Peaks Island, Maine: Diamond Pass Publishing, 2000.

Brandes, Kathy M. *Maine Handbook*: Moon Publications, 1998.

Maine Geographic Series: Hiking, vols. I, II, and III. Yarmouth, Maine: DeLorme Publishing, 1999.

The Maine Atlas & Gazetteer. Yarmouth, Maine: DeLorme Publishing, 1999.

We have endeavored to include the best possible selection of activities for each chapter, but inevitably, some items get left out and new things yet to come are not included here. We apologize for any errors and omissions.

This book presents information in many of the chapters by geography. Our geographical divisions are along county lines.

Southern Maine: Cumberland and York Counties
Mid-Coast Maine: Knox, Lincoln, Sagadahoc, and Waldo Counties
Down East Maine: Hancock and Washington Counties
Central Maine: Androscoggin and Kennebec Counties
Western Maine: Franklin, Oxford, and Somerset Counties
Northern Maine: Aroostook, Penobscot, and Piscataquis Counties

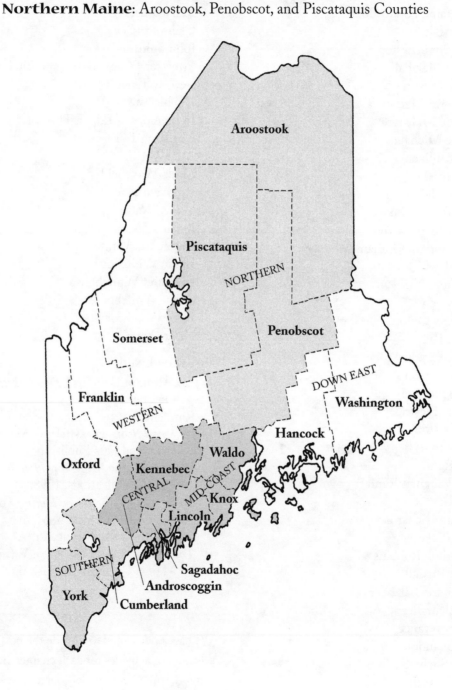

Contents

A detailed table of contents is given on the opening page of each chapter.

Chapter 1   **The Performing Arts** . . . 1

Chapter 2   **Beaches** . . . 11

Chapter 3   **Boating** . . . 19

Chapter 4   **Books** . . . 29

Chapter 5   **Things to Cook** . . . 39

Chapter 6   **Crafts** . . . 53

Chapter 7   **Fairs, Festivals, and Special Events** . . . 65

Chapter 8   **Great Ideas from Famous Maine Folks** . . . 73

Chapter 9   **Hiking** . . . 81

Chapter 10   **Historic Sites and Forts** . . . 97

Chapter 11   **Islands** . . . 105

Chapter 12   **Lighthouses** . . . 113

Chapter 13   **Museums** . . . 121

Chapter 14   **One of a Kind** . . . 131

Chapter 15   **Parks, Preserves, and Sanctuaries** . . . 137

Chapter 16   **Picking Fruit** . . . 149

Chapter 17   **Fun Places to Visit** . . . 157

Chapter 18   **Skiing and Snowboarding** . . . 163

Chapter 19   **Trains, Planes, and Things that GO!** . . . 169

Chapter 20   **Web Sites** . . . 173

chapter 1

The Performing Arts

Southern Maine ... 2

Arundel Barn Playhouse, Arundel ... 2

The Booth Theatre/Booth Productions,
Ogunquit ... 2

Bowdoin College, Brunswick ... 2

Deertrees Theatre and Cultural Center,
Harrison ... 2

Hackmatack Playhouse, Berwick ... 3

Maine State Music Theatre, Brunswick ... 3

Maritime Productions, Kennebunkport ... 3

Ogunquit Playhouse, Ogunquit ... 3

Sanford Maine Stage Company/
Pine Tree Players, Springvale ... 4

Schoolhouse Arts Center at
Sebago Lake ... 4

The Theater Project, Brunswick ... 4

University of Southern Maine, Gorham ... 4

The Greater Portland Area ... 5

Center for Cultural Exchange, Portland ... 5

Children's Theatre of Maine, Portland ... 5

Cumberland County Civic Center,
Portland ... 5

Lyric Music Theater, South Portland ... 5

Maine State Ballet, Westbrook ... 5

Merrill Auditorium, Portland ... 6

Portland Ballet Company, Portland ... 6

Portland Opera Repertory Theater,
Portland ... 6

Portland Stage Company, Portland ... 6

Portland Symphony Orchestra,
Portland ... 6

Mid-Coast Maine ... 7

Belfast Maskers, Belfast ... 7

Camden Civic Theater, Camden ... 7

Carousel Music Theatre,
Boothbay Harbor ... 7

Center for the Arts at the Chocolate
Church, Bath ... 7

National Theatre Workshop of the
Handicapped, Belfast ... 7

Down East Maine ... 7

Acadia Repertory Theatre, Somesville ... 7

Deck House Cabaret Theater,
Southwest Harbor ... 8

University of Maine, Machias ... 8

Western Maine ... 8

Celebration Barn Theatre,
South Paris ... 8

Lakeside Youth Theater, Rangeley ... 8

Lakewood Theater, Skowhegan ... 8

Oddfellow Theater, Buckfield ... 8

Central Maine ... 9

Augusta Civic Center, Augusta ... 9

Bates College, Lewiston ... 9

Colby College, Waterville ... 9

Gaslight Theatre, Hallowell ... 9

Johnson Hall Performing Arts Center,
Gardiner ... 9

The Public Theatre, Lewiston ... 9

The Theater at Monmouth,
Monmouth ... 10

Northern Maine ... 10

Maine Center for the Arts, Orono ... 10

Penobscot Theatre Company, Bangor ... 10

University of Maine/Maine Masque
Theatre, Orono ... 10

Maine-ly Music!, Bangor Symphony
Orchestra, Bangor ... 10

The Performing Arts

Many of Maine's theaters offer a variety of plays, musicals, and music and dance concerts. Some are designed especially for children, while others are suitable as family entertainment.

Southern Maine

Arundel Barn Playhouse

53 Old Post Road, Arundel
Box office: (207) 985-5552
For more information, visit
www.arundelbarnplayhouse.com

This professional, summer music theatre in the Smith sisters' restored 1888 New England farm barn offers five plays per season, some of which are suitable for children. It's located just off Route 1 near Kennebunk and Kennebunkport. Call for reservations and schedule.

The Booth Theatre/ Booth Productions

5 Beach Street, Ogunquit
Box office: (207) 646-8142
For more information, visit
www.boothproductions.com

In residence from June to September at the Betty Doon Motor Hotel, just a short walk from the Ogunquit Beach, Booth Productions provides community theater, youth summer camp programs, and a summer repertory company. Services include summer theater training, summer stock for young performers, Theater Training for grades 7 to 12 and college, workshops, performances for special groups, and rentals of costumes and backdrops. For workshop information before June, call the Worcester, Massachusetts, office at (508) 797-9277.

Bowdoin College

Pickard Theater, Maine and Bath
Streets, Brunswick
Ticket information: (207) 725-3375
Administrative office: (207) 725-3322
For more information, visit
http://www.summermusic.org/ or
http://academic.bowdoin.edu/
theaterdance/index.shtml

One of Bowdoin College's summer programs is the Bowdoin Summer Music Festival, Inc., which comprises a music school, a concert series featuring internationally acclaimed guest artists and the festival's renowned faculty, and the nationally recognized Gamper Festival of Contemporary Music. Approximately two hundred gifted performers of high school, college, and graduate school levels participate in a concentrated six-week program of instrumental and chamber music and composition studies with faculty composed of teacher-performers from the world's leading conservatories. The festival runs from June to August.

Besides student and faculty performances, the Theater and Dance Department sponsors concerts and plays by nationally known dance companies. Some performances may interest children. Call or check the Web site for a schedule.

Deertrees Theatre and Cultural Center

Deertrees Road, Harrison
Box office: (207) 583-6747
For more information, visit
www.deertreestheatre.org

Since 1936, the famous and the unknowns, Broadway stars and local would-be actors, world-acclaimed musicians and aspiring students have graced the theatre's stage. Today Deertrees is operated as a nonprofit performing arts center and is home to the Sebago Long Lake Chamber Music Festival, the Deertrees Theatre Festival, the Deertrees Children's Mornings, the Backstage Art Gallery, and the Salt Lick Cafe.

Hackmatack Playhouse

538 Route 9, Berwick
Call (207) 698-1807
For more information, visit
www.hackmatack.org

Hackmatack's regular adult schedule usually contains some plays and musicals suitable for children. The Playhouse also offers drama camps for kids ages 9 to 12 for five weeks in the summer. The children produce and are guaranteed a part in the play they perform at camp's end. For the Hackmatack Children's Theater, adult actors perform a series of plays for children during July and August, usually on Fridays and Saturdays. Call for drama camp prices and play schedule.

Maine State Music Theatre

Pickard Theater, Maine and Bath
Streets, Brunswick
Call (207) 725-8769
For more information, visit www.msmt.org

Maine's only professional musical theater presents plays during the summer, many of which are suitable for young people. No children under the age of four are allowed at any plays except the Children's Theater productions. Two productions specifically for children are held annually for one day each.

Maritime Productions

Kennebunkport Marina, Ocean Avenue,
Kennebunkport
Reservations: (877) 933-0707
For more information, visit
http://www.cacruises.com/theatre_cruise.htm

Leaving from the same dock as Cape Arundel Whale Watch tours, Maritime Productions offers true tales of intrigue, horror, and haunted lighthouses as outdoor adventure theater aboard the *Deep Water II*. Directors say the plays are not suitable for children under six or the squeamish, but feel the professional performances create exciting, intelligent escapism and outdoor adventure on the high seas. Ticket prices include the boat ride, play, snacks, and soft drinks.

Ogunquit Playhouse

10 U.S. Route 1, Ogunquit
Box office: (207) 646-5511
Other info: (207) 646-2402
For more information, visit
www.ogunquitplayhouse.org

Established in 1933, the Ogunquit Playhouse mounts special Kids' Korner shows for children on selected Saturdays, July through September. Two of the four offerings are the result of intensive week-long workshops where children of all ages learn stagecraft and then mount a full-scale production on the main stage. Saturday children's productions are often accompanied by additional events, such as the Mad Hatter's Tea Party picnic held in 2001 to complement the kids' production of "Alice in Wonderland." Most plays and musicals in the regular production schedule are suitable for children. Musical concerts are scheduled some Sunday nights. Call for schedule.

Sanford Maine Stage Company-Pine Tree Players

Beaver Hill Road, Springvale
(From Route 109/Main Street in Sanford, proceed north and turn right onto Mill Street, which becomes Beaver Hill Road)
Call (207) 324-9691
For more information, visit
www.sanfordmainestage.org

This community theater stages musicals, non-musicals, and children's theater from April to December and offers a low cost, four-week Children's Summer Theater Workshop for children ages 7 to 12. The workshop covers everything from acting to stage work to juggling. Call the box office for more information.

Schoolhouse Arts Center at Sebago Lake

Richville Road, Standish
Call (207) 642-3743
For more information, visit
www.schoolhousearts.org

The Schoolhouse Arts Center at Sebago Lake is a community arts school and theater located in the old Standish High School in Sebago Lake Village within walking distance to Big Sebago Lake. This year-round, nonprofit, publicly supported organization is dedicated to arts education and the presentation of the arts. The center also offers an alternative to traditional summer camp with a fun and varied program of courses designed to expose children to the arts. Among the teachers are experienced actors, directors, dancers, choreographers, musicians, writers, and visual artists. At least one theater production per year is geared toward younger child actors, with several other productions offering acting and technical support roles to older children.

The Theater Project

14 School Street, Brunswick
Box office: (207) 729-8584
For more information, visit
www.theaterproject.com

A recipient of the New England Regional Theater Conference Citation for Achievement in Theater, this nonprofit community-based organization caters to all ages. The Theater Project has provided innovative, entertaining performances, has designed programming for members of the community with special needs, and has taught theater to thousands of children from Maine to the Middle East and beyond. The Theater Project includes the Young People's Theater—a longstanding program for elementary through middle school actors that includes classes and productions by young actors.

University of Southern Maine

McCormack Performing Arts Center, Morrill Avenue, Gorham
Summer Session Office: (207) 780-5617
For more information, visit
www.usm.maine.edu/summer/smta.htm

The University's Southern Maine Theatre Academy, a resident camp, offers junior high and high school age students a basic understanding of performance concepts and skills needed to create a stage production, such as voice, movement, and acting techniques. Students engage in performance exercises that enhance acting talent and develop imagination, confidence, self-awareness, and communication skills. At the conclusion of the camp, participants put on a performance.

The Greater Portland Area

Center for Cultural Exchange

One Longfellow Square, Portland
Call (207) 761-0591 ext. 100
For more information, visit
www.centerforculturalexchange.org

All the events sponsored by the Center for Cultural Exchange are open to children and are family-friendly. The exchange brings in musicians and dancers from around the world who appear in concerts open to the public. Sometimes a community dinner is held around the event. The exchange also offers Kinder-Culture for kids 3 to 8, with hands-on activities that include art, puppetry, story exchanges, and dance—all focusing on the theme of diversity. Sometimes artists in residence hold workshops open to all ages. Poetry readings and open fiddle nights are regular attractions. Call for schedules, prices, and times.

Children's Theatre of Maine

317 Marginal Way, Portland
Call (207) 878-2774 for program or
workshop information
Call (207) 828-0617 for ticket information

The Children's Theatre of Maine (CTM) is a 76-year-old institution dedicated to providing educational and entertaining theater experiences for children and adults alike. Traditionally, CTM has scheduled several series yearly, including Theatre for Young Audiences, The Family Favorites Series, and a New Play Series. One component of the New Play Series is the annual statewide Young Playwrights' Contest in which young writers can see their plays come to life on stage. CTM also hosts an annual Shakespeare Festival in the spring, in which high schools from around the state gather to perform works of the Bard. CTM also produces an annual summer production of Shakespeare in the Park, a free performance by students of CTM's Maine Summer Dramatic Institute.

In addition to these various productions, CTM offers workshops for children twice a year and runs summer camp programs: Creative Arts I and II (suitable for children ages 4 to 10) and The Jester's Troupe (for children ages 11 to 14).

Cumberland County Civic Center

One Civic Center Square, Portland
Call (207) 775-3438
24-hour hotline (207) 775-3825
For more information, visit
www.theciviccenter.com

Home to the Portland Pirates, the Cumberland County Civic Center is also the venue for many main stage music acts and specialty performances such as *Sesame Street on Ice* and the circus. It is conveniently located in the heart of downtown Portland.

Lyric Music Theater

176 Sawyer Street, South Portland
Box office: (207) 774-2435

Frequently plays in the regular adult schedule are also suitable for children, and often children appear in the cast. Formerly known as the Lyric Theater, the company offers four musicals from September through May. Call for schedule and reservations.

Maine State Ballet

91 Forest Street, Westbrook
Call (207) 856-1663
For more information, visit
www.mainestateballet.org

The Maine State Ballet, in cooperation with the Maine State School for the Performing Arts, performs full-length ballets and one-act productions in Portland's Merrill Auditorium (see below). They also perform *The Nutcracker* during the holiday season.

Merrill Auditorium

City Hall, 20 Myrtle Street, Portland
For information, call (207) 874-8200
For tickets, call PortTix at (207) 842-0800
For more information, visit
www.pcagreatperformances.org

Merrill Auditorium in downtown Portland offers a variety of Portland Concert Association Great Performances events, mostly musical, ranging from classical concerts to jazz soloists, tap-dancing revues, and touring Broadway shows. Educational events feature dance company residencies and master classes, and include performances open to the public. PortTix, the box office at Merrill Auditorium, is the ticketing agent for all PCA Great Performances events.

Portland Ballet Company

517 Forest Avenue, Portland
For info and tickets call (207) 772-9671
For more information, visit
www.portlandballet.org

The Portland Ballet, founded in 1985, includes the School of Ballet and the Portland Ballet Company. The school holds classes for children as young as four. Some of the company's past performances have included *Carnival of the Animals, Cinderella, Peter and the Wolf,* and *Sleeping Beauty.* Every December, the Portland Ballet Company performs *Victorian Nutcracker* to commemorate the famed Victoria Mansion in Portland.

Portland Opera Repertory Theater

437 Congress Street, Portland
Call (207) 879-7678

The Portland Opera Repertory Theater performs two productions a year at the Merrill

Auditorium during July. English super-titles appear above the stage to help the audience better understand the performance. In July, an outreach program is also offered for younger artists that includes the staging of an opera sung in English, in full costume and accompanied by the piano.

Portland Stage Company

25A Forest Avenue, Portland
Box office: (207) 774-0465
Administrative office: (207) 774-1043
For more information, visit
www.portlandstage.com

The company puts on five main stage productions during its fall through spring season, but from late November until just before Christmas, *A Christmas Carol,* by Charles Dickens, is always performed. One night in September is Pay-What-You-Can Night, when select tickets are available to patrons at any amount they can afford. Also, half-price Rush Tickets are subject to availability and are released one hour prior to the curtain time of each performance.

Portland Symphony Orchestra

477 Congress Street, Portland
PSO Info: (207) 773-6128
For tickets call PortTix at (207) 842-0800
For more information, visit
www.portlandsymphony.com

The Portland Symphony Orchestra offers 35- to 40-minute Kinderkonzerts for children ages 3 to 7 throughout the state. The PSO also offers Youth Concerts (grades 3 to 6), petting zoos for instruments (K through 5), *Meet the Maestro* (K through 12 and adults), open dress rehearsals, and performances with comedians and mimes.

Mid-Coast Maine

Belfast Maskers

Railroad Depot, Front Street, Belfast
Call (207) 338-9668
For more information, visit
www.belfastmaskers.com

This year-round community theater initially performed in churches, schools, and the library, but now has a somewhat permanent home in a former railroad depot. The Maskers bill themselves as an eclectic, adventuresome, and entertaining bunch of actors, directors, and stagehands who enjoy nothing more than creating wonderful performances for all ages and stages. Many of their plays are suitable for children. Call for schedule and age range.

Camden Civic Theatre

29 Elm Street, Camden
Call (207) 236-2281

The 30-year-old Camden Civic Theatre mounts its four annual productions in the renovated Camden Opera House on Route 1 in the heart of town, from March through December. Many of the plays are suitable for older children, and many children are cast in parts.

Carousel Music Theatre

Townsend Avenue, Boothbay Harbor
Call (207) 633-5297 or (800) 757-5297
For more information, visit
www.boothbaydinnertheatre.com

Since 1975, the Carousel Music Theatre has offered dinner theater in Boothbay Harbor from mid-May to mid-October. Most of the musical offerings are suitable for older children who can stay up late enough to enjoy it. Youthful professional actors, dancers, and singers perform a little "Old-Time Vaudeville, some Old-Time Broadway, and a lot of Old-Time Show Biz in a Turn-of-the-Century Atmosphere."

Center for the Arts at the Chocolate Church

798 Washington Street, Bath
Phone/Box Office (207) 442-8455
For more information, visit
www.chocolatechurcharts.org

The Chocolate Church sponsors a variety of plays, musical concerts, and other performances, and some would be enjoyable for children.

National Theatre Workshop of the Handicapped

96 Church Street, Belfast
Call (207) 338-6894

Founded in 1977, this national workshop offers learning experiences for both adults and children with disabilities. From late June until early September, they offer ten-day workshops for both able-bodied children and those with disabilities. The workshop activities include theater games, acting, and improvisation, as well as a performance at the end of the workshop period.

Down East Maine

Acadia Repertory Theatre

Route 102, Somesville, Mt. Desert Island
Call (207) 244-7260

This summer stock theater stages a blend of non-musical comedies, mysteries, and dramas from the 4th of July weekend through Labor Day. One play just for children runs all summer, while other plays on the regular schedule are suitable for older children.

Deck House Cabaret Theater

Great Harbor Marina, Southwest Harbor, Mt. Desert Island
Call (207) 244-5044

The Deck House Cabaret Theater features Broadway musical numbers mid-June to September. No productions are specific for children, but all are suitable for children who can stay up late enough and sit still long enough to enjoy them.

University of Maine, Machias

9 O'Brien Avenue, Machias
Call (207) 255-3313 ext. 284
For more information, visit
www.umm.maine.edu/

Productions at the UM Machias campus offer a wide range of plays from Shakespeare to comedy. The UMM Readers' Theatre also offers productions that include local legends and tales of the sea.

Western Maine

Celebration Barn Theatre

190 Stock Farm Road, South Paris
Call (207) 743-8452
For more information, visit
www.celebrationbarn.com

Founded in 1972 by mime Tony Montanaro, the Celebration Barn Theatre is both a performance center and a school where students study in areas as diverse as mime, mask, movement, fight coordination, juggling, voice, acrobatics, and clowning. Throughout the summer, performances are scheduled in all of these varied disciplines.

Lakeside Youth Theater

Main Street, Rangeley
Call (207) 864-5000

The Lakeside Youth Theater offers low-cost film festivals, many aimed at children. The theater has a 30-foot screen with a Dolby Surround Sound system, reclining seats, popcorn, candy, and sodas. Call for movies and dates. In the past, Lakeside has hosted an independent film festival on Thursday nights. Live entertainment includes a comedy festival.

Lakewood Theater

Beach Road (Lake Wesserunsett), Skowhegan
Call (207) 474-7176
For more information, visit
www.lakewoodtheater.org

In the nation's oldest summer theater, founded in 1900, the Lakewood Jesters perform excellent theater for children during four productions in July and August. Lakewood also offers a Young Performers camp in two four-week sessions, for the very young through high school age. At the end of camp, children perform their play. Much of Lakewood's regular summer lineup—including musicals, comedies, and light dramas (presented Thursdays through Saturdays)—is suitable for older children.

Oddfellow Theater

Route 117, Buckfield
Box office: (207) 336-3306
For more information, visit
www.oddfellow.com

The Oddfellow Theater hosts family-oriented productions suitable for children. A regular early evening show runs the first Saturday of each month. Entertainment includes jugglers, folk singers, vaudevillians, and other concerts.

Central Maine

Augusta Civic Center

76 Community Drive, Augusta
Call (207) 626-2405
For more information, visit
www.augustaciviccenter.org

The Civic Center hosts a wide variety of events, many suitable or planned for children.

Bates College

163 Wood Street, Lewiston
Call (207) 786-6381
For more information, visit
http://abacus.bates.edu/Faculty/theater/

Bates offers a broad selection of plays, dance and musical performances, and dance festivals throughout the year. Summer festivals include the American College Dance Festival and The Bates Dance Festival, covering every style of dance from tap to jazz and improvisation. Dance concerts include performances by Bates College Dancers and other companies. Plays range from Shakespeare to new works. Call or check the Web site for a comprehensive schedule and age suitability.

Colby College

4000 Mayflower Hill Drive, Waterville
Box office: (207) 872-3358
Info: (207) 872-3388
For more information, visit
www.colby.edu/theater

The Colby College Department of Theater and Dance offers a wide variety of theater, music, and dance events during the year. Many are suitable for older children; the box office will provide information on age suitability.

Gaslight Theatre

City Hall, 1 Winthrop Street, Hallowell
Box office: (207) 626-3698
For more information, visit
http://www.gaslighttheater.org/

Continually operating since 1977, this all-volunteer community theater stages four productions a year, most of which are comedies or musicals suitable for children.

Johnson Hall Performing Arts Center

280 Water Street, Gardiner
Call (207) 582-7144
For more information, visit
www.johnsonhall.org

This historic hall is the scene of many musical concerts and plays by touring companies. Johnson Hall is also the venue for Reader's Theater and Open Book Players. They give several performances year-round.

The Public Theatre

Ritz Theatre building, corner of Lisbon and Maple Streets, Lewiston
Box office: (207) 782-3200,
or (800) 639-9575
Business office: (207) 782-2211
For more information, visit
www.thepublictheatre.org/

Aside from the shows it produces, this professional theater company is dedicated to promoting the interactive possibilities of live entertainment. It offers students, teachers, and their regular audience opportunities to participate in thought-provoking discussions, allowing them to respond to the issues addressed in the plays presented. Their Educational Outreach Program includes a special student internship as well as a student matinee program.

The Theater at Monmouth

Cumston Hall, Route 132, Monmouth
Box office: (207) 933-9999
Business office: (207) 933-2952
For more information, visit
www.theateratmonmouth.org

Housed in an historic old opera house in the center of town, the company offers one play just for children in matinees during the week and on weekends in the summer. In spring, children's matinees are held during the week so school groups may attend. Some productions on the regular schedule are suitable for older children.

Northern Maine

Maine Center for the Arts

University of Maine campus, Orono
For tickets call (207) 581-1755,
or (800) 622-8499
For more information, visit
www.ume.maine.edu/~mca

The Maine Center for the Arts hosts a wide variety of events, presenting classical and contemporary music, dance, theater, comedy, and lectures. Most are held in the modern 1,629-seat Hutchins Concert Hall, and many are suitable for children.

Penobscot Theatre Company/ Maine Shakespeare Festival

183 Main Street, Bangor
Box office: (207) 942-3333
Administrative office: (207) 947-6618
For more information, visit
http://ptc.maineguide.com/

Professional Shakespearean actors teach acting, improvisation, and production at summer day camps held for children ages 7 to 12 and 13 to 18. The Maine Shakespeare Festival is held outdoors on the banks of the Penobscot River from mid-July to mid-

August. Penobscot Theatre Company also offers intern programs for high school kids to work on the adult plays and with children in day camp. Penobscot Theatre Company produces at least two plays for children each summer.

University of Maine/ Maine Masque Theatre

Hauck Auditorium and Pavilion Theater, Orono
Call (207) 581-4702
For more information, visit
www.umaine.edu/mainemasque/

Maine Masque, the university theater group within the School of Performing Arts, offers a new show every other week in Hauck Auditorium. Serious and well-known contemporary dramas, as well as various student-written productions, are often performed. Generally, the faculty directs and students perform. Some productions are suitable for children. Call for schedule and suitability. Check out more experimental works in the Pavilion Theater.

Maine-ly Music!

Bangor Symphony
44 Central Street, Bangor
BSO Youth Orchestra: (207) 989-2104
    or (800) 639-3221
Bangor Symphony Orchestra:
    (207) 942-5555 or (800) 639-3221
For more information, visit
www.bangorsymphony.com

The nation's oldest symphony orchestra offers Youth Orchestra and Ensemble concerts and other educational music events throughout the year and throughout the state in schools and other venues. Regular BSO concerts are usually given in the Maine Center for the Arts on the Orono campus of the University of Maine. *The Nutcracker* is performed annually with the Robinson Ballet Company.

chapter 2

Beaches

Southern Maine ... 12

Crescent Beach, Cape Elizabeth ... 12

East End Beach, Portland ... 12

Ferry Beach, Western Beach,
  Scarborough ... 12

Ferry Beach State Park, Saco ... 12

Fort Foster Beaches, Kittery Point ... 13

Long Sands Beach, York ... 13

Moody Beach, Wells ... 13

Ogunquit Beach, Ogunquit ... 13

Old Orchard Beach and Surfside,
  Old Orchard Beach ... 13

Parsons Beach, Kennebunkport ... 13

Scarborough Beach State Park,
  Scarborough ... 13

Sebago Lake State Park, Casco ... 14

Short Sands Beach, York ... 14

Singing Sands Beach, Long Island,
  in Casco Bay ... 14

Tassel Top Beach, Raymond ... 14

Thomas Point Beach, Brunswick ... 14

Wells Beach, Wells ... 14

Willard Beach, South Portland ... 15

Winslow Memorial Park, Freeport ... 15

Mid-Coast Maine ... 15

Birch Point State Park, Owls Head ... 15

Crescent Beach, Owls Head ... 15

Damariscotta Lake State Park,
  Jefferson ... 15

Lake St. George State Park, Liberty ... 15

Lincolnville Beach, Lincolnville ... 15

Pemaquid Beach, Pemaquid ... 16

Popham Beach, Phippsburg ... 16

Reid State Park, Georgetown ... 16

Swan Lake State Park, Swanville ... 16

Down East Maine ... 16

Jasper Beach, Machiasport ... 16

Lamoine Beach, Lamoine ... 17

Roque Bluffs Beach, Roque Bluffs ... 17

Sand Beach, Bar Harbor ... 17

Shackford Head State Park, Eastport ... 17

Central Maine ... 17

Peacock Beach State Park, Richmond ... 17

Range Ponds State Park,
  Poland Spring ... 18

Western Maine ... 18

Mount Blue State Park, Weld ... 18

Northern Maine ... 18

Peaks-Kenney State Park,
  Dover-Foxcroft ... 18

Beaches

Maine is not a state known for extensive beaches. Even the native Mainer may only be able to name a few. Yet it is the overall rocky character of Maine's coast that makes the state's few sandy beaches so special. Each has its own personality. There are hopping summer beach communities like Old Orchard Beach; private and infrequently visited beaches where the waves come roaring in every day, and calm, tranquil, warm beaches on the shores of lakes and at the mouths of rivers. You will also find beaches of pebbles or crushed shells as well as coarse or fine white sand. This diversity makes each beach a unique place to treasure.

Southern Maine

Crescent Beach

Crescent Beach State Park
Route 77, Cape Elizabeth

Bordering Seal Cove in Cape Elizabeth, this beach presents visitors with the classic Maine seacoast atmosphere. The star attraction of the park, the fine sand and pebble beach, covers almost a mile and looks out onto lobster and fishing boats anchored in the cove. Richmond Island protects the beach and makes the waters comparatively quiet and calm. Seashells and rock formations add a little more distinctiveness to this beach. Visitors will find ample parking, a snack bar, changing areas, restrooms, picnic areas, and grills.

East End Beach

Eastern Promenade, Portland

The City of Portland's only public beach, the East End Beach (just off the Eastern Promenade on the easternmost end of the Portland Peninsula), offers changing rooms, restrooms, a few picnic tables, and a superb view of Casco Bay. No lifeguard or food available. Parking is limited.

Ferry Beach, Western Beach

Route 207, Prouts Neck, Scarborough

Almost a mile in length, these adjacent beaches are located on the easterly side of the protected mouth of the Scarborough River. While it offers no spectacular views of the Atlantic or huge waves, the setting makes the water temperature much warmer in comparison to that of many other Maine beaches. There is a small parking area with some restroom facilities.

Ferry Beach State Park

95 Bay View Road, Saco
(207) 283-0067
Open Memorial Day to September 30

Not to be confused with Ferry Beach in Scarborough (above), Ferry Beach State Park is located in Saco, just south of Old Orchard. This 117-acre state park provides access to more than two and a half miles of white sand beaches between the Saco River and Pine Point. The Ferry Beach State park facility provides lifeguards, changing areas, picnic areas, grills, and nature trails. This is an all-around great beach for families.

Fort Foster Beaches

Pocahontas Road, Kittery Point
(207) 439-2182 (gatehouse)

Three beautiful sand beaches are found at Fort Foster: Pier Beach, Whaleback Beach, and Rocky Beach. Among the features the three have access to are picnic tables, restrooms, and grills. Additionally, the fort offers a playground, nature trails, grassy fields, and a pier, plus scenic views of Portsmouth Harbor, Whaleback Lighthouse, the Isles of Shoals, and across to New Hampshire. Lifeguards are not provided.

Long Sands Beach

Long Beach Avenue (U.S. Route 1A),
York Beach

This sandy beach stretching from York Harbor to Nubble Light has a designated surfing area. There is metered parking along the beach. Food is available at the shops across the street. Changing areas and toilets are available near Oceanside Avenue. Lifeguards are on duty.

Moody Beach

Bourne Avenue, off U.S. Route 1, Wells
Wells Chamber of Commerce:
(207) 646-2451

Moody Beach is a continuation of Ogunquit Beach (see below). Public restrooms and lifeguards are available. One end of the beach offers rocky tide pools.

Ogunquit Beach

U.S. Route 1, Ogunquit
Ogunquit Chamber of Commerce:
(207) 646-2939

This long, straight beach occupies the entire coast of the town of Ogunquit and is made up of some of the finest white sand one can find in Maine. Nearly three miles in length, it offers all the amenities that many expect at a beach: boardwalks, a snack bar, changing facilities, and restrooms. Parking is available for a small fee.

Old Orchard Beach and Surfside

Route 9, Old Orchard Beach
Old Orchard Beach Chamber
of Commerce: (800) 365-9386

The entire coastline of this community is occupied by this beach. At times, this wide strip of fine, white sand is just as much a carnival as it is a beach. With nearby rides, arcades, and food vendors along the boardwalk, this is not your typical quiet Maine beach experience. Ample parking is available for a nominal fee.

Parsons Beach

Route 9, Kennebunkport

This mile of fine, white sand is quiet and peaceful. You are more likely to find walkers and great fishing here than body surfing and boardwalks. There are no facilities offered, and parking is limited. This kind of quiet and undeveloped beach is a rare find on the active southern coast of Maine.

Scarborough Beach State Park

Route 207, Scarborough

Located on the ocean side of the same peninsula as Ferry Beach in Scarborough, this mile-long barrier beach of white sand abuts a freshwater marsh. It offers great views of the Atlantic, good fishing, picnic tables, changing facilities, grills, and a bath house. Parking is available for a small fee.

Sebago Lake State Park

11 Park Access Road, off Route 302, Casco
Park office: (207) 693-6613 during park season
Casco Parks & Recreation Dept.: (207) 693-6231, off-season
Open May 15 through October 1

The park's 1,400 acres feature sandy beaches along Maine's second largest lake. Explore the extensive woodlands, ponds, and bogs, or swim, sport fish, camp, or boat at this popular Maine destination. Picnic facilities, a boat ramp, lifeguards, and bath houses are all available.

Short Sands Beach

York Beach, York
Off Route 1A, north of York Beach
Greater York Region Chamber of Commerce: (207) 363-4422

This sandy beach offers a myriad of amenities, many of them family oriented: a large bathhouse, outside shower, playground, basketball courts, limited shade under the pavilion, metered parking, and benches along the boardwalk on the beach. Shops and restaurants are available within walking distance, and private parking lots are nearby. Concerts are held on summer evenings. No snack bar. Lifeguards on duty.

Singing Sands Beach

South Beach, Long Island, in Casco Bay

Take the Casco Bay Lines ferry to Long Island. (Casco Bay Lines is located at the corner of Franklin and Commercial Streets, Portland. Visit _www.cascobaylines.com_ and click on "sailing schedule," or call (207) 774-7871 for ferry departure times.) A 15-minute (half-mile) walk across the island from the bay side, where the ferry docks, to the ocean side will bring you to South Beach. Also known as Singing Sands, the beach and cove are named after the unique sound the sand makes under your feet. Beachgoers can wander to a smaller offshore island at low tide.

Tassel Top Beach

Route 302, Raymond, across from Raymond Shopping Center
Raymond Town Hall: (207) 655-4742
Open Memorial Day through Labor Day

The State Planning Office has identified Tassel Top as "one of the eight most outstanding beaches in the organized towns of the state," and "the largest undeveloped sand beach remaining on Sebago Lake." Picnic tables and grills are available, but there is no lifeguard. A park ranger is on duty during beach hours.

Thomas Point Beach

29 Meadow Road, Brunswick
Park office: (207) 725-6009

While this is a small beach, the location on tidal water overlooking the New Meadows River makes it a protected spot to swim. An adjoining campground set on 85 acres offers many amenities, including a snack bar, gift shop, playground, arcade, numerous picnic tables, softball and volleyball areas, and overnight accommodations. There is a small entrance fee.

Wells Beach

U.S. Route 1, Wells

This two-mile-long stretch of smooth, white sand is a classic summer resort beach. With motels and lots of activity on the boardwalk, the small village of Wells comes alive in the summer. A nearby saltwater marsh offers good bird watching. There are changing rooms and restrooms at the beach. Parking is available for a small fee.

Willard Beach

**Myrtle Avenue or Willard Street,
South Portland**

Nearly a mile long, Willard Beach is sandwiched between the Southern Maine Technical College campus and Fisherman's Point. Its views of the Spring Point Lighthouse and the Portland ship channel appeal to families, as do its fine sand and gentle surf. There are restrooms and limited parking available.

Winslow Memorial Park

**Staples Point Road, South Freeport
Park Office: (207) 865-4198 in summer**

This 90-acre park includes a gentle, sandy beach surrounded by the Harraseeket River and Casco Bay. Amenities include picnic tables, campsites, playground, tidal boat launching site, and restrooms. A small entrance fee is charged.

Mid-Coast Maine

Birch Point State Park

**Off Route 73, Owls Head
Bureau of Parks and Lands:
    (207) 941-4014
Open Memorial Day through Labor Day**

A little extra effort is required to find this park. In Owls Head, south of Rockland, turn east off Route 73 onto North Shore Drive and take your first right onto Ash Point Drive. Take the right immediately after the Knox County Regional Airport, and the road will guide you to the park. Once there, you can photograph spectacular views of Penobscot Bay and the nearby islands, plus two lighthouses. This crescent-shaped sand and rock beach is a lovely spot to swim; however, there are no lifeguards. Access is free and parking is limited.

Crescent Beach

Crescent Terrace, Owls Head

This popular swimming beach is located near a summer colony and offers fine views of Penobscot Bay. From South Shore Drive, turn east onto Birchmont Road, left onto Bellevue Street, and right onto Crescent Terrace. When the tide is right, there is more than 3,000 feet of sandy shoreline here to enjoy, but very little parking.

Damariscotta Lake State Park

**8 State Park Road, off Route 32, Jefferson
Park office: (207) 549-7600
Open Memorial Day through Labor Day**

This fine sand beach has lifeguards as well as a group-use shelter, picnic tables, and grills. An old-fashioned playground with several swings is next to the beach.

Lake St. George State Park

**Route 3, Liberty
Park office: (207) 589-4255
Open May 15 through September 30**

Swim in this popular, crystal-clear lake or relax on the lawn at the lake's edge. Located on the northwest shore of the lake, you'll find restrooms, campsites, hiking, fishing, boat and canoe rentals, and a lifeguard.

Lincolnville Beach

U.S. Route 1, Lincolnville

This half-mile-long beach is located about 4 miles north of Camden on Route 1, next to the Islesboro Ferry landing. Nestled in the town of Lincolnville, it is a popular summer location close to restaurants, stores, and nearby Camden Hills State Park. Limited free parking is available.

Pemaquid Beach

**Pemaquid Loop Road, off Route 130,
Pemaquid
Damariscotta Region Chamber
of Commerce: (207) 563-8340**

This is a crescent-shaped sand beach tucked in a small cove near Pemaquid Harbor and Fort William Henry, a short walk away. In addition to swimming, you can tour the fort and the excavated remnants of the early settlement of Pemaquid and enjoy beautiful views of Johns Bay.

Popham Beach

**10 Perkins Farm Lane, Phippsburg
Park office: (207) 389-1335
Open April 15 to October 30**

Located less than ten miles south of Bath, near the end of the Phippsburg peninsula, this fine sand beach is a rare find in mid-coast Maine. Popham Beach overlooks the mouth of the Kennebec River and has an unobstructed view of the Atlantic. Rarely crowded, this two-mile-long beach abuts dunes and, in places, rock outcroppings with tide pools. The beach is part of a 529-acre state park that offers bath houses, grills, freshwater showers, and picnic areas.

Reid State Park

**About 2 miles south of Route 127 on
Seguin Island Road, Georgetown
Park office: (207) 371-2303**

Reid State Park actually has two adjacent beaches, aptly named Mile Beach and Half Mile Beach. It is the beaches that draw more than 80,000 people to the park each year, yet they never feel crowded. The two large swathes of sand and dunes are separated by a rocky stretch that is more typical of the Maine coast. Located on the end of the Georgetown peninsula, Reid State Park offers crashing waves and bold, open ocean vistas. Beachside accommodations include charcoal grills, bath houses, freshwater showers, picnic areas, and a snack bar. Ample parking is available.

Swan Lake State Park

**100 West Park Lane, off Frankfort Road
about a mile and a half east of Route
141, Swanville
Park office: (207) 525-4404
Open Memorial Day through Labor Day**

Enjoy the shores of Swan Lake, where you can swim at the sandy beach. Sixty-seven acres of land make up the park, and one can find picnic facilities, a playground, and group shelter there. Shoreline fishing is very popular because of the abundance of game fish. A lifeguard is available, and there are toilet and changing facilities.

Down East Maine

Jasper Beach

Jasper Beach Road, Machiasport

Named for the polished red volcanic stones commonly found here, Jasper Beach is framed by bedrock and abuts freshwater and saltwater lagoons and a salt marsh. To find this unusual beach, drive east from Machias on Rte. 92, which becomes Machias Road when you enter Machiasport. Travel several miles to Howard Cove and watch for Jasper Beach Road on your left. A limited parking area is provided.

Lamoine Beach

23 State Park Road, off Route 184, Lamoine
Park office: (207) 667-4778
Open May 15 through October 15

Eight miles southeast of Ellsworth, in Lamoine Beach State Park, is where this mile-and-a-half-long beach can be found. Enjoy nice views of Mt. Desert Island and the mountains of Acadia National Park from here. Picnic facilities and a boat ramp are available. The park also offers campsite areas, hot showers, a saltwater fishing pier, and a playground.

Roque Bluffs Beach

145 Schoppee Point Road, off Roque Bluffs Road, Roque Bluffs
Park office: (207) 255-3475
Open May 15 to September 30

Located six miles south of U.S. Rte. 1 in the university town of Machias, Roque Bluffs State Park contains one of eastern Maine's few coastal swimming beaches. The beach is small, with fine sand and pebble areas that slope gradually into the water. Dunes separate the ocean from a unique 66-acre freshwater pond where visitors can swim or picnic. One parking area has a deck that looks out over the beach, with views of islands and the Gulf of Maine. This open view, however, emphasizes the unprotected nature of this beach in any weather. Dramatic sunrises can be seen by early risers. Parking and toilet facilities are available, along with a picnic area and children's playground.

Sand Beach

Acadia National Park
Park Loop Road, Bar Harbor
Park office: (207) 288-3338

Located in a cove between two high ledge outcroppings, this unusual beach is formed primarily out of crushed shell, not sand, despite its name. It looks out onto a ledge of Mt. Desert's famed pink granite. Numerous hiking trails lead from the beach deeper into Acadia National Park. Although the beach is protected from rough seas, the water temperature does not get much above 50 degrees in the summer. This beach is a wonderful place to go while visiting Acadia. There are parking and restroom facilities, and a lifeguard is on duty in the summer.

Shackford Head State Park

Deep Cove Road, west of Route 190, Eastport

Cony Beach, as it is known to the locals, is just one reason to come to Shackford. Located on an undeveloped peninsula with protected coves, high trails, and two fossil beds, this park offers beautiful views of Cobscook Bay and Broad Cove once you've hiked in a short distance from the park entrance. The sand/pebble beach is great for those who like to just walk or search for shells or old warship artifacts. (Between 1901 and 1920, five Civil War–era ships were towed here and burned.) One of the nation's most eastern points, Shackford Head State Park offers a small parking area and limited facilities, but is not staffed.

Central Maine

Peacock Beach State Park

Route 201, Pleasant Pond, Richmond
Park office: (207) 582-2813
Open Memorial Day through Labor Day

Ninety-three acres of recreation land borders the shores of the aptly named Pleasant Pond. Enjoy picnicking or swimming from the small beach. Lifeguards are available.

Range Ponds State Park

31 State Park Road, Poland Spring
Park office: (207) 998-4104
Open May 15 through October 15

Located southwest of Lewiston-Auburn, Range Ponds State Park is a seasonal day-use park with recreation centered around Lower Range Pond. Just footsteps away from the long, sandy beach are modern bath houses. Picnicking, hiking, and playing baseball at the nearby field are all popular activities. The State Park Road is accessed from the north by Empire Road and from the south by Poland Spring Road.

Western Maine

Mount Blue State Park

Webb Lake area, off West Road, Weld
Park office: (207) 585-2347
Open May 15 through October 1

Swim in the popular Webb Lake or lounge on sandy Webb Beach at the smaller of the two areas that make up Mount Blue State Park. The Webb Lake portion of the park also offers a boat launch site as well as an amphitheater and nature center for educational talks and environmental displays. Restrooms are provided, and shelter is available for large groups.

Northern Maine

Peaks-Kenney State Park

500 State Park Road, off Route 153
(Greely Landing Road),
Dover-Foxcroft
Park office: (207) 564-2003
Open May 15 through September 30

The beach at Peaks-Kenney State Park is located on the shores of pristine Sebec Lake, known for its cool, deep waters. The park surrounds the lake's South Cove and offers picnicking, swimming, fishing, boat rentals, and hiking. A lifeguard is provided.

chapter 3

Boating

Southern Maine...20

Atlantic Seal Cruises, South Freeport...20

Bayview Cruises, Portland...20

Cape Arundel Cruises,
    Kennebunkport...20

Casco Bay Lines, Portland...20

First Chance and *Second Chance*,
    Kennebunkport...20

Lucky Catch Cruises, Portland...21

Maine Island Kayak Company,
    Peaks Island...21

Olde Port Mariner Fleet, Portland...21

Scotia Prince, Portland...21

Songo River Queen II, Naples...21

Mid-Coast Maine...22

Annie McGee, Belfast...22

Appledore II, Camden...22

Balmy Days Cruises, Boothbay
    Harbor...22

Cap'n Fish's Cruises,
    Boothbay Harbor...22

The Captain's Watch Sail Charter,
    Harpswell...22

Hardy Boat Cruises, New Harbor...23

Maine Maritime Museum, Bath...23

Maine Windjammer Association, Camden,
    Rockland, Rockport...23

Monhegan Boat Line, Port Clyde...23

Schooner Yacht *Wendameen*, Rockland...23

Down East Maine...24

Acadia Bike and Canoe, Bar Harbor...24

Bar Harbor Whale Watch Company,
    Bar Harbor...24

The Cat, Bar Harbor...24

Isle au Haut Boat Company,
    Stonington...24

Maine Maritime Academy, Castine...24

The *Margaret Todd*, Bar Harbor...24

Robertson Sea Tours and Adventures,
    Milbridge...25

The *Sea Princess*, Northeast Harbor...25

Whale Watcher, Inc., Bar Harbor...25

Central Maine...25

Belgrade Lakes Mail Boat,
    Belgrade Lakes...25

Maine Wilderness Tours, Belgrade...25

North Country Rivers,
    East Vassalboro...26

Western Maine...26

Adventure Bound Rafting, Caratunk...26

Bethel Outdoor Adventure, Bethel...26

Downriver Guide Service, Farmington...26

The Mountain House, Oquossoc...26

Moxie Outdoor Adventures,
    The Forks...26

Saco River Canoe & Kayak,
    Fryeburg...27

Northern Maine...27

Allagash Canoe Trips, Greenville...27

The Birches Resort Wilderness
    Expeditions, Rockwood...27

Katahdin Cruises, Greenville...27

Moosehead Adventures, Greenville...27

New England Outdoor Center,
    Millinocket...28

Northwoods Outfitters, Greenville...28

Boating

Southern Maine

Atlantic Seal Cruises

Town Wharf, South Freeport
(207) 865-6112
For more information, visit
www.inusa.com/tour/me/portland/seal.htm

Seal watch cruises, fall foliage cruises, and charters are all available from the town wharf in Freeport. *Atlantic Seal* offers a special Eagle Island adventure tour that includes a stop at the home of Admiral Peary as well as time to explore the island itself. (You can read more about Eagle Island in Chapter 11.)

Bayview Cruises

184 Commercial Street, Portland
(207) 761-0496
For more information, visit
www.cascobaybiz.com/bayview/home.html

Bayview offers six different sightseeing trips a day, including a seal-watch tour and a tour of the Casco Bay area that focuses on Portland Head Light. All tours are narrated, and there is a snack bar on board. On Sundays a brunch tour is also available. Bayview Cruises is located next to the Bayview Restaurant, a seafood restaurant that welcomes children.

Cape Arundel Cruises

Kennebunkport Marina, Kennebunkport
(207) 967-5595
For more information, visit
www.cacruises.com

Cape Arundel offers two different cruising options for families—a traditional whale watch and a somewhat unusual sightseeing cruise from Kennebunkport Harbor. The scenic cruise is under two hours and focuses on the historic islands in the area. It offers a rare view of former President Bush's estate on Walker's Point as well as plenty of nature watching.

Casco Bay Lines

Commercial and Franklin Streets, Portland
(207) 774-7871
For more information, visit
www.cascobaylines.com

Casco Bay Lines is the oldest ferry service in America. Although the ferries are mainly used by island inhabitants for transportation to and from the mainland, several cruises are open to the general public. The hourly trips to Peaks Island are the best bet for those with young children. There are bike rentals available on the island, as well as a few shops and restaurants. Other island destinations serviced by the ferry include Chebeague Island, Great Diamond Island, and Long Island. (To read more about several of the Casco Bay islands, see Chapter 11.)

First Chance and *Second Chance*

4A Western Avenue, Lower Village, Kennebunk
(207) 967-5507 or (800) 767-BOAT
For more information, visit
www.firstchancewhalewatch.com

On a whale-watch cruise aboard the *First Chance,* look for humpback, minke, finback, and pilot whales or perhaps see a dolphin or a shark. Sightings are guaranteed on the half-day trips aboard this 72-foot custom whale-watch boat. A scenic cruise awaits you aboard the *Second Chance,* where you can get an up-close look at fishermen hauling their lobster traps.

Lucky Catch Cruises

170 Commercial Street, Portland
(207) 233-2026
For more information, visit
www.luckycatch.com

Lucky Catch offers a traditional tour of Casco Bay while giving a glimpse into the life of a Maine lobsterman. Five tours run daily, and each lasts about an hour and a half. Children will be able to see the process of hauling and setting lobster traps. The different touring options include a seal watch and White Head passage tour. Every tour gives an intimate view of the Maine coast and its traditions.

Maine Island Kayak Company

70 Luther Street, Peaks Island
(207) 766-2373
For more information, visit
www.maineislandkayak.com

MIKCO's Casco Bay half-day tour is a perfect way to introduce children and families to sea kayaking. The company is located on Peaks Island, a 15-minute ferry ride from Portland. (See Casco Bay Lines, page 20.) All equipment, including safety gear, is provided. Civil War forts and bird sanctuaries that are otherwise inaccessible are explored. Mondays are specified as family days, with discounts for children, but families are welcome any day of the week.

Olde Port Mariner Fleet

Commercial Street, Portland
(207) 775-0727
For more information, visit
www.marinerfleet.com

There are several kinds of trips offered through Olde Port Mariner Fleet, including scenic cruises, lobstering cruises, and dinner cruises. The narrated scenic cruises are excellent for viewing Casco Bay.

Scotia Prince

Portland International Ferry Terminal,
468 Commercial Street, Portland
(207) 775-5616 or (800) 341-7540
For more information, visit
www.scotiaprince.com

The *Scotia Prince* ferry departs nightly from Portland and arrives in Yarmouth, Nova Scotia, the next morning. After a one-hour layover, the ship returns to Portland. The sailing time is about 11 hours each way, which shaves off about 14 hours of driving between the two ports. There is a full restaurant on board, as well as a casino and snack bar. In addition, there are plenty of children's activities, including special shows and events.

Songo River Queen II Cruises

Route 302, The Causeway, Naples
(207) 693-6861
For more information, visit
www.songoriverqueen.com

The *Songo River Queen II* is a replica of a Mississippi paddleboat that offers two separate cruising options. The first is a two-and-a-half-hour cruise operating through the Songo Lock system on the Crooked River to Sebago Lake. The second cruise, a one-hour trip, makes its way across Long Lake. Both cruises operate on a daily basis during the peak summer season and offer a relaxing and unique adventure that highlights the atmosphere and wildlife of Naples. The *Songo River Queen II* also runs fall foliage cruises in the Sebago Lake area.

Mid-Coast Maine

The *Annie McGee*

12 Anderson Street, Belfast
(207) 338-6338
For more information, visit
www.anniemcgee.com

The *Annie McGee* is a schooner offering daily Penobscot Bay excursions by charter. The schooner can hold a party of six, and each day sail is personalized and different. A catered menu is available for an additional fee. The *Annie McGee* is unusual because very few charter ships are available for day packages. This flexibility allows you to design your own voyage and see the sights you desire.

Appledore II

0 Lily Pond Drive, Camden
(207) 236-8353
For more information, visit
www.appledore2.com

Come aboard this 86-foot schooner for a two-hour day sail around lighthouses and islands on a boat that has sailed around the world. Often you'll spot marine life such as seals and porpoises as you cruise in western Penobscot Bay. Snacks are available.

Balmy Days Cruises

On the waterfront in Boothbay Harbor
(207) 633-2284
For more information, visit
www.balmydayscruises.com

Balmy Days' harbor tour aboard the *Novelty* is a quick cruise through Boothbay Harbor, with views of lobstering boats, coves, and marinas. The tour stops at Squirrel Island, offering a glimpse of one of Maine's oldest summer colonies. The company offers a supper cruise geared toward families. You can also take in a sail aboard *Bay Lady*, a Friendship sloop, or hop aboard *Balmy Days* for an all-day adventure to Monhegan Island, 12 miles out to sea.

Cap'n Fish's Cruises

65 Atlantic Avenue, Boothbay Harbor
(207) 633-6606
For more information, visit
www.capnfishmotel.com

Although the most popular cruises offered by this family-owned company are the whale watches, there are several other options that are also perfect for children. The seal-watch cruise navigates around small islands in order to provide views of seals on their ledges. The Pemaquid Point cruise provides a nice view of the historic light and several other classic Maine lighthouses.

The Captain's Watch Sail Charter

2476 Cundy's Harbor Road, Harpswell
(207) 725-0979
For more information, visit
http://home.gwi.net/~cwatch/sail.htm

The 37-foot *Symbion* is available for charters ranging from one afternoon to five days. Captain Ken Brigham is willing to teach passengers to take control of the sloop, instructing on sea charts and the newest sailing technologies available on the *Symbion*. Day sails can accommodate six passengers and can last from three hours to a full day. The options for these day cruises include a sail to Eagle Island, Seguin Island, or various open-water sails. Passengers are encouraged to bring their own picnics.

Hardy Boat Cruises

**Route 32, Shaw's Fish and Lobster
Wharf, New Harbor
(800) 2PUFFIN**

*For more information, visit
www.hardyboat.com*

Hardy Boat's Lighthouse Cruise is offered in the early evenings—giving passengers sunset views of an historic lighthouse and the coastline. The tour lasts only an hour, and children are welcome. Hardy Boat is also known for great puffin cruises to Eastern Egg Rock and a Monhegan Island ferry service. The fall coastal cruise offers foliage views, seal watching, and a historical tour of the Muscongus Bay islands.

Maine Maritime Museum

**243 Washington Street, Bath
(207) 443-1316**

*For more information, visit
www.bathmaine.com*

The Maine Maritime Museum is most typically known for nautical exhibits and shipyard tours, but it also offers many different cruises throughout the summer and fall tourist season. The dates for the cruises are limited, so it is best to check with the museum before making plans. The cruises include a family cruise to the Boothbay Aquarium, a cruise to Seguin Island, and a fall foliage cruise.

Maine Windjammer Association

**P.O. Box 317P, Augusta
(800) 807-WIND**

*For more information, visit
www.sailmainecoast.com*

Take part in the quintessential Maine experience: sailing the ocean for 3- or 6-day cruises in a traditional tall ship! The Maine Windjammer Association boasts 14 tall ships in their fleet operating out of Camden, Rockland, and Rockport. They range in size from 46 to 132 feet on deck. You can participate in all aspects of sailing, including hoisting sails, navigating, and taking your turn at the wheel, or you can relax on deck or in a single, double, or triple cabin. At night the windjammers drop anchor, so you can explore some of Maine's picturesque islands. Planning ahead is required for this adventure. Call for reservations.

Monhegan Boat Line

**Port Clyde, on the pier next to
the Port Clyde General Store
(207) 372-8848**

*For more information, visit
www.monheganboat.com*

The Monhegan Boat Line has two boats in its fleet. The first, the *Elizabeth Ann,* was built in 1995 specifically for this run and features a heated cabin. She sails to Monhegan, offering lighthouse views as well as passenger service to the island—the home of 75 year-round residents and the Monhegan Museum (located in a lighthouse). The second boat, the *Laura B.,* was built as a T-57 during WWII and originally sailed in the Pacific. The *Laura B.* is available for charters as well as providing early morning service to Monhegan. Both boats offer amazing views of Monhegan in an intimate setting with enough space to allow families to enjoy the voyage.

Schooner Yacht *Wendameen*

**On the harbor in Rockland
(207) 594-1751**

*For more information, visit
www.schooneryacht.com*

Enjoy an overnight cruise aboard the 67-foot schooner, where you can help sail or just lie back and relax. Spend the night anchored in a quiet cove. Comfortable and fast, the *Wendameen* sails daily. Captain Neal Parker has written a book about how he restored this historic vessel: *Wendameen: The Life of an American Schooner* (Down East Books, 2002).

Down East Maine

Acadia Bike and Canoe

48 Cottage Street, Bar Harbor
(800) 526-8615
For more information, visit
www.acadiafun.com

Acadia offers canoe and bike rentals in addition to guided sea-kayaking trips. The company is known for its experienced guides and small group trips. There are several trips available, and the family half-day tour focusing on the wildlife of Mt. Desert Island is perfect for those with children ages 8 and up. Acadia will also custom-design tours for groups.

Bar Harbor Whale Watch Company

1 West Street, Bar Harbor
(207) 288-2386
For more information, visit
www.whalesrus.com

The Bar Harbor Whale Watch Company operates four different boats offering whale, seal, and puffin sighting opportunities. Most notable is the *Friendship V,* one of the fastest whale-watching boats in the country. Because of the *Friendship*'s catamaran design, there is little rocking or pitching—excellent for children with motion sickness tendencies. Bar Harbor Whale Watch claims the best sighting record in Bar Harbor for the past 11 years.

The Cat

121 Eden Street, Bar Harbor
(207) 288-3395
For more information, visit
www.catferry.com

The Cat is the fastest car ferry in North America, providing transportation between Bar Harbor and Yarmouth, Nova Scotia, in just under three hours. There are many things for families to enjoy on board, such as the children's films shown in the movie lounge or the kid-friendly food in the café. *The Cat* offers several different day trips to Yarmouth as well, including a biking trip or a seaside tour once you get there. Overnight packages are also available.

Isle Au Haut Boat Company

Sea Breeze Avenue, Stonington
(207) 367-6516
For more information, visit
www.isleauhaut.com

Come aboard the Isle au Haut mail boats and escape to a remote, offshore portion of beautiful Acadia National Park, or sit back and relax on a wonderful sightseeing excursion around some of the many islands in upper Penobscot Bay.

Maine Maritime Academy

Pleasant Street, Castine
(207) 326-4311
For more information, visit
www.mainemaritime.edu

The T.S. *State of Maine* serves as a training ship for the students of Maine Maritime Academy and several months during the year travels to Iceland, Germany, Russia, Bermuda, and elsewhere. The public can tour this impressive ship (almost 500 feet in length) when she is in port. Call ahead.

The *Margaret Todd*

27 Main Street, Bar Harbor
(207) 288-4585
For more information, visit
http://www.downeastwindjammer.com/
margaret—todd.html

The *Margaret Todd* is a beautiful four-masted, red-sailed schooner that offers tours out of Bar Harbor. Designed by owner and captain

Steven Pagels, the 151-foot vessel sets sail three times daily in season, offering unparalleled views of Acadia National Park.

Robertson Sea Tours and Adventures

Milbridge Marina, Bayview Street, Milbridge
(207) 546-3883
For more information, visit
  www.harborlightsweb.com/robertson/
  index.html

There are several cruise options aboard this traditional down-east fishing boat owned and operated by experienced lobsterman and captain James Robertson. The lighthouse cruise is among the most popular and offers close views of three historic lights. Other cruises include lobstering demonstrations and wildlife expeditions.

The *Sea Princess*

Town Marina, 18 Harbor Drive, Northeast Harbor
(207) 276-5352
For more information, visit
  www.barharborcruises.com

The *Sea Princess* offers tours of Acadia National Park as part of the park's Naturalist Program. The three-hour tour includes a stop at the Islesford Museum. There is also a sunset dinner cruise available, which includes a meal stop at the Isleford Dock Restaurant.

Whale Watcher, Inc.

1 West Street, corner of West and Maine, next to the Town Pier, Bar Harbor
(207) 288-3322 or (800) 508-1499
For more information, visit
  www.acadiainfo.com/whalewatcher.htm

Board the *Whale Watcher* for a three-and-a-half-hour adventure into the Gulf of Maine in search of great whales. The vessel, which is over 105 feet in length, leaves Bar Harbor through the Porcupine Islands, past Egg Rock Lighthouse and Acadia National Park, and ventures some 20 miles out to sea. An experienced naturalist answers questions and provides information on whales, other marine mammals, and the many varieties of sea birds that you may encounter.

Central Maine

Belgrade Lakes Mail Boat

Belgrade Lakes
(207) 495-7716

The Belgrade Lakes Mail Boat offers cruises for families on a 24-foot pontoon mail boat providing a view of the rustic Belgrade Lakes area. Great Pond was the inspiration for the movie *On Golden Pond,* and the cruise includes some history on this subject. The cruises leave daily from the Belgrade Lakes Post Office on Main Street. Custom cruises on Great Pond are also available.

Maine Wilderness Tours

RR2, Belgrade
(207) 465-4333
For more information, visit
  www.mainewildernesstours.com

Maine Wilderness Tours offers numerous recreation options in the central Maine region. Some of the day trips are perfect for children. On the canoe trip, guides and equipment are included, and the trip down Belgrade Stream concludes with a full lobster picnic. Day fishing trips are also available to families. Kayaking trips on Belgrade Lake offer opportunities for bird watching, hiking, and swimming.

North Country Rivers

East Vassalboro
(888) 348-8871
For more information, visit
www.ncrivers.com

North Country offers several types of rafting packages, including customized whitewater trips. The minimum age for a North Country passenger is 10 years. The company runs trips every day from April to October, including both overnight and day excursions on the Penobscot, Kennebec, and Dead Rivers.

Western Maine

Adventure Bound Rafting

Route 201, Caratunk
(207) 672-4300
For more information, visit
www.adv-bound.com

Adventure Bound Rafting designs custom family trips ranging from one-day to weeklong excursions. Trips can include rafting and kayaking, ropes courses, climbing-wall practice, and hikes to Moxie Falls, Maine's highest waterfall. The Adventure Bound sports complex near the Kennebec River has a heated pool and a 24-person hot tub, allowing families to relax after an eventful day on the river. Overnight accommodations are available.

Bethel Outdoor Adventure

Route 2, Bethel
(207) 824-4224
For more information, visit
www.betheloutdooradventure.com

Bethel Outdoor Adventure has several boating and cruising options. At their center, you can rent kayaks and canoes, hire Registered Maine Guides, and sign up for a guided pontoon-boat ride. The trips vary in length and location. The pontoon ride on Lake Umbagog boasts moose sightings and views of bald eagle nests.

Downriver Guide Service

Farmington
(207) 634-3688
For more information, visit
www.downriverguideservice.com

Downriver is a small, family-run guide service that customizes canoe day trips on the Kennebec River. The trips can include a variety of activities, including swimming and tubing, fishing, and observing wildlife and flora. The trips cater to children of all ages, and child care is available for very young children.

The Mountain House

Route 4, Oquossoc
(207) 864-5661
For more information, visit
www.etravelmaine.com/mooselod

For an interesting look at the Rangeley Lake area and its wildlife, Mountain House offers boat tours on Rangeley and Mooselookmeguntic Lakes led by Registered Maine Guides. They operate a 24-foot pontoon boat on Rangeley Lake and a 15-foot Scout boat on Mooselookmeguntic.

Moxie Outdoor Adventures

Lake Moxie Camp, off Route 201,
The Forks
(800) 866-6943
For more information, visit
http://wild-rivers.com/aaa/vacation.html

Moxie Outdoor Adventures' rafting department leads whitewater day trips down the Kennebec, Dead, and Penobscot Rivers. The lower river trips on the Kennebec, with class III rapids, are options for children as young as 4. The split-trip option on the Kennebec is perfect for families with children over the age of six—older children can raft the wilder water in the upper Kennebec Gorge and meet up with the rest of the family at the lower stretch of river. Lunch is provided, and there is time to swim in the calmer waters. Family trips in inflatable kayaks are offered on the Dead River and include a picnic lunch. Inflatable kayak trips are available on the Lower Kennebec as well—a seven-mile calm stretch ideal for families. Camping and guided overnights are available on all three rivers.

Saco River Canoe & Kayak

Route 5, Fryeburg
(207) 935-2369

Explore the beautiful Saco River, nestled in the foothills of the majestic White Mountains in the charming village of Fryeburg. Enjoy a leisurely one-day trip around Mt. Tom to Walker's Bridge, an overnight journey downriver to Lovewell's Pond in Brownfield, or a three-day trip ending in Hiram.

Northern Maine

Allagash Canoe Trips

Greenville
(207) 237-3077
For more information, visit
  www.allagashcanoetrips.com

Get away from it all by canoe-camping in the north woods of Maine and eastern Canada. A guided trip gives you the opportunity to enjoy a relaxed adventure with plenty of free time and no worries about logistics, meal preparation, decision making, camp chores, and transportation. Guides can teach you about the North Country, canoeing, and camping (how to use a setting pole in shallow rapids, for example, or how to bake fresh breads before an open fire).

The Birches Resort Wilderness Expeditions

Off Routes 6/15, Moosehead Lake,
  Rockwood
(800) 825-9453
For more information, visit
  www.birches.com

The Birches Resort is located amid 11,000 acres of wilderness and offers many family oriented trips, including inner-tube float adventures and boat rentals. Whitewater rafting trips are also available for the whole family. One of the resort's most popular attractions is the moose cruise on Moosehead Lake.

Katahdin Cruises

North Main Street, Greenville
(207) 695-2716
For more information, visit
  www.katahdincruises.com

Katahdin Cruises offers several cruising options on Moosehead Lake. The antique steamboat S.S. *Katahdin* has several decks, narrated tours, and a galley. Cruises vary in time and content, and the ship is available for private charters and cruises. The cruises depart from the Moosehead Marine Museum. The *Katahdin* itself is the main exhibit of the museum, which also houses many exhibits on steamboating history. A fireworks cruise is available on the Fourth of July.

Moosehead Adventures

Birch Point Road, Greenville
(207) 695-4434
For more information, visit
  www.kynd.net/~kayak/

Moosehead Adventures employs Registered Maine Guides for customized kayaking tours. Tours are available on Moosehead Lake as well as several surrounding ponds and rivers. Wildlife observed in the area includes moose and loons. Some kayaking trips include hikes on Mt. Kineo. Family tours with tandem kayaks are popular. Beginners are welcome.

New England Outdoor Center

Medway Road, Millinocket
(800) 766-7238

For more information, visit www.neoc.com

New England Outdoor Center is a whitewater outfitter serving the Kennebec and Penobscot River regions. The base facilities include a family restaurant, fully equipped lakeside cabins, and a charming bed and breakfast. Take out a canoe on the lake for free or soak in a hot tub.

Northwoods Outfitters

Maine Street, Greenville
(207) 695-3288

For more information, visit www.maineoutfitter.com

Northwoods offers guided and self-guided canoe, kayak, and fishing trips in the Moose-head Lake region. Moose safaris are available, as are moonlight kayak trips and island hops. The equipment available for rent includes kayaks, canoes, personal flotation devices (PFDs), paddles, and camping gear.

chapter 4

Books

Introduction...30

A Celebration of Maine Children's Books...30

Picture Books...30

Ages 3 and up...30

Ages 4 and up...32

Ages 5 and up...32

Ages 6 and up...34

Ages 7 and up...35

Ages 8 and up...35

Ages 9 and up...37

Ages 12 and up...37

Books for all ages...37

Books

The following list is a selection of children's books about Maine. The titles listed include many favorites, organized first by age level, then by author. *A Celebration of Maine Children's Books* (see listing), by Lynn Plourde and Paul Knowles, was a useful resource in choosing books for our list, as was the Children's Bookseller at Borders in South Portland, who provided the age-level recommendations. However, we are sure that there are other excellent Maine books we have missed, and some about to be published as this list goes to print. We hope that our selection shares Maine's unique charm and spirit and that these books will continue to be enjoyed by parents, grandparents, and visitors to our great state.

PLOURDE, LYNN AND
KNOWLES, PAUL

A Celebration of Maine Children's Books

1998, University of Maine Press

This listing of 185 Maine children's books includes related activities, as well as author and illustrator biographies. The descriptions are rich and informative and serve as an invaluable guide for teachers, parents, and anyone who wants to know about the wealth of Maine children's books available.

Picture Books

AGELL, CHARLOTTE

Mud Makes Me Dance in the Spring

I Wear Long Green Hair in Summer

Wind Spins Me Around in the Fall

Slide Into the White of Winter

1994, Tilbury House

Offering a playful look at Maine's four seasons, these four small picture books are ideal for the very young.

I Swam with a Seal

1995, Gulliver Books, Harcourt Brace

This picture book, written in rhyme with simple drawings, is a delightful way for young children to learn about Maine animals.

Ages 3 and Up

COONEY, BARBARA

Island Boy

1988, Viking

This picture book has the feel of a biography as it tells the life story of an island boy who leaves for the mainland, but returns to his true place on the island to live out his life as a fisherman. Cooney based this story on a real person and depicted the life of a fisherman in detailed text and paintings.

Miss Rumphius

1982, Viking

Miss Rumphius has received the American Book and Lupine awards and is a multigenerational favorite. Miss Rumphius is a memorable character who lives an independent life, traveling and living by the sea. She finds a wonderful way "to make the world a more beautiful place." Cooney based this character on a real person who used to plant lupine seeds along the Maine coast.

MCCLOSKEY, ROBERT

Blueberries for Sal

1948, Penguin Putnam

A favorite children's story for more than 50 years, this story features Sal, who goes blueberrying with her mother, and Little Bear, who goes blueberry hunting with *his* mother. The fun begins when they get lost and follow each other's mothers.

Burt Dow, Deep-Water Man

1963, Viking

Burt Dow is a retired Maine fisherman who convinces a whale to temporarily swallow him and his boat, the *Tidely-Idely,* in order to be saved from a big storm. A funny adventure that takes place in a colorful Maine sea setting.

One Morning in Maine

1952, Viking (hardcover); Penguin Putnam (paperback)

Follow a young Maine girl in her daily life on the Maine coast as she loses a tooth, goes on a boat ride, and visits with community members in Bucks Harbor.

PLOURDE, LYNN

Moose, of Course

1999, Down East Books

This book is packed with the kind of silly action that young children love. A boy heads north to see a moose and has numerous adventures along the way. In the end, the moose finds him! The language play ("bonkity bonk") adds to the pleasure of this book.

Pigs in the Mud in the Middle of the Rud

1997, Blue Sky Press/Scholastic Trade

Maine humor in the vein of comedian Tim Sample appears in this very funny book ("rud" is a local way of saying "road"). Maine is known for having a mud season, and in this story Grandma and her family cannot drive down the "rud" because pigs and a variety of country animals are blocking the way. The language play helps to make this a highly entertaining book.

SMITH, HARRY W.

ABC's of Maine

1980, Down East Books

This delightful alphabet book features typical Maine objects, scenes, and characters.

SMITH, MAGGIE

Counting Our Way to Maine

1995, Orchard Books

This book follows a family's vacation trip to Maine. On each page there are things to count, all the way to twenty.

Ages 4 and up

APPELBAUM, DIANA

Cocoa Ice

1997, Orchard Books

The trade in Caribbean cocoa and Maine ice a century ago links two girls and their families.

BROWN, MARGARET WISE

The Little Island

1947, Doubleday

This Caldecott Award winner from the 1940s tells about seasonal changes, with reflections on the nature of an island.

CHETKOWSKI, EMILY

Mabel Takes the Ferry

1995, J.N. Townsend Publishing

Mabel, a delightful character based on Chetkowski's real dog, has an adventure when she takes a ride by herself on a ferryboat to a Maine island. The setting includes nice local details.

HOPKINSON, DEBORAH

Birdie's Lighthouse

1997, Simon & Schuster

This fictional picture-book diary is based on the real lives of brave female members of lighthouse keepers' families who lived 150 years ago. Beautifully illustrated, this tall and narrow book reminds one of the special architecture of lighthouses.

ROCKWELL, ANNE

Ferryboat Ride!

1999, Crown Publishers; reprint ed. 2000, Random House

This book would make a delightful take-home memory for anyone who has ridden on a ferry. Detailed watercolors support the narration of a young girl who describes her ride.

SHETTERLY, SUSAN HAND

Shelterwood

1999, Tilbury House

A girl learns about the Maine woods when she spends the summer with her grandfather.

Ages 5 and up

BACON, JOY

Oliver Bean's Halloween

1998, Windswept House Publishers

This is a charming book that captures elementary school life in a small Maine town.

BENSON, ROSIE

Fessic the Eddy School Cat

1999, self-published

This sweet story is based on a real-life event in which a cat was adopted by a Maine elementary school in Edgecomb.

HASSETT, JOHN AND ANN

Moose on the Loose

1987, Down East Books

Max the Moose satisfies his curiosity about people through humorous escapades during a visit to Bangor, Maine.

HOLMAN, DORIS ANNE

Come with Me to the Sea

1998, self-published

Vibrant watercolors splash across the pages of this poetic picture book that takes readers on a visit to Maine's coast.

JACOBSEN, JENNIFER

Moon Sandwich Mom

1999, Albert Whitman & Co.

When his artist mom is too busy to play, a young fox leaves home to spend time with the moms of other animals. In the end he finds out which mom is best for him. Native Maine animals are the characters in this humorous picture book.

LASKY, KATHRYN

Marven of the Great North Woods

1997, Harcourt

This picture book captures the feel of logging camps in the North American woods a century ago through beautiful pictures by local artist Kevin Hawkes. The story is about young Marven, who is sent to a logging camp to avoid exposure to a deadly flu.

MACDONALD, AMY

Little Beaver and the Echo

1990, G.P. Putnam's Sons

Little Beaver's echo answers his call for friends. As he searches for the voice, he meets wonderful Maine animals who befriend him. This book has outstanding watercolor illustrations.

MALLET, DAVID

Inch by Inch: The Garden Song

1995, HarperTrophy

This is a whimsically illustrated interpretation of Maine native Dave Mallet's famous song.

MCCLOSKEY, ROBERT

Time of Wonder

1957, Penguin Putnam

Whether readers have ever visited a Maine island or not, they will be charmed by this gorgeous book with large, colorful illustrations that speak of daily island life, changes in weather, and preparations for an impending storm. This is a wonderful book for the whole family.

ROOP, PETER AND CONNIE

Keep the Lights Burning, Abbie

1985, Carolrhoda Books

One of the best accounts written of Abbie Burgess, a lighthouse keeper's daughter who, in the mid-1800s, tended the lighthouse during a fierce storm while her father was away. Abbie's heroism is well presented in this book for early readers.

RYDER, JOANNE

A House by the Sea

1994, William Morrow & Co.

A boy imagines what it would be like to live in a house by the sea. While not specific to the Maine coast, this book is illustrated by popular Maine illustrator Melissa Sweet.

SCARPINO, JANE

Nellie, the Lighthouse Dog

1993, Windswept House Publishers

A wire-haired fox terrier saves the day at Maine's Marshall Point Lighthouse.

Ages 6 and up

BAILER, DARICE

Puffin's Homecoming: The Story of an Atlantic Puffin

1993, Soundprints

This is a science book about an Atlantic puffin who comes home to the same Maine island each spring.

BERNIER, EVARISTE

Baxter Bear and Moses Moose

1990, Down East Books

Baxter is a Maine black bear with a problem: he collects hats and needs a hat rack. Moses the Moose also has a problem: his feet are cold! In this humorous picture book the two meet and find a way to help each other.

GIBBONS, GAIL

Gulls, Gulls, Gulls

1997, Holiday House

Beacons of Light: Lighthouses

1990, William Morrow & Co.

Anyone who summers on the Maine coast will appreciate the information included in these two colorfully illustrated books.

IPCAR, DAHLOV

Lobsterman

1962, Random House; reprint ed. Down East Books

An artistically illustrated story of a boy who grows up to become a lobster fisherman. More of Ipcar's art can be seen in Maine museums.

My Wonderful Christmas Tree

1999, Down East Books

Imaginatively illustrated, this holiday poem depicts scenes of a Maine farm on a winter night.

MATHER, KAREN

Silas the Bookstore Cat

1994, Down East Books

Silas is based on a real cat that used to live in a small bookstore in Brunswick. This book tells of his interactions with a boy who visits the store, and has a message to encourage young readers.

WEINBERGER, JANE

Cory, the Cormorant

1993, Windswept House Publishers

A young cormorant is befriended by a well-meaning grandmother.

Stormy

1985, Windswept House Publishers

A storm petrel finds a burrow on Great Duck Island.

Wee Peter Puffin

1984, Windswept House Publishers

The words and music for the poem "There Once Was a Puffin" are included in this colorful book about the puffins of Matinicus Rock.

Ages 7 and up

ALVORD, DOUGLAS

Sarah's Boat

1994, Tilbury House

Exciting story about a 12-year-old girl training for a sailboat race on the coast of Maine. It includes diagrams and technical information about sailing.

DODD, ANNE WESTCOTT

The Story of the Sea Glass

1999, Down East Books

A grandmother and her granddaughter go walking along the Maine coast and discover beautiful sea glass. As they walk, the grandmother tells a story from her own childhood. This book contains beautiful watercolors and directions for making sea glass sun-catchers.

POCHOCKI, ETHEL

A Penny for a Hundred

1996, Down East Books

Set in Aroostook County during World War II, this book describes a cross-cultural friendship between a youngster in a Maine potato-farming family and a German P.O.W. when workers from the prison camp were sent to help with the fall harvest.

Rosebud and Red Flannel

1991, Henry Holt & Co.; reprint ed. 1999, Down East Books

A symbolic love story takes place between a pair of red flannel long-johns and an elegant nightgown. They find themselves hung out on a clothesline when a snowstorm blows in.

Ages 8 and up

BRUCHAC, JOSEPH

Gluskabe and the Four Wishes

1995, Cobblehill Books/Dutton

Gluskabe is a mythical Great-Spirit helper in Maine Native American Abenaki mythology. In this tale, Gluskabe grants wishes to four men who make a journey to his island. One of the men learns the meaning of patience and unselfish wishes.

CERULLO, MARY

Lobsters, Gangsters of the Sea

1994, Cobblehill Books

Lobsters, lobstering, and lobster lore are thoroughly explained in this book of colorful photographs.

FAZIO, WENDE

Acadia National Park (True Book series)

1998, Scholastic Library Publishing

An informational overview of the park's history, geography, and wildlife. Includes activities and photos.

FENDLER, DONN

Lost on a Mountain in Maine

1939, 1992, William Morrow & Co.; several reprint editions available from other publishers

The dramatic account of a 12-year-old boy who spent nine days lost on Mount Katahdin.

LAFAYE, A.

Strawberry Hill

1999, Simon & Schuster; reprint ed. 2000, Aladdin Library

An intermediate novel about a young teenage girl who gets to know an isolated native in the small Maine town where she summers with her family.

LEVIN, BETTY

Island Bound

1997, Greenwillow Books

Two teens encounter adventure and suspense on a haunted Maine island.

MARTIN, JACQUELINE BRIGGS

Snowflake Bentley

1998, Houghton Mifflin Company

Tells the life story of Wilson Bentley of Vermont, who discovered a way to photograph snowflakes. It has won the Lupine and Caldecott awards and captures the essence of New England with its beautiful woodcuts by Mary Azarian.

MASON, CHERIE

Wild Fox: A True Story

1993, Down East Books

This enthralling story is based on Mason's true-life interactions with an injured fox pup who regularly returned to her yard.

MCMILLAN, BRUCE

Grandfather's Trolley

1995, Candlewick Press

Photographer McMillan shows life in a small Maine town at the turn of the century using techniques that create old-fashioned–looking photos. The story follows a trolleyman and his granddaughter, for whom he always saves a seat.

THORSON, KRISTINE AND ROBERT

Stone Wall Secrets

1998, Tilbury House

A boy and his grandfather learn about the geology and early settlers while they repair a stone wall.

VAUGHAN, MARCIA

Abbie Against the Storm

1999, Beyond Words Publishing, Inc.

Abbie Burgess, the real-life daughter of a lighthouse keeper, tended the light by herself during a fierce storm while her father was away. Captures the drama and power of Abbie's story.

Ages 9 and up

Books for all ages

BENEDUCE, ANN KAY

A Weekend with Winslow Homer

1993, Rizzoli International Publications

Introduces children to the artist Winslow Homer, who spent much of his later life working and living in Prout's Neck, just south of Scarborough.

SHEPARD, STEVEN

Fogbound

1993, Landmark Editions

A 13-year-old Maine student wrote this intermediate-level novel. Set on the coast of Maine, it is a suspenseful tale with a message.

SIMPSON, DOROTHY

Island in the Bay

1956, Lippincott; reprint ed. 1993, Blackberry Books

This novel for young adults is a suspenseful coming-of-age story that takes place in a fishing community modeled on Criehaven.

Ages 12 and up

FLEISCHMAN, PAUL

Whirligig

1998, Henry Holt & Co.

The story of a 16-year-old boy who kills a young girl in a car accident. Given an unusual sentence by the girl's father, he travels to the four corners of the United States, including Maine, to build whirligigs in her honor.

CARPENTER, MIMI

What the Sea Left Behind

1981, Down East Books

Beachcombers will appreciate this nature book, which presents various treasures from the Maine ocean in beautiful paintings.

DEAN, JULIA

A Year on Monhegan Island

1995, Ticknor and Fields

Photographer Dean shows us life on Monhegan Island, including scenes in a one-room schoolhouse, the beginning of lobstering season, and the summer tourist season. Winner of the Lupine Award in 1995.

DIETZ, LEW

The Story of Andre

1979, Down East Books

The life of Maine's most famous and most personable seal, who traveled each year from the New England Aquarium in Boston to Rockport Harbor, Maine.

ENGFER, LEEANNE

Maine (part of the *Hello, USA* series)

1991, Lerner Publications

This fact-filled book of photographs is a great overview of Maine's geography, history, points of interest, and trivia.

HARRINGTON, TY

Maine: America the Beautiful

1992, Children's Press

This book is a great compilation of facts and photographs. Clearly written, and a good reference for people of all ages who want to know more about our wonderful state.

JENECZKO, PAUL

Brickyard Summer

1989, Orchard Books

Poet and teacher Paul Janeczko describes his childhood in the mill town of Lewiston in this collection of original poems.

OWENS, MARY BETH

Be Blest: A Celebration of Seasons

1999, Simon & Schuster

Inspired by a prayer of Saint Francis of Assisi, this book describes the beauty of Maine's dramatic seasons.

chapter 5

Things to Cook

With Blueberries...40

Blueberry Smoothie...40
Blueberry Buckle...40
Blueberry Muffins...40
Blueberry Dump-It Cake...41
Blueberry Kuchen...41
Blueberry Poppy Seed Coffee Cake...41
Blueberry Cookie "Pizza"...42

Cookies and Candy...42

Colossal Cookies...42
Sunflower Blossom Cookies...42
Chocolate Raspberry Pretzel Cookies...43
Easy Reindeer Cookies...43
Grandma's Potato Candy...43
Whoopie Pies...44
Maine Needhams...44

Breakfast...44

Nona Angela's Pancakes...44
Puffin Eggs...45
Maine Monkey Bread...45
Raspberry and Lemon Yogurt Muffins...45
Happy-Face Toast...45
On-the-Go Maine Burrito...46
Spider Rolls...46

Main Meal...46

Peanut Butter Pasta Salad...46
Stone Soup...47
Potato Soup...47
Hobo Potatoes...47
Campfire Corn on the Cob...48
Zucchini "Pizza"...48

Desserts...48

Fresh Apple Cake...48
Old-Fashioned Maine Apple Crisp...48
Homemade Applesauce...49
Autumn Baked Apples...49
Indian Pudding...49
Sea Moss Pudding...50
Chocolate Raspberry Dream Cake...50
Ice Cream in a Baggie...50
Snow "Ice Cream"...50

Gifts from the Kitchen...51

Cinnamon Ornaments...51
Ana's People Chow...51
Dog Biscuits...51
Hot Chocolate Mix...51
Bean Soup Mix in a Mason Jar...52
Vegetable Bean Soup...52

Things to Cook

With Blueberries

Blueberry Smoothie

Makes 2 servings. You'll need a blender for this recipe.

1 banana, cut in slices
$^1/_2$ cup washed blueberries (or use $^1/_2$ cup raspberries or 6 large strawberries)
$1^1/_2$ cups vanilla yogurt
1 cup milk
2 tablespoons sugar

STEPS

1. Put all ingredients in blender.
2. Blend until smooth.

Blueberry Buckle

2 cups flour
$^3/_4$ cup sugar
$^1/_2$ teaspoon salt
1 teaspoon baking powder
$^1/_4$ cup butter, softened
$^1/_2$ cup milk
1 egg
2 cups Maine blueberries (fresh or frozen)

TOPPING

$^1/_3$ cup flour
1 teaspoon cinnamon
$^1/_2$ cup sugar
$^1/_2$ stick softened butter

STEPS

1. Preheat oven to 350°.
2. Sift together flour, sugar, salt, and baking powder and stir well.
3. Add butter, milk, and egg and mix well.
4. Carefully fold in blueberries.
5. Pour into greased 9-inch square pan.
6. In a small bowl, stir together the first 3 topping ingredients. Add butter and mix with fingers until crumbly.
7. Top the batter with this mixture.
8. Bake for 40 to 50 minutes, until toothpick comes out clean. Cool 5 to 10 minutes before serving.

Blueberry Muffins

Makes 8 large or 12 small muffins.

2 cups sifted flour
$^1/_2$ teaspoon salt
3 teaspoons baking powder
$^1/_2$ cup sugar
1 cup milk
2 teaspoons lemon juice
1 egg, well beaten
$^1/_4$ cup oil
1 cup blueberries (fresh or frozen)

STEPS

1. Preheat oven to 375°.
2. Sift flour, salt, baking powder, and sugar together in one bowl.
3. In a second bowl, beat together egg, milk, oil, and lemon juice.
4. Add liquid ingredients to dry ingredients and stir briefly (until damp but still lumpy).
5. Fold in berries gently.
6. Fill paper-lined or greased muffin tins three-quarters full.
7. Sprinkle tops with cinnamon and sugar and bake for 25 minutes or until golden in color.

Blueberry Dump-It Cake

1 can blueberry pie filling

1 small box yellow cake mix (enough to make one 8- or 9-inch layer)

1 stick (½ cup) butter or margarine

1 cup chopped pecans

STEPS

1. Preheat oven to 350°.
2. Spread blueberry pie filling into 8-inch square baking dish that has been sprayed with non-stick vegetable spray.
3. Sprinkle dry cake mix on top.
4. Melt butter or margarine in small saucepan and pour evenly over the cake mix.
5. Sprinkle pecans over top.
6. Bake 45 minutes.

Blueberry Kuchen

1 cup flour

2 tablespoons sugar

Pinch of salt

½ cup butter (firm)

1 tablespoon white vinegar

3 cups blueberries

¾ cup sugar

2 tablespoons flour

Dash of cinnamon

STEPS

1. Preheat oven to 400°.
2. Combine first 5 ingredients in a bowl with clean fingertips until crumbly.
3. Press into bottom and sides of small springform pan (a 9-inch square pan works, too).
4. Combine 2 cups of the berries with the sugar, flour, and cinnamon. Pour into pan.
5. Bake for about 45 minutes, until crust is brown. Remove from oven and sprinkle last cup of berries over top while still hot.
6. Serve warm or cooled with whipped cream.

Blueberry Poppy Seed Coffee Cake

⅔ cup sugar

½ cup margarine (softened)

2 teaspoons grated lemon rind

1 egg

1½ cups flour

2 tablespoons poppy seeds

½ teaspoon baking soda

¼ teaspoon salt

½ cup sour cream

TOPPING

2 cups fresh or frozen Maine blueberries (washed and drained)

⅓ cup sugar

2 teaspoons flour

¼ teaspoon nutmeg

STEPS

1. Preheat oven to 350°.
2. Combine sugar and margarine and beat until light and fluffy.
3. Add lemon and egg and mix well.
4. In another bowl, combine flour, poppy seeds, baking soda, and salt and mix well.
5. Add to the sugar mix alternately with sour cream.
6. Spread batter across bottom and sides of 9-inch round or square greased and floured cake pan.
7. Mix all topping ingredients together and place on top of batter.
8. Bake for 45 minutes or until crust is golden.

Blueberry Cookie "Pizza"

CRUST

Pre-made frozen piecrust (thawed),
or substitute prepared pizza dough

TOPPING

Raspberry or strawberry jam

Chocolate chips

Blueberries

Nuts (peanuts or almonds)

Flaked coconut

STEPS

1. Coat 12-inch pizza pan or cookie sheet with cooking spray.
2. Press piecrust or pizza dough onto the pan.
3. Bake according to dough directions.
4. Once crust has cooled, spread raspberry preserves evenly over cooked crust to within 1 inch of the edge. Sprinkle chocolate chips, blueberries, nuts, and flaked coconut evenly over the preserves.
5. Cut the cookie "pizza" into wedge-shaped slices.

Cookies and Candy

Colossal Cookies

Kids love these! No flour! Makes approximately 6 dozen 2-inch cookies.

1 stick ($^1/_2$ cup) margarine (softened)

$1^1/_2$ cups sugar

$1^1/_2$ cups brown sugar

4 eggs

$2^1/_2$ teaspoons baking soda

2 teaspoons vanilla

18-oz. jar crunchy peanut butter

6 cups oatmeal (either quick-cooking or regular oats will work)

12-oz. package chocolate chips

STEPS

1. Preheat oven to 350°.
2. In very large bowl, beat together the first 6 ingredients.
3. Add peanut butter and oatmeal by cupfuls.
4. As mixture becomes sticky, add chocolate chips. Mix well.
5. Drop by heaping spoonfuls on greased cookie sheet. Bake for 12 to 15 minutes. Cool before removing from pan.

Sunflower Blossom Cookies

Makes about 3 dozen

$1^3/_4$ cups flour

1 teaspoon baking soda

$^1/_2$ teaspoon salt

$^1/_2$ cup butter

$^1/_2$ cup peanut butter

$^1/_2$ cup sugar

$^1/_2$ cup brown sugar

1 egg

2 tablespoons milk

1 teaspoon vanilla

Hershey Kisses (9-oz. bag)

STEPS

1. Preheat oven to 375°.
2. Combine first 3 ingredients in small bowl.
3. In a large bowl, cream together next 4 ingredients.
4. Add egg, milk, and vanilla to the butter and sugar mixture.
5. Add the flour mixture to the creamed mixture and mix well.
6. Shape into balls and place on ungreased cookie sheet.
7. Bake for 8 minutes. Remove from oven and press unwrapped Hershey Kiss into center of each cookie.
8. Return to oven and bake $2^1/_2$ minutes more.
9. Cool thoroughly before removing from cookie sheet.

Chocolate Raspberry Pretzel Cookies

Submitted by Chef Barelman, Executive Chef on the MS Maasdam, *a cruise ship that visited Maine for the first time in 1999. This German chef works in the metric system. We have made the conversions for you. A piping kit (often sold in grocery stores in the frosting section) is helpful for this recipe, but not required.*

Makes about 2 dozen

> *500 grams of flour* = 2 cups plus 3 table-spoons
>
> *250 grams unsalted butter* = 2 sticks plus 1½ tablespoons
>
> *200 grams confectioners' sugar* = ¾ cup plus 2 tablespoons
>
> 2 whole eggs
>
> *225 grams chocolate chips* = 1 cup
>
> 1 small jar raspberry jam

STEPS

1. Preheat oven to 180° C (375° F).
2. Cream butter and sugar. Add eggs. Gradually add flour.
3. Pipe dough onto cookie sheets in any pretzel shape desired, or roll dough in small, ¼-inch-thick logs and twist to desired shape. Try to make the individual "pretzels" consistent in shape as much as possible.
4. Bake for 15 minutes; watch closely. Cool for 10 minutes.
5. Stick 2 pretzels together with raspberry jam to make cookies.
6. Melt 1 cup chocolate chips, uncovered, in microwave on high for 1 minute. Stir well. Continue microwaving in 10-second intervals until completely melted, stirring after each interval until smooth.
7. Dip an end of each cookie in melted chocolate and let cool until chocolate is firm.

Easy Reindeer Cookies

Makes 30 cookies

> 20-oz. package refrigerated sliceable peanut butter cookie dough
>
> 60 small round (2-inch) pretzel twists
>
> 60 semisweet chocolate morsels
>
> 30 red candy-coated chocolate pieces

STEPS

1. Preheat oven to 350°.
2. Put dough in freezer for 15 minutes.
3. Cut dough into 30 quarter-inch-thick slices. Place 4 inches apart on ungreased cookie sheets.
4. Using your fingers, pinch the edge of each slice at 10 o'clock and 2 o'clock on the circle to make a shallow dent.
5. Press a pretzel into each "pinch" to make the antlers. Press in chocolate morsels for eyes.
6. Bake for 9 to 11 minutes, or until lightly browned. Remove from oven and press in red candy for nose.
7. Cool on cookie sheets for 2 minutes; transfer to wire racks to cool.

Grandma's Potato Candy

Makes 6 servings

> 1 Maine potato, baked
>
> 1½ cups confectioners' sugar
>
> ⅔ cup peanut butter
>
> ⅔ cup chocolate morsels

STEPS

1. Mash potato. Add enough confectioners' sugar to make the consistency of stiff cookie dough.
2. Roll out to a ⅛-inch-thick rectangle.
3. Spread with peanut butter. Melt chocolate bits and spread over the peanut butter.
4. Roll up jellyroll-style and cut into half-inch slices.

Courtesy of the Maine Potato Board, Presque Isle, Maine.

Whoopie Pies

Makes 8 to 10 pies.

6 tablespoons shortening
1 cup sugar
1 egg
1 cup milk
1 teaspoon vanilla
2 cups flour
1½ teaspoons baking soda
5 heaping tablespoons cocoa
1 teaspoon salt

FILLING

¾ cup shortening
¾ cup confectioners' sugar
6 tablespoons Marshmallow Fluff
1 teaspoon vanilla

STEPS

1. Preheat oven to 375°.
2. In large bowl, cream sugar and shortening.
3. Mix in the rest of the ingredients.
4. Drop on greased cookie sheet by heaping teaspoon.
5. Bake for 10 minutes. Cool on wire rack.
6. Mix filling ingredients with beater until fluffy.
7. Put 2 cookies together with filling between to make pies.

Maine Needhams

Hot wax used in this recipe! Adult supervision suggested.

¾ cup mashed potato
½ teaspoon salt
2 pounds confectioners' sugar
1 stick (½ cup) butter
½ pound flaked coconut
2 teaspoons vanilla
12-oz. package chocolate chips
4 squares unsweetened chocolate
½ cake (2 oz.) paraffin wax

STEPS

1. Peel and cook enough Maine-grown potatoes (about 2 or 3) to make ¾ cup mashed potato. Do not use salt and pepper when making the mashed potatoes; just add the milk and butter you normally would. Set aside.
2. Melt butter in top of large double boiler. When it's melted, add the mashed potatoes, confectioners' sugar, coconut, vanilla, and salt. Mix well.
3. Spread out mixture on a buttered cookie sheet or pan and place in refrigerator to harden. When hard, cut into small squares to dip into the chocolate mixture.
4. Using your just-cleaned double boiler, melt the paraffin wax. When melted, stir in the unsweetened chocolate and the chocolate chips until all is melted and smooth.
5. Using a slotted spoon or tongs, dip each square of hardened potato mixture into the chocolate mixture and place on waxed paper to cool.

Breakfast

Nona Angela's Pancakes

2 cups flour
5 teaspoons baking powder
1 teaspoon salt
¼ cup sugar
2 eggs
1 or 2 individual-size fruit yogurt of choice
2 cups milk
2 tablespoons vegetable oil

STEPS

1. Mix all ingredients together with a whisk and allow the batter to set for an hour before cooking, if you can wait! If not, go to it—the pancakes always taste good!

Puffin Eggs

Cream of Wheat cereal

Canned peach halves, one per eater

As many saucers or plates as you have eaters

STEPS

1. Cook the Cream of Wheat, following the directions on the box.
2. Pour warm cereal into the saucers.
3. Top with one peach half in the center.
4. Serve while warm with maple syrup or milk.

Maine Monkey Bread

3 packages refrigerated, ready-to-bake biscuits

$1/2$ cup sugar

1 tablespoon cinnamon

$1/2$ cup chopped pecans or walnuts (optional)

SAUCE

$1^1/4$ sticks of butter or margarine

$2/3$ cup sugar

2 teaspoons water

2 teaspoons cinnamon

STEPS

1. Preheat oven to 350°.
1. Bring all the *sauce* ingredients to a boil over low heat in a small saucepan; remove from heat.
2. Combine the $1/2$ cup sugar and the 1 tablespoon cinnamon in a separate dish.
3. Cut each biscuit into quarters.
4. Roll each biscuit piece in the sugar and cinnamon mixture. Place evenly to cover the bottom of an ungreased bundt pan.
5. Pour $1/3$ of the sauce over the biscuits and spread a few of the nuts.
6. Repeat this procedure until all the biscuits have been placed in the bundt pan with the sauce poured over them.
7. Bake for 30 minutes. Remove from the oven and immediately turn over onto a large plate to cool.

Raspberry and Lemon Yogurt Muffins

Makes 1 dozen

2 cups all-purpose flour

$1/2$ cup sugar

1 teaspoon baking powder

1 teaspoon baking soda

$1/2$ teaspoon salt

2 large eggs, beaten lightly

1 (8-oz.) container lemon-flavored yogurt

$1/4$ cup unsalted butter, melted and cooled to room temperature

1 teaspoon grated lemon peel

1 teaspoon vanilla extract

$1^1/2$ cups fresh or frozen raspberries

STEPS

1. Preheat oven to 400°.
2. Combine first 5 ingredients in large bowl.
3. In another bowl, combine next 5 ingredients and mix well.
4. Stir wet mixture into large bowl until just moistened. Do not overmix. Gently fold in raspberries.
5. Fill paper-lined or greased muffin tins three-quarters full.
6. Bake for 18 to 20 minutes.

Happy-Face Toast

You will need paper cups and new paintbrushes for this recipe.

Bread for toasting

Butter

Milk

Food coloring in several colors

STEPS

1. Pour milk in paper cups. Use as many cups as needed for different colors. Add food coloring to each.
2. Paint a face or design on each piece of bread. Toast. Lightly butter. Munch away!

On-the-Go Maine Burrito

1 egg

1 tablespoon milk

1 slice American cheese

1 to 2 tablespoons of salsa

1 small tortilla

1 slice ham (optional)

STEPS

1. Break egg directly into a small microwave-safe bowl (a ramekin works great). Add milk, and lightly beat egg and milk together with a fork or whisk.
2. Place in microwave and cook on High for approximately 1 minute and 20 seconds, or until desired doneness.
3. Warm tortilla in microwave for 10 seconds.
4. Place hot scrambled egg in the middle of the tortilla.
5. Put slice of cheese on top of egg and spoon salsa over cheese. Add ham if desired.
6. Fold bottom of tortilla up onto egg and then fold each side over to form a roll-up. Place in a napkin to catch leaks, or use a small paper cup as a holder.

Spider Rolls

Makes 12 spiders

1 package (1 lb. 9 oz.) frozen Parker House Roll dough, thawed

1 large egg, beaten to blend

¼ cup black sesame seeds or poppy seeds

STEPS

1. To make each spider, use 2 rolls. Dip clean kitchen scissors in flour. Then cut the first roll into 4 equal strips.
2. With floured hands or on a floured board, roll or stretch each strip into a log about 4½ inches long.
3. On a greased 12 x 15–inch baking sheet, set logs parallel to each other, about ¼-inch apart. Bend each log slightly on both ends to resemble spider legs.
4. Cut the second roll apart, making 1 piece

about twice as large as the other. Shape each piece into a smooth ball.
5. Set balls, touching each other, on top of the legs, forming body and head. Gently press on body and head, sticking them onto the legs.
6. Repeat to make remaining spiders, spacing them about 2 inches apart on pan. Cover lightly with plastic wrap.
7. Let rise in a warm place until puffy, 10 to 15 minutes, while you preheat the oven to 350°.
8. Brush dough lightly with beaten egg and sprinkle evenly with sesame or poppy seeds.
9. Bake until golden brown, about 20 minutes. Transfer to racks and let cool.

Main Meal

Peanut Butter Pasta Salad

2 packages ramen noodles

½ cup broccoli

½ to 1 cup carrots (to taste)

½ cup scallions

Cooked chicken chunks (optional)

DRESSING

3 tablespoons rice vinegar

2 tablespoons soy sauce

2 tablespoons peanut butter

⅓ cup olive oil

1 package of seasoning from ramen noodles

STEPS

1. Cook noodles for 3 minutes in boiling water. Set aside.
2. While noodles are cooking, put carrots and broccoli in food processor to cut into very small pieces. Use scissors to snip scallions in quarter-inch pieces.
3. Put all dressing ingredients in a small bowl and whisk to mix well.
4. Drain and rinse noodles. Place in mixing bowl. Add carrots, broccoli, and scallions. Top with dressing and mix.
5. Chill well and serve.

Stone Soup

2 carrots, scraped

2 celery stalks, washed

2 potatoes, peeled

1 medium onion, peeled

1 large, clean Maine stone!

1 (28-oz.) can tomatoes

3 cups chicken broth

1 teaspoon salt

1 bay leaf

$1/4$ teaspoon pepper

$1/2$ cup alphabet pasta

STEPS

1. Cut the carrots, celery, potatoes, and onion into bite-sized pieces. Put them into the pot.
2. Add the stone, tomatoes, chicken broth, salt, bay leaf, and pepper. Mix well.
3. Cook on medium-high heat. When the soup starts to boil, turn down to low and cover the pot. Simmer for 30 minutes.
4. Add the pasta and cook for 10 minutes more.
5. Let the soup cool a bit. Ladle into bowls, removing the bay leaf and stone, and serve.

Potato Soup

Serves 4 to 6

4 large baking potatoes, peeled and cubed

1 cup finely chopped onion

3 tablespoons olive oil

3 cans chicken or vegetable stock (15 oz. each)

1 teaspoon thyme

1 cup milk

2 cups finely grated cheddar cheese, divided

Salt and pepper to taste

STEPS

1. Heat oil in a medium stockpot over medium heat.
2. Add chopped onions and sauté until soft (about 5 minutes).
3. Add potatoes, 2 cans of the stock, and the thyme.

4. Cover and simmer over medium heat until potatoes are tender, about 20 minutes, stirring often. Add more stock if necessary.
5. With a large spoon or a potato masher, lightly mash potatoes, leaving small chunks. Taste and add salt and pepper if necessary. Soup should be thick.
6. Add milk and 1 cup of the cheese and continue to heat over low heat until heated through. *Once milk is added, do not let soup boil again.*
7. Serve in large mugs and sprinkle with remaining cheese, if desired. This soup freezes well.

Hobo Potatoes

7 slices bacon

3 large potatoes

$1/2$ teaspoon salt

$1/2$ teaspoon pepper

1 large onion

$1/2$ pound cheddar cheese, cubed

1 stick butter or margarine, cubed

STEPS

1. Preheat oven to 350°.
2. Fry bacon in pan and drain on paper towels. When cool enough to touch, crumble bacon into small pieces.
3. Peel potatoes, slice them $1/4$-inch thick and place on foil. Sprinkle with salt and pepper and the bacon.
4. Peel onion and cut into thin slices; put on top.
5. Sprinkle cheese and butter or margarine cubes over potato/bacon mixture.
6. Wrap foil up tightly in one large bundle and place on a cookie sheet.
7. Bake for 40 minutes, or until fork-tender.

Campfire Corn on the Cob

6 to 8 freshly picked ears of corn, husked

Large aluminum foil bags (Reynolds Hot Bags)

$1/4$ cup water

Salt

Butter

STEPS

1. Place ears of corn inside foil bag in a single layer. Sprinkle with water and season with salt.
2. Fold top of foil bag and seal securely. Place bag directly on hot grill rack over campfire or barbecue grill.
3. Grill for approximately 8 minutes, then turn bag over (using pot holders) and continue cooking approximately 8 more minutes, or until desired tenderness is reached.
4. Season with butter and salt.

Zucchini "Pizza"

This is a great recipe, especially for using those extra large zucchini that grow to be the size of a small baseball bat.

Large zucchini

Pizza sauce

Cheese

Toppings of your choice: salami, green pepper, black olives, etc.

STEPS

1. Preheat oven to 350°.
2. Wash zucchini.
3. Working the long way, slice the zucchini into long, flat strips, $1/2$-inch thick.
4. Lay the strips on a cookie sheet that has been lightly sprayed with cooking spray. This is your pizza "crust."
5. Layer on your favorite pizza sauce, cheese, and toppings of your choice.
6. Bake for about 15 to 20 minutes until cheese is melted and bubbly.

Desserts

Fresh Apple Cake

$1^1/_2$ cups oil

2 cups sugar

3 eggs

1 teaspoon baking soda

1 teaspoon salt

3 cups flour

1 teaspoon cinnamon

1 teaspoon vanilla

3 cups peeled, chopped apples

1 cup chopped walnuts

OPTIONAL GLAZE

$1^1/_2$ cups brown sugar

1 cup evaporated milk

$1/_2$ cup butter

STEPS

1. Preheat oven to 325°.
2. Combine all cake ingredients except apples and nuts. Mix well.
3. Stir in apples and nuts.
4. Pour into a greased 9 x 13-inch pan and bake in preheated oven for 45 minutes.
5. Cool, and if desired, top with glaze. Refrigerate.
6. To make glaze: Combine all glaze ingredients in saucepan, heat to boiling, and pour over cooled cake.

Old-Fashioned Maine Apple Crisp

6 medium McIntosh apples, peeled, cored, and sliced

2 tablespoons sugar

4 teaspoons flour

1 teaspoon cinnamon

$1/_8$ teaspoon nutmeg

1 teaspoon lemon juice

$3/_4$ cup all-purpose flour

1 cup rolled oats

$3/_4$ cup firmly packed brown sugar

$1/_2$ cup margarine or butter, softened

STEPS

1. Preheat oven to 375°.
2. Peel, core, and slice apples into large bowl; set aside.
3. In small bowl, combine sugar, 4 teaspoons flour, cinnamon, and nutmeg. Sprinkle over fruit, and place fruit mixture in ungreased 2-quart, oven-safe casserole. Sprinkle with lemon juice.
4. In medium bowl, combine $^3/_4$ cup flour, oats, and brown sugar.
5. Use a pastry cutter and cut in butter/margarine until crumbly.
6. Sprinkle crumb mixture over fruit and pat lightly.
7. Bake for 35 to 45 minutes or until top is golden brown and fruit is tender.

Homemade Applesauce

The number of apples you use is determined by the amount of sauce you want to make. Three quarts of cut-up apples will make about $1^1/_2$ quarts of strained applesauce.

Maine-grown apples
Water
Salt
Sugar
Nutmeg
Cinnamon

STEPS

1. Wash the apples, quarter them, cut out the blossom and stem end and any blemishes, but do not peel.
2. Put apples in saucepan, add about 1 cup water and a sprinkle of salt. Cover pan, bring to a boil. Lower heat and cook about 15 minutes, or until apples are soft.
3. Using a wooden spoon, press the apples through a sieve. Keep pressing until you have every bit of goodness from the fruit. (You can also use a food mill for this.)
4. Add $^1/_2$ to 1 cup granulated sugar, a shake of nutmeg, and a shake of cinnamon. Serve hot or cold. Put extra in freezer.

Autumn Baked Apples

Fresh apples (one per serving)
Maple syrup
Butter
Walnuts
Raisins
Cinnamon

STEPS

1. Preheat oven to 350°.
2. Core apples, leaving a bit of apple in bottom of core hole to prevent contents from leaking during baking.
3. Fill hole of each apple with a small piece of butter, walnuts, raisins, syrup, and cinnamon.
4. Bake in greased 8 x 8-inch glass pan covered with foil for 45 minutes or until soft.

Indian Pudding

The Native Americans taught the English settlers the importance of corn (or maize) when they first arrived. This recipe is easy to put together but has a long cooking time. It tastes great with a scoop of vanilla ice cream on top.

1 cup yellow corn meal
$^1/_2$ cup dark molasses
$^1/_2$ cup sugar
$^1/_4$ cup butter
$^1/_4$ teaspoon baking soda
2 eggs
$1^1/_2$ quarts hot milk

STEPS

1. Preheat oven to 250°.
2. Mix all ingredients with half of the hot milk.
3. Bake uncovered in oven in a well-greased stone crock (a bean pot or large oven-safe casserole dish with cover will also work) until mixture boils. (Check every half hour until it reaches boiling point.)
4. Stir in remaining milk.
5. Bake, covered, for 5 to 7 hours.

Sea Moss Pudding

¹⁄₃ to ¹⁄₂ cup Irish Moss
(Chondrus crispus. *This is the source of the carrageenan used to thicken commercial ice cream and other products.*)

1 pint milk

¹⁄₄ cup sugar

STEPS

1. Pick up Irish Moss on the shore (or purchase at a natural foods store). It comes in small, leafy pieces—no pods—and color will range from light red-brown to beige. Rinse thoroughly to remove sand, etc. Let dry.
2. Simmer milk and moss in top of double boiler about 15 minutes.
3. Strain, add sugar, and chill (it will thicken as it cools). Serve with cream and any desired sweetening.

Irish Moss.

Chocolate Raspberry Dream Cake

Angel food cake mix

1 small jar raspberry jam

1 cup whipping cream

1 cup confectioners' sugar

¹⁄₂ cup unsweetened cocoa powder

1 teaspoon vanilla

Fresh raspberries for garnish, if desired

STEPS

1. Bake an angel food cake according to package directions.

2. When cake is cool, cut into 3 layers using serrated knife.
3. Frost between middle layers with a thin coating of jam.
4. Using a chilled metal or glass bowl and beaters, whip the cream until just thickened.
5. Add the sugar, cocoa, and vanilla and continue whipping until firm peaks form.
6. Frost top and sides with this chocolate whipped cream mixture.
7. Garnish with fresh raspberries. Refrigerate until served.

Ice Cream in a Baggie

For this recipe you will need both a small Ziploc baggie and a gallon-size Ziploc bag. Makes one serving.

1 tablespoon sugar

¹⁄₂ cup milk

¹⁄₂ teaspoon vanilla, coffee, chocolate, or strawberry syrup to taste

Ice

6 tablespoons salt

STEPS

1. Put sugar, milk, and flavored syrup into the small baggie.
2. Fill the gallon baggie halfway with ice and salt.
3. Place small baggie inside the large one. Shake 5 minutes, and—amazingly—you'll get ice cream.

Snow "Ice Cream"

You must make this very quickly and eat it immediately.

Clean, newly fallen snow

Cream

Vanilla

Granulated sugar

STEPS

1. Mix cream and vanilla together (cream should be flavored to taste; that is why no proportions are given).

2. After collecting snow, put layers of it into a large chilled bowl, sprinkling sugar on each layer. Fold flavored cream into snow, being sure not to let the cream pool in the bottom of the bowl. Toss snow constantly; it will freeze the cream.

Gifts from the Kitchen

Cinnamon Ornaments

NOTE: Although they are yummy smelling, these ornaments are not meant to be eaten.

8 ounces powdered cinnamon

1 pound applesauce (use a high quality)

STEPS

1. Starting with small amounts, mix cinnamon and applesauce until it reaches cookie-dough consistency.
2. Take a lump the size of an orange and flatten with your hand to $1/4$-inch thickness.
3. Cut with cookie cutter.
4. Place on cookie sheet, lined with waxed paper, and let dry for 1 week, turning every day. (Or bake at 150° for 3 to 4 hours.)

Ana's People Chow

1 box (13 oz.) Golden Grahams cereal

1 small jar (8 oz.) smooth peanut butter

1 bag (16 oz.) milk chocolate bits

1 stick butter

3 cups confectioners' sugar

STEPS

1. Mix and melt peanut butter, chocolate bits, and butter together (until just melted).
2. In large bowl, mix the Golden Grahams and melted ingredients until cereal is coated.
3. Put confectioners' sugar in a large plastic bag, spoon in the coated cereal, and shake until the mix is coated with the confectioners' sugar. It will be kind of clumpy and good!

Dog Biscuits

$3/4$ cup beef broth

$1/3$ cup margarine

$1/2$ cup powdered milk

1 egg

1 teaspoon salt

1 tablespoon sugar

3 cups whole wheat flour

STEPS

1. Preheat oven to 350°.
2. Mix together warmed beef broth and margarine.
3. Stir in powdered milk, salt, sugar, and egg.
4. Add flour a little at a time, mixing well each time. Knead well. Mixture will be very stiff. Add more flour if necessary.
5. Roll to $1/2$-inch thickness and cut into any shapes you like.
6. Cook on greased baking sheet for 45 to 50 minutes. Biscuits will be hard and dry when cool.

Courtesy of the Animal Welfare Society, Inc., W. Kennebunk, Maine.

Hot Chocolate Mix

25 ounces instant nonfat dry milk

16 ounces chocolate drink powder, such as Nestlé Quik

6 ounces nondairy creamer

4 ounces powdered cocoa

$7/8$ pound of confectioners' sugar

STEPS

1. Mix all ingredients together in large bowl.
2. Store mix in tight container.
3. The mix can also be given as a gift—put cocoa mix into cloth bags or glass jars, tied with a ribbon and instructions for mixing.

Instructions for mixing: For each cup of hot chocolate, mix $1/4$ cup of mix with 6 ounces of hot water.

Bean Soup Mix in a Mason Jar

4 teaspoons each of garlic powder and dried basil

1 cup each of 8 different types of dried beans (lentils, kidney beans, lima beans, chickpeas, white beans, split peas, barley, etc.)

4 pint-size Mason jars

STEPS

1. Layer beans into Mason jars one kind at a time.
2. Sprinkle with 1 teaspoon of garlic powder and 1 teaspoon basil.
3. Seal jar and affix a copy of the following recipe. Jars can be decorated as you desire.

Vegetable Bean Soup

2 cups bean soup mix

8 cups water

1 (28-oz.) can tomatoes

3 cups of fresh, frozen, or canned vegetables (celery, carrots, corn, peas, potatoes, etc.)

Salt and pepper to taste

STEPS

1. Put soup mix, water, and canned tomatoes into a large pot and bring to a boil.
2. Reduce the heat and simmer for 2 hours, stirring occasionally.
3. Add vegetables and cook for another 20 to 30 minutes, or until vegetables are tender.
4. Season with salt and pepper to taste.

chapter 6

Crafts

From Woods and Fields ... 54

Maine Nature Weaving ... 54
Birdfeeders ... 55
Wildflower Bookmarks ... 55
Maine Leaf Placemats ... 55
Birdhouse from a Gourd ... 56
Balsam Fir Pillows or Bags ... 56
Maine Collage ... 56
Forest Terrarium ... 57
Maine Shadow Boxes ... 57
Nature's T-Shirts ... 57
Pinecone Ornaments ... 57

From the Seashore ... 58

Beach Bracelet ... 58
Sea Glass Suncatchers ... 58
Driftwood Mobile ... 58
Sand Pictures ... 58
Seashore Decorated Picture Frames ... 59
Maine Treasure Box ... 59
Seashell Wreaths ... 59
Shell Soap Dish ... 59
Maine Sea Creatures ... 60
Seashell Ornaments ... 60
Message on a Rock ... 60
Monster Rocks ... 60
Rock Sculptures ... 61
Hot Rocks ... 61

One of a Kind ... 61

Maine Potato Prints ... 61
Gift Bag ... 61
Pretzel Log Cabin ... 62
Surprise Ball from Maine ... 62

The Basics ... 62

Homemade Play Dough ... 62
Cornstarch Cookie Ornaments ... 63
Bubble-Blowing Liquid ... 63

Crafts

From Woods and Fields

Maine Nature Weaving

The weavings look beautiful when you are done. Work together in groups of two.

YOU WILL NEED:

    Chair (school or kitchen)

    2 sticks or pieces of driftwood long enough to span the width of the chair legs

    Masking tape

    Collect different colored and textured reeds, twigs with berries, seed pods, corn stalks, etc., in nearby fields and along roadsides, near marshes, back yards, etc. Seaweed and moss are great too.

    String or twine

    Lots of weaving materials from nature

    Glue gun

    Drop cloth or old sheet or newspaper (for under chair while weaving)

    Shells, acorns, etc., to accent the weavings at the end

STEPS

1. Place drop cloth on floor. Set chair upside-down on the drop cloth. The bottoms of the chair legs will help support your frame.
2. Securely attach each stick to the bottom of the chair legs with masking tape so they are parallel to each other (refer to illustration).
3. Referring to the second illustration, tie 10 strings between the sticks, alternating sides (1 left, 1 right, 1 left, 1 right) until all your strings are tied and ready for weaving. (Check to make sure the strings are taut and knotted well.)
4. Weave your reeds, seed pods, berries on twigs, corn stalks, etc. through the strings. Alternate colors, textures, sizes, etc. Weave tightly until no more of the large pieces will fit.
5. Fill in loose spaces by weaving in seaweed and moss (or smaller pieces of weaving materials) so that once the weaving is hung, the materials don't loosen up and fall out or hang crooked.
6. Make a hanger for each weaving by tying an additional string to each end of the top stick.
7. With an adult's help, use the glue gun to attach shell or acorn decorations, if desired.
8. Remove from chair legs and hang. They look so great that folks don't think kids made them, and they last forever.

Caution: An activity using weeds, etc., may affect people with allergies.

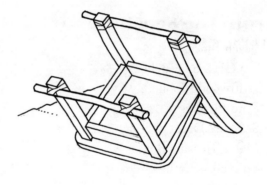

Step 2.

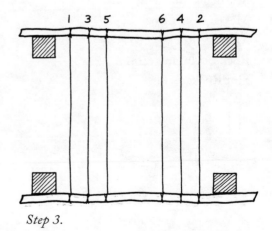

Step 3.

Birdfeeders

VERSION I

YOU WILL NEED:

Pinecones
Twine
Peanut butter
Birdseed

STEPS

1. Spread a thick layer of peanut butter on the whole pinecone (messy, but fun).
2. Roll pinecone in birdseed.
3. Hang with twine from tree branches.

VERSION II

YOU WILL NEED:

Milk container (plastic gallon or cardboard half-gallon)
Scissors
String
Stickers

STEPS

1. Cut openings in milk carton as shown in picture below.
2. Decorate with stickers as desired.
3. Attach string to hang feeder.
4. Fill with modest amount of seed.
5. Hang outside in a tree near a window where you can watch the birds!

Milk carton birdfeeder.

Wildflower Bookmarks

YOU WILL NEED:

Wildflowers (lupine, fiddlehead, etc.) 3 inches long
2 pieces of waxed paper, 2 by 5 inches, for each bookmark
Hot iron (an old one, as waxed paper may leave a residue)
Old cloth to protect work surface
Stickers and crayons for decorating bookmarks when completed

STEPS

1. Have an adult plug in the iron and heat it up.
2. Place one piece of waxed paper on a table covered by an old cloth for protection.
3. Place wildflower in the center and place second sheet of waxed paper on top.
4. Press hot iron to waxed paper to stick top sheet to bottom.
5. Allow time to cool and decorate as desired with stickers and crayons.

Caution: Adult supervision required. Hot iron needed for this project.

Maine Leaf Placemats

YOU WILL NEED:

Burlap
Fall leaves
Glue
Clear contact paper

STEPS

1. Take burlap and cut into a rectangle the size of a placemat.
2. Have kids arrange dried leaves on burlap as desired.
3. Glue leaves to burlap and let dry flat.
4. When dry, cover placemats with clear contact paper to laminate.

Birdhouse from a Gourd

YOU WILL NEED:

Dry, smooth-surfaced gourd, 8 to 12 inches in length
2 sticks about 8 to 10 inches in length
Ice pick
Clear lacquer
Raffia

STEPS

1. Mark holes on gourd for perches ($\frac{1}{4}$- to $\frac{1}{2}$-inch diameter) and entrance (1 inch diameter). One perch should be near top of gourd, the other lower down.
2. Use an ice pick to punch out these holes.
3. Shake out seeds from gourd.
4. Push sticks into holes for perches.
5. Paint surface with lacquer.
6. Tie securely with raffia at top perch for hanging.

From Discover Maine through Handicraft, *by Emma J. MacDonald and Cynthia M. Ayer. Published 1974 by the Maine Dept. of Educational and Cultural Services.*

Gourd birdhouse.

Balsam Fir Pillows or Bags

YOU WILL NEED:

Cloth cut in 5- by 10-inch rectangles
Dry, fragrant balsam needles (or pine needles)
Needle
Thread

STEPS

1. Collect balsam needles, dry or fresh work fine. (One way to capture lots of needles is to shake your Christmas tree onto an old sheet outside when you are taking it down.)
2. Fold cloths in half with right sides together. Sew up 2 sides.
3. Turn right-side out and stuff with balsam or pine needles.
4. You can either leave enough room at the top to tie a ribbon around the open end to make a bag, or fill the bag full and sew up the open side to make a pillow.

Maine Collage

YOU WILL NEED:

Bag to hold your treasures
Found items from Maine woods: pinecones, acorns, ferns, leaves, flowers, seeds, bark fallen from trees, pieces of wood, small rocks, etc.
9- by 12-inch piece of cardboard or poster board
Glue or glue gun

STEPS

1. Take all of your treasures that you have collected out of your bag and put them on a tray.
2. Glue them to the cardboard in shapes or freeform to create an interesting picture.

Forest Terrarium

YOU WILL NEED:

**Mosses and miniature plants and soil
from the woods**

**Jar or small glass container that can be
covered with a glass top**

Small mirror

Small pebbles (¹/₄-inch)

Larger stones (¹/₂-inch or bigger)

STEPS

1. Take your child for a hike in the woods. Bring along a small shovel or knife and a basket or plastic bag to hold your collection. Be on the lookout for mosses and small plants. When collecting small plants, be sure to include enough soil to keep the root ball intact.

2. When you have what you need (be sure not to take too much—a little goes a long way), come home and arrange your materials to form a little garden in the container you have chosen.

3. Use the pebbles to create a pathway, the mirror for a pond, and larger stones for the "boulders."

4. If you do this in late summer or early fall, and keep it lightly watered, your terrarium will last a long time. The covered containers do not often need watering.

Maine Shadow Boxes

YOU WILL NEED:

Empty notecard boxes with clear plastic lids
Construction paper
Treasures from beach combing
Glue

STEPS

1. Line notecard box with construction paper in appropriate color for what child wants to make (blue for sky or sea, green for grass, brown for soil).

2. Have child make picture or design as desired and glue materials in box (twigs and sea glass for flowers, shells and twigs for sailing ships, "hinged" clam shells for sea gulls).

3. Place transparent cover over box and tape together.

Nature's T-Shirts

This is a sunny-day project.

YOU WILL NEED:

**100-percent colored cotton T-shirt (not
white or black)**

**Plastic bag folded to the size of the inside
of T-shirt**

**Leaves, shells, and other objects from
nature with interesting shapes**

**Solution of 50 percent bleach and
50 percent water mixed in a spray bottle**

Bucket of cold water

STEPS

1. Slide a plastic bag between the layers of the shirt to protect back layer from the bleach solution. Lay shirt flat on the grass.

2. Place leaves, shells, and other objects you collected in an interesting way on the front of the shirt.

3. Spray bleach solution around edges of leaves, shells, etc.

4. Let the shirt sit in direct sun for a minute.

5. Dunk in a bucket of cold water and thoroughly rinse out the bleach.

6. Lay flat in the sun to dry.

Pinecone Ornaments

YOU WILL NEED:

Pinecones
White glue
White glitter
Old toothbrushes or artist brushes
Newspapers
Narrow ribbon (color of your choice)

STEPS

1. Take a walk in the woods in autumn to gather bags of pinecones. Try to find ones with stems still attached.

2. Let cones dry for a day or two.

3. Spread newspaper on work surface.

4. Pour glue onto an old plate.

5. Dip brush in glue and, holding cone by stem, paint the glue liberally on top side of

outer edges all around, using downward strokes. Don't worry about applying it evenly.

6. Still holding cone, sprinkle it with white glitter and shake off excess.
7. Set on newspaper to dry.
8. When dry, tie colored ribbon onto stem and make a loop large enough to fit over a tree bough. If used as Christmas tree decorations, the cones will sparkle when tree lights are on.

From the Seashore

Beach Bracelet

YOU WILL NEED:

Narrow masking tape or duct tape ($\frac{1}{2}$- or 1-inch wide)

Small, lightweight treasures: shells, feathers, sea glass, dried seaweed, pretty leaves, etc.

STEPS

1. Cut masking tape long enough to circle wrist with ends overlapping one inch. Make it large enough to slip on and off easily.
2. Stick tape together in a loop, sticky side out.
3. Decorate with treasures.

Sea Glass Suncatchers

YOU WILL NEED:

Large or small pieces of white sea glass
Watercolor paints
Paintbrush
Water

STEPS

1. Paint your own design on one side of the sea glass.
2. Let dry.
3. Prop on windowsill and enjoy.

Driftwood Mobile

YOU WILL NEED:

Sea glass
Crab shells
Sea urchins
Mussel shells
Seaweed
Piece of driftwood, 2 feet long
Scissors
Fishing line or cotton string

STEPS

1. Choose a piece of driftwood about 2 feet long.
2. Attach one piece of fishing line or yarn to one end of the driftwood, then tie the other end of the line or yarn to the other end of the driftwood.
3. Hang the driftwood at eye level.
4. With additional line or yarn, attach your treasures to the driftwood. Use varying lengths of line or yarn so your treasures will hang at differing heights. Adjust placements so mobile will balance the way you want it to.

Sand Pictures

YOU WILL NEED:

Sand
Colored chalk
White or craft glue
Paper plate or sheet of thick paper
Paper bowls, one for each color you plan to use

STEPS

1. Put some sand in a bowl.
2. Rub chalk in the sand to color it and mix in.
3. Brush glue onto desired places on the paper plate or sheet. (The sand will stick where the glue is.)
4. Sprinkle the colored sand onto the glue, then shake excess sand back into the bowl.
5. Repeat with other colors to achieve the desired effect.

Seashore Decorated Picture Frames

YOU WILL NEED:

A bag of small-sized sea treasures collected along the shore

Low-temperature glue gun and glue sticks

Picture frames—clear plastic or colored wooden frame (blue or green make a nice background), or make your own from cardboard

Newspaper

STEPS

1. Spread sea treasures out on a tray so you can see and grab them easily.
2. Arrange treasures on a flat surface the way you want them to look on the frame.
3. Glue treasures to frame. If the frame will stand on top of a bureau or table, make sure the treasures do not project too far past the lower edge.
4. Let dry for 24 hours.

Caution: Adult supervision required for glue gun.

Maine Treasure Box

YOU WILL NEED:

Cardboard box with cover

Masking tape, 1 inch wide

Enamel paints

Brushes

Clear shellac (thinned)

Glue or glue gun

Treasures from the woods or shore

STEPS

1. Attach a strip of masking tape where the cover is to be attached to box. (The tape will act as a hinge for the cover.)
2. Shellac the top and sides of the box and let dry thoroughly.
3. Paint the top and sides of the box, using bright enamel paint, and let dry.
4. Decorate the box with your treasures using glue or glue gun.

Caution: Adult supervision required for glue gun.

Seashell Wreaths

YOU WILL NEED:

Cardboard

All types of shells and shore treasures

Sand

Glue

Ribbon

STEPS

1. Go to the shore and gather shells, sand, and treasures.
2. Cut cardboard rings of desired wreath size and shape—small to make ornament-sized wreath, larger for decorative wreath.
3. Glue treasures to cardboard ring.
4. Fill in around treasures with sand poured onto glue spots.
5. Attach ribbon on top as a bow and on back as a hanger.

Shell Soap Dish

YOU WILL NEED:

Large clam shell

Enamel paint and brush

Plastic sandwich bag

Ribbon

Small bar of decorative soap

STEPS

1. Clean the shell carefully.
2. Paint the inside. Gold paint looks pretty, or use a color of your choice to go with the soap you select.
3. When dry, place the soap on the shell. Package your shell in a plastic bag tied with a ribbon if giving as a gift.

Maine Sea Creatures

YOU WILL NEED:

Driftwood, shells, sea glass, rocks, pinecones, and any other treasures desired

Glue gun

Plastic wiggle eyes

STEPS

1. Use driftwood as your base and assemble treasures on the driftwood in shapes to make imaginary sea creatures.
2. Glue on shells or sea glass to make a face. Add wiggle eyes.

This idea can be adapted to make a name plaque (see below).

STEPS

1. Using the flat driftwood as a base, outline in pencil the letters of the child's name.
2. Glue on treasures over the outlined letters.

Seashell Ornaments

YOU WILL NEED:

Shells

Sand dollars

Paint

Brushes

Glitter

Glue

Narrow ribbon (¼-inch)

STEPS

1. Collect the shells and sand dollars at the beach.
2. Put them in a pail overnight in a solution of 75 percent water and 25 percent bleach.
3. Place them in the sun the next day to dry.
4. When dry, paint them your favorite color.
5. When the paint is dry, use the glue to put on the glitter.
6. Cut pieces of ribbon long enough to make a bow. Put glue in the middle of the ribbon and glue to the shell or sand dollar. Let dry, then tie a bow so you can hang it.

Message on a Rock

YOU WILL NEED:

Round or oval flat-topped rocks, 2 to 3 inches in size

Crayons

Newspapers

Cookie sheet

Potholders

Oven

STEPS

1. Put rocks on cookie sheet and heat in oven for 2 hours at 250°.
2. Using potholders, remove a rock and place it on a thick layer of newspapers.
3. Write with crayons special words such as *love, courage, friendship,* or *beauty*.
4. Set to cool for 24 hours.

Monster Rocks

YOU WILL NEED:

Maine rocks, 2 to 3 inches in long

Acrylic paint

Wiggle eyes

Chenille pipe cleaners

Glitter

Sequins

Glue

STEPS

1. Paint rocks in one or several colors to resemble monsters.
2. When dry, glue on eyes and curled chenille pipe cleaners for antennae.
3. Glue on glitter and sequins to finish your creation.

This is a fun project to accompany by reading Where the Wild Things Are, *by Maurice Sendak.*

Rock Sculptures

YOU WILL NEED:

Rocks

Sand

STEPS

1. Select a flat rock as your base.
2. Place a little pile of sand on it and carefully balance another rock, even a very round one, on the sand.
3. Blow away the extra sand.
4. Try adding another rock on top in the same way. You must go slowly and carefully, being patient about finding the balance, but you can build gravity-defying stacks of rocks that will amaze everyone.

Hot Rocks

YOU WILL NEED:

Smooth Maine rocks, 3 to 5 inches in size

Lots of crayons (this is a good project for using up old crayons)

Newspapers

Cookie sheet

Potholders

Oven

STEPS

1. Preheat oven to 250° F.
2. Place rocks on a cookie sheet and heat for 2 hours.
3. Using potholders, remove a rock and place it on a thick layer of newspapers. Leave the rest of the rocks in the oven to stay hot until you are ready to color them.
4. Pick your favorite crayon colors and color on the rock. The crayons will melt on contact. *Use lots of crayons*, coloring one layer of color over another. Accent with gold, silver, or glitter crayons.
5. Leave to set for 24 hours, then buff with soft cloth.

These are quick to do and lots of fun. Make great gifts. Can be used as paperweights.

One of a Kind

Maine Potato Prints

YOU WILL NEED:

1 large Maine potato

Sharp paring knife

Tempera paint (color of your choice)

Aluminum pie pan

Non-glossy paper (color of your choice)

Smock or old shirt

Newspapers

STEPS

1. Have a child put on a smock and place newspapers on table.
2. With a sharp paring knife, have an adult cut the potato in half and carve a shape (circle, diamond, or letter for an initial) into the flat surface of the potato.
3. Cut away excess potato so that the shape sticks out $1/4$- to $1/2$-inch.
4. Pour small amount of paint in pie tin.
5. Place paper for picture on top of newspapers.
6. Dip potato, cut side down, into paint and press onto paper.
7. Repeat across paper, decorating as desired.
8. Allow to dry.

Caution: Adult assistance required for handling knife.

Gift Bag

YOU WILL NEED:

Gingerbread man cookie cutter

Brown paper lunch bag

Piece of gingham cloth

Ribbon or rickrack

Small colorful buttons

Glue

STEPS

1. Trace cookie cutter on cloth, then cut out the gingerbread man shape.
2. Glue cut cloth onto the bag.

3. Glue buttons on for eyes, nose, and mouth.
4. Trim with ribbon or rickrack.
5. Put your favorite Maine treasure in the bag to give to a special person.

Pretzel Log Cabin

YOU WILL NEED:

Small, skinny pretzel sticks
Softened cream cheese
Shredded mini-wheat cereal
Half-pint milk cartons
Small crackers

STEPS

1. Wash and dry inside and outside of milk cartons.
2. Frost outside of cartons with cream cheese.
3. Press pretzels onto sides of cartons, cutting to fit.
4. Cover roof with shredded wheat to make roof shingles.
5. Attach cracker doors and windows using more cream cheese.
6. Display for all to admire.

Surprise Ball from Maine

YOU WILL NEED:

A bag of leftover yarn or rolls of crepe paper
Special treasures from shore, woods, or even your child's junk drawer
1 very small bottle of bubble-blowing liquid
Ribbon

STEPS

1. Tie different-colored yarns together to make one very long, continuous piece, or use crepe paper.
2. Wrap yarn or crepe paper tightly around bottle of bubbles, tucking in treasures every so often as you go along.
3. When you have wrapped enough yarn or crepe paper to make a 5-inch ball, tuck in the end.
4. Tie a decorative ribbon around the ball, finishing with a bow.

The Basics

Homemade Play Dough

VERSION I

YOU WILL NEED:

2½ cups flour
½ cup salt
2 packages Kool-Aid
3 tablespoons oil
2 cups boiling water

STEPS

1. Mix dry ingredients together.
2. Add oil and boiling water. Mix well with a spoon. Dough may be a little sticky. If so, more flour can be added.
3. Allow to cool before playing with this dough. (Note: Hands may become stained while using.)
4. Store in an airtight container.

VERSION II

YOU WILL NEED:

1 cup flour
1 tablespoon vegetable oil
1 cup water
½ cup salt
2 tsp. cream of tartar
Food coloring (optional)

STEPS

1. Mix all ingredients together in a medium-size saucepan.
2. Add food coloring if desired.
3. Cook over low to medium heat until mixture forms a ball. Stir occasionally while cooking.
4. Remove from pan and knead well. *Parents should do this step, as dough is still quite hot at this point.* The more the dough is kneaded, the silkier and more elastic it becomes.
5. Store in refrigerator in a Ziploc bag or covered container.

Cornstarch Cookie Ornaments

YOU WILL NEED:

1-pound box of baking soda
1 cup corn starch
1¹/₄ cups water
Cookie cutters
String for hanging

STEPS

1. Mix first 3 ingredients in a saucepan and cook over medium heat. The mixture will form a ball like pie dough.
2. Let cool several minutes.
3. Roll out dough and cut with cookie cutters.
4. Make hole in each cookie with a toothpick.
5. Place on a cookie sheet to dry overnight. Do not bake.
6. Paint or color with marker.
7. Put string through hole to hang.

Bubble-Blowing Liquid

YOU WILL NEED:

1 cup warm water
¹/₄ cup liquid dish detergent
1 teaspoon glycerin (get this at the drugstore)
Pinch of sugar
Few drops of food coloring

STEPS

1. Mix all ingredients together in a plastic bottle.
2. Use any bubble-making apparatus to blow lots of bubbles.

chapter 7

Fairs, Festivals, and Special Events

Fairs by Date...66

Fairs by Town...67

Festivals and Special Events...68

Fairs, Festivals, and Special Events

Maine's 26 agricultural fairs are a rich part of its history. In fact, the Skowhegan Fair, in its 185th year in 2003, is the oldest agricultural fair in the United States. Most all fairs are advertised as family oriented. Activities for children go well beyond the carnival midway and can include 4-H activities, games, animal exhibits, cooking contests, arts and crafts, and more.

The fair season starts July 1 in Houlton and ends the first week of October in Fryeburg, with Maine's largest fair. The Common Ground Fair, held in September at the Maine Organic Farmers and Gardeners Association headquarters in Unity, is unique in its celebration of sustainable rural living. You won't find a midway here, but there is a lot to appeal to kids, including a special children's area, a garden parade, an apple pie contest, and a Youth Enterprise Zone.

Our listing of fairs is presented twice: first, in date order, then in alphabetical order by town. Fair dates are determined by when Labor Day falls each September, but they are approximately the same time yearly. Brochures with all fair dates are available from the Maine Association of Agricultural Fairs, P.O. Box 200, Litchfield, ME 04350. You can also call (207) 268-4631 or visit the Web site at www.maineagriculturalfairs.org/.

Fairs by Date

Note: Fairs do not necessarily run for a full week. Check the fair you are interested in for the specific dates of operation. Fairs are usually named after the town they are held in. If that is not the case, or if the fair is known within the region by a different name, we have noted that after the location in parentheses.

Week in which fair operates	Location
The first week of July	Houlton
The second week of July	Ossippee (Valley Fair)
The second and third week of July	Pittston
The fourth week of July	North Waterford (World's Fair)
The end of July, beginning of August	Bangor (State Fair)
The end of July, beginning of August	Presque Isle (Northern Maine)
The first week of August	Athens
The first week of August	Monmouth
The second week of August	Topsham
The second and third week of August	Skowhegan
The third and fourth week of August	Union
The fourth week of August	Acton
The fourth week of August	Piscataquis
The end of August, beginning of September	Windsor
The first week of September	Blue Hill

The first week of September.................................Springfield
The second week of September ....Clinton (Lion's Fair)
The second week of September ....Litchfield
The second and third week of September.............Oxford
The third week of September ....New Portland (Lion's Fair)
The third and fourth week of September.............Farmington
The fourth week of September ....Unity (Common Ground Fair)
The fourth week of September ....Cumberland
The first week of October...................................Fryeburg

Fairs by Town

Note: Fairs are usually named after the town they are held in. If that is not the case, or if the fair is known within the region by a different name, we have noted that after the location in parentheses. Fairs do not necessarily run for a full week. Check the fair you are interested in for the specific dates of operation.

Location	Week in which fair operates
Acton	The fourth week of August
Athens	The first week of August
Bangor	The end of July, beginning of August
Blue Hill	The first week of September
Clinton (Lion's Fair)	The second week of September
Cumberland	The fourth week of September
Farmington	The third and fourth week of September
Fryeburg	The first week of October
Houlton	The first week of July
Litchfield	The second week of September
Monmouth	The first week of August
New Portland (Lion's Fair)	The third week of September
North Waterford (World's Fair)	The fourth week of July
Ossippee Valley Fair	The second week of July
Oxford	The second and third week of September
Piscataquis	The fourth week of August
Pittston	The second and third week of July
Presque Isle (Northern Maine Fair)	The end of July, beginning of August
Skowhegan	The second and third week of August
Springfield	The first week of September
Topsham	The second week of August
Union	The third and fourth week of August
Unity (Common Ground Fair)	The fourth week of September
Windsor	The end of August, beginning of September

Festivals and Special Events

Maine offers a multitude of festivals, events, and celebrations in all shapes, sizes, and forms that reflect the rich heritage and the natural resources of the state. From the hundreds of events held each year, we have carefully selected events that are unique and enjoy a history of success.

This list is organized by the month in which the event is typically held. No specific dates are provided because they change somewhat every year. Please call ahead for the event you are interested in to find out the exact date and any other details you may need.

FEBRUARY

Camden: **Annual U.S. Toboggan Championship**
(207) 236-3438

More than 250 teams compete at the Camden Snow Bowl.

Caribou: **Winter Carnival**
(207) 498-6156

Features the Snow Goddess festival and downhill canoe races.

MARCH

Fort Kent: **Annual Mardi Gras**
(800) 733-3563

Snowmobile parade, pageant, and more.

Fort Kent: **Annual Can-Am Crown Sled Dog Races**
(800) 733-3563

30-, 60-, and 250-mile races.

Maine: **Maine Maple Sunday**
(207) 287-3491

Held the fourth Sunday in March at maple syrup farms across the state.

Greater Portland Area: *People, Places & Plants* **Spring Flower Show**
(207) 829-4783 or 800 251-1784; www.ppplants.com

A breath of spring, beautiful gardens, booths, and a special children's section.

APRIL

Boothbay Harbor: **Annual Fishermen's Festival**
(207) 633-2353

Competitions, trap-hauling races, and more. Great spectator fun.

MAY

Greenville/Rockwood: **Moosemainea**
(207) 695-2702

A month-long moose celebration with canoe racing, biking, rowing, fly-casting championship, antique auto parade, and more.

Kennebunk/Kennebunkport: **May Day Festival**
(207) 967-0857

Maypole dancing; carriage and wagon rides.

Lewiston/Auburn: **Annual Maine State Parade**
(207) 828-6666

The largest parade in Maine.

JUNE

Biddeford: **La Kermesse Festival**
(207) 282-2894

Maine's largest Franco-American festival, with a block party, entertainment, and cultural events.

Boothbay Harbor: **Annual Windjammer Days**
(207) 633-2353

Majestic windjammers sail into the harbor amid much fanfare; street parade, fireworks.

Camden: **Mid-Coast Soap Box Derby**
(207) 236-2119

Kids compete in soap box derby races with the hope of making it to the world championship held in Ohio in August.

Houlton: **Soap Box Derby**
(207) 532-7522

Kids compete in soap box derby races with the hope of making it to the world championship held in Ohio in August.

Madawaska: **Acadian Festival**
(207) 728-7000

Entertainment, cultural displays, parade.

Portland: **Annual Old Port Festival**
(207) 772-6828

Parade, performers, and 10 stages with rock, folk, comedy, country, and jazz performances in the heart of Portland.

Rockland/North Haven: **Great Schooner Race**
(800) 807-9463

Enjoy a day of tall ship racing at North America's largest annual gathering of tall ships.

Wiscasset: **Strawberry Festival**
(207) 882-7184

A fifty-year tradition with lots of berries, an auction, crafts, and children's games.

JULY

Augusta: **Family Festival/ Children's Day at Capitol Park**
Augusta Chamber of Commerce
(207) 623-4559

Pony rides, games, and performances for kids.

Bailey Island: **Tuna Tournament**
(207) 833-5531

Prizes and trophies.

Bar Harbor: **Native American Festival**
(207) 288-3519

Celebrating Native American culture including arts and crafts, basket sales, demonstrations, and traditional food.

Bath: **Annual Heritage Days**
(207) 443-9751

Maritime festival, parade, midway, and fireworks.

Bethel: **Western Maine Gem and Mineral Festival**
(207) 665-2759

A special show right in the heart of gem country.

Boothbay: **Antique Auto Days**
 (207) 633-2353

A weekend of fun, including a wonderful antique auto parade of old cars through town.

Fort Fairfield:
Annual Potato Blossom Festival
 (207) 472-3802

A parade, midway, and the crowning of the Maine Potato Blossom Queen.

Jonesport: **Lobster Boat Races and Fourth of July Celebration**
 (207) 497-5417

One of the most exciting races of the lobster boat racing summer circuit.

Maine: **Open Farm Day**
 (207) 786-0637 or (800) 287-1458

A statewide event in which farms across Maine invite the public to participate in the experience of a real-life working farm. Many farms offer special events like hayrides and tours.

Ogunquit: **Sand Building Contest**
 (207) 646-3032

Enter to win or simply watch as adults and children create objects in the sand.

Pittsfield: **Annual Central Maine Egg Festival**
 (207) 487-5282

In celebration of the brown egg industry, this fair offers games, crafts, booths, a Scholarship Pageant, and fireworks.

Rangeley:
Annual Logging Festival
 (207) 864-5595

Includes Burying of the Beans, a Biscuit Bake, Little Miss and Mr. Woodchip contest, and a parade.

Rockland: **Schooner Days & North Atlantic Blues Festival**
 (207) 596-0376 or (800) 562-2529

Parade of sail, water events, fireworks, and more.

Yarmouth: **Annual Clam Festival**
 (207) 846-3984

Lots of clams to eat, plus a parade, midway, music, crafts, and food.

AUGUST

Bath:
Annual Bluefish Tournament
 (207) 443-9751

Northern New England's largest saltwater fishing tournament, open to all New England fishermen. It takes place rain or shine.

Brunswick:
Annual Maine Highland Games
 (207) 364-3063

Traditional Scottish events at Thomas Point Beach Park, including dancing, bagpipes, clan and society tents, games, and arts and crafts.

Brunswick:
Annual Bluegrass Festival
 (207) 725-6009

Four days of great music including international, national, and local performers at Thomas Point Beach Park.

Brunswick:
Annual Maine Arts Festival

(207) 772-9012

Maine's largest art and cultural event, with all-Maine craftspeople, artists, and performers. Held at Thomas Point Beach.

Houlton: **Potato Feast Days**

(207) 534-4216

Parade of dolls, dance, entertainment, and crafts.

Lewiston/Auburn: **Annual Great Falls Balloon Festival**

(207) 782-8961

One of the largest hot air balloon festivals in New England, plus a concert and children's activities.

Machias: **Wild Blueberry Festival**

(207) 255-6665

Fish fry, parade, music, and crafts.

Old Orchard Beach:
Annual Beach Olympics

(207) 934-2500

Sand sculptures, games, and music.

Perry: **Sipayik Indian Days Celebration**

(207) 853-2600

Indian culture, folklore, and dances.

Rangeley:
Annual Blueberry Festival

(207) 864-2283

Jams, muffins, pies, and entertainment for kids.

Rockland:
Annual Maine Lobster Festival

(800) LOB-CLAW

Lobsters, maritime events, parade, entertainment, and the coronation of the Maine Sea Goddess.

Wilton: **Annual Blueberry Festival**

(207) 778-4726

Parade, races, fireworks, and more.

York: **Mt. Agamenticus Jazz and Blues Festival**

(207) 363-1040

Day-long jazz and blues, jug band, kid's tent.

SEPTEMBER

Camden:
Annual Windjammer Weekend

(800) 807-9463

The largest single gathering of windjammers, including sail parades, music, and fireworks.

Cornish: **Annual Apple Festival**

(207) 625-7447

Food, arts and crafts booths, an antique car parade, a 5K run, and children's games.

Freedom:
Annual Healing Arts Festival

(207) 336-2065

Gathering of unity, peace, and spiritual development at Hidden Valley Camp.

Eastport: **Annual Salmon Festival**

A salmon dinner is the highlight of this event, which includes a fishing derby, walking and boat tours, crafts, and educational booths.

Greenville:
International Seaplane Fly-In

(207) 695-4571 or (207) 695-2991

Demos appeal to kids who like planes.

OCTOBER

Boothbay:
Annual Fall Foliage Festival

(207) 633-4743

Fun, food, entertainment, and crafts.

Bradley: **Living History Days**

(207) 581-2871

Traditional crafts and a reenactment of early pioneer life.

Fort Kent:
Annual Scarecrow Festival

(800) 733-3563

Scarecrow building contest, parade, and barn dance.

Medway: **Haunted Trolley Ride**

(207) 723-4443

Ride the trolley on a scary journey.

NOVEMBER

York Beach: **Lighting of the Nubble**

(207) 363-1040

Watch this lighthouse glow with holiday spirit, music, and Santa too!

DECEMBER

Boothbay Harbor:
Harbor Lights Festival

(207) 633-2353

A lighted boat parade at dusk, Santa, and a living creche.

Camden: **Christmas by the Sea**

(207) 236-4404

Wagon rides, Santa, a Christmas house tour, and entertainment.

Kennebunkport: **Christmas Prelude**

(207) 967-0857

Santa arrives by lobster boat. Lighting of a lobster-pot–decorated tree, caroling, and holiday cheer.

Livermore: **Christmas at Norlands**

(207) 897-4366

An old-fashioned holiday celebration.

Portland: **New Year's Portland**

(207) 772-9012

Performances, parade, food, and fireworks.

chapter 8

Great Ideas from Famous Maine Folks

Former First Lady Barbara Bush,
Exploring Maine's Tidal Pools ...74

Governor John Baldacci, First Lady Karen
Baldacci, and Jack Baldacci,
Biking at Acadia National Park ...74

Former Governor Angus S. King Jr.,
and former First Lady Mary J. Herman,
*Building Maine Sea Treasure
Sculptures* ...74

U.S. Senator Olympia J. Snowe and
former Governor John R. McKernan,
Creating an ABC Book About Maine ...74

U.S. Senator Susan M. Collins,
*Gathering Sea Glass and Friendship
Stones* ...75

U.S. Representative Tom Allen,
*Learning to Identify Birds Found
in Maine* ...75

Mrs. Caspar Weinberger,
Creating Sweet Modeling Clay ...75

The family of Betty Noyce,
Creating Periwinkle Jewelry ...76

Cindy Blodgett, former University of
Maine basketball star,
Cooking Grandma's Chop Suey ...76

Rick Charrette, Children's Singer
and Entertainer,
Hiking Douglas Mountain in Sebago ...76

Leon (L.L. Bean past president)
and Lisa Gorman, *Enjoying Favorite
Vistas at Acadia National Park* ...76

Dr. Craig Hurwitz (Medical Director
for Maine Children's Cancer Program),
Mrs. Hurwitz, and Hutch Hurwitz,
*Visiting Little Chebeague Island
in Casco Bay* ...76

Julie Russem, Maine Children's Cancer
Program cofounder, and daughter Nina,
Night Skiing in Maine ...77

Dr. Steve Blattner, Maine Children's
Cancer Program cofounder,
Walking the Beach with Your Dog ...77

Jim King and John Scott, Founders of
Stonewall Kitchens,
*Baking Buried Treasure Cupcakes and
Zebra Bars* ...77

David Santoro, WGME-Channel 13
Chief Meteorologist, *Building
Weather Instruments* ...78

Steve Romanoff, leader of the singing
group Schooner Fare,
Visiting Vinalhaven Island ...80

Great Ideas from Famous Maine Folks

Idea:
Exploring Maine's Tidal Pools
From: Former First Lady Barbara Bush

"Exploring tidal pools with parents or grandparents is one of life's great pleasures. Under rocks are such a treasure trove of starfish, crabs, sea urchins, and tiny bait. In the pools one is certain to find a variety of seaweed, sea glass, and numerous interesting things. The time spent outside climbing rocks and discovering these jewels of pools with loved ones is priceless—but completely free of charge—and I recommend it highly."

Idea:
Biking at Acadia National Park
From: Governor John Baldacci, First Lady Karen Baldacci, and Jack Baldacci

"Acadia is a beautiful spot, with many activities that are fun for the family to do together. We enjoy the bike trails. Be sure to eat a good breakfast or lunch before you begin, and bring water along, too. Be on the lookout for wildlife and seals and whales offshore."

Idea: ## Building Maine Sea Treasure Sculptures
From: Former Governor Angus S. King Jr. and former First Lady Mary J. Herman

"Spend spring and early summer collecting seashells, driftwood, and treasures along the shore."

YOU WILL NEED:

Glue gun (adult supervision required)
Fishing line
Scissors
Tape measure

STEPS
1. Heat glue gun.
2. Arrange seashells and other items collected to make sculptures.
3. Glue and let dry.
4. Alternately, you can use the fishing line to hang the treasures from driftwood to make a mobile.

Idea: ## Creating an ABC Book About Maine

From: U.S. Senator Olympia Snowe and former Governor John R. McKernan
Create a book of people, places, and things that are unique to Maine. This is a great way for children and adults to learn all about Maine—its people, communities, and resources. This activity allows parents and children to use a variety of research tools, such as the library, Internet, first-person interviews, etc.

Begin with any letter of the alphabet and select a person, place, or thing from Maine. Example: F could stand for Farnsworth Museum, which is located in Rockland, Maine. Call to find out the hours of operation. Take a drive to Rockland and tour the museum. The Farnsworth is best known for its extensive collection of art by three generations of Wyeths. It is also home to works by William and Marguerite Zorach.

While you're in Rockland, you can also research other letters, such as W, for windjammer. Rockland, and neighboring Camden and Rockport, are home to the Maine Windjammer Fleet. The Victory Chimes is the oldest wooden windjammer in the country and has been granted the National Historic Landmark designation.

Other examples might be: P, for potato from Aroostook County, or A, for the Androscoggin River, which flows between the twin cities of

Auburn and Lewiston; or B, for Biddeford, home to La Kermesse, one of the state's largest Franco-American heritage festivals.

Take photographs, pick up free brochures, or purchase postcards of the things you see. Back at home, assemble your information alphabetically in a scrapbook format. Be creative—use photos, pictures that the children have drawn, poems or short stories that the children have written about their experiences. The scrapbook can be as simple as pieces of colored paper bound with ribbon or a ring binder where pages are inserted into clear plastic protective covers.

Idea: Gathering Sea Glass and Friendship Stones

From: U.S. Senator Susan M. Collins

"Go to the beach with an adult and take a bucket along. You will be searching in the sand and among the rocks. Be sure to search the high-water mark, the low-water mark, and in the water! You are looking for pieces of colored glass (green, brown, clear, or lucky pink) and for stones—friendship stones!

The sea glass should be cloudy in color and have no rough edges. It should feel smooth as can be when you rub it in your hands. If it isn't smooth, put it back. It isn't sea glass yet!

Your friendship stone should have at least one solid white line going all the way around, with no cracks or breaks in the line."

Idea: Learning to Identify Birds Found in Maine

From: U.S. Representative Tom Allen

"Birds have different songs, and it's a challenge to learn to identify them. Any time of day can be okay for observing, but early morning is best for seeing small birds. Walk quietly or sit patiently near bushes or trees and watch and listen. If birds are nearby, you can try to bring them closer by

making pssh sounds while you stand near a bush or tree. Try different rhythms, like pssh . . . . pssh-pssh . . . . pssh, and see what works best. Many small birds will be curious and come closer."

Idea: Creating Sweet Modeling Clay

From: Mrs. Caspar Weinberger

INGREDIENTS REQUIRED:

¼ cup Maine mashed potatoes
1 teaspoon vanilla
1 box of powdered sugar
Food coloring—red, green, and yellow
Toothpicks
Extras you might like: melted chocolate, M&Ms, grated coconut, pecan halves, chopped walnuts, or chocolate chips

STEPS

1. Warm the mashed potatoes.
2. Add vanilla flavoring.
3. Work in the powdered sugar until the mixture feels like play dough. You may need less than one whole box of sugar.
4. Take small amounts of your "dough" and make animal shapes or worms, adding the food coloring and kneading it in to get the color you desire.
5. Dip toothpick into color to make designs, eyes, noses, mouths, and other markings. Place each finished product on a cookie sheet lined with waxed paper.
6. Now is the time to add any extra trimmings you may choose.
7. Place in refrigerator to set for 2 hours.

Idea: Creating Periwinkle Jewelry

From: The family of Betty Noyce

Pendred Noyce shared a remembrance of summers growing up on the coast of Maine with her mother, Elizabeth Noyce, a noted philanthropist who generously supported a wide range of causes in Maine.

Pendred remembers her experiences by the sea, and particularly "collecting periwinkle shells which were then strung together with needle and thread, making a necklace or bracelet for each of the children. Yellow was the favorite color of this classically fine Maine jewelry."

Note: Often the ocean makes natural holes in the shells for stringing together; if not, drill small holes.

Idea: Cooking Grandma's Chop Suey

From: Cindy Blodgett, former University of Maine Basketball Star

INGREDIENTS:

- **1 lb. hamburger**
- **Small can of mushrooms**
- **Salt and pepper to taste**
- **1 small box elbow pasta**
- **1 can of Campbell's Tomato Soup**

STEPS

1. Cook the hamburger in a frying pan and add mushrooms, salt, and pepper.
2. Boil the pasta until cooked, then drain.
3. Mix the pasta and the cooked hamburger together. Then add the tomato soup. Mix thoroughly and serve.

This is a quick and easy meal that kids can make and enjoy eating, too!

Idea: Hiking Douglas Mountain in Sebago

From: Rick Charrette, Children's Singer and Entertainer

"Why is it fun? Even if you are thinking that you are not crazy about hiking, I am quite certain you will enjoy this adventure. Begin at the base of Douglas Mountain [found on map 4, C4 in De-lorme Publishing's Maine Atlas and Gazetteer]. Hike a short distance through the woods, then over some open ledges. In about 10 to 15 minutes, you will reach the summit. A stone tower awaits you at the top. You will want to step inside and climb the circular stone staircase to the top. Look all around. On a clear day, you will see spectacular views of the White Mountains, Pleasant Moun-tain, and Sebago Lake. Have a picnic with your family and friends.

Wear comfortable shoes or hiking boots. You may want to carry a small backpack with snacks, water, camera, and binoculars."

Idea: Enjoying Favorite Vistas at Acadia National Park

From: Leon (L.L. Bean past president) and Lisa Gorman

"Take a few days to visit Acadia National Park and explore its beauty. Walking the carriage roads of Acadia National Park is a great way to exercise both body and mind! There are over fifty miles of gravel roads with no cars allowed. Enjoy the beautiful scenery!"

Idea: Visiting Little Chebeague Island in Casco Bay

From: Dr. Craig Hurwitz (Medical Director for Maine Children's Cancer Program), Mrs. Hurwitz, and Hutch Hurwitz

Little Chebeague offers a wonderful walk through history. At low tide, you can get there from Great Chebeague by going across what is known as The

Hook. The island was cleared by settlers in the eighteenth century and used for farming and fishing. After the Civil War, it attracted Maine Civil War veterans, who held their eleventh reunion camping in the pastures. In 1865 a hotel and "bowling saloon" were built there, and the island became a resort area for several years. The U.S. Navy took over the island in 1942, and it became a recreational area for sailors. Now only the frameworks of some of the original homes remain. The island offers a beautiful walking tour with many plaques that detail the history.

Idea: **Night Skiing in Maine**

From: Julie Russem, Maine Children's Cancer Program cofounder, and daughter Nina

"We discovered night skiing at Shawnee Peak [in Bridgton]. Tickets are about half the cost of a regular day ticket, and the French fries are superb. We have skied during full moons, blue moons, and blizzards; and I know we have made new favorite family memories."

Idea: **Walking the Beach with Your Dog**

From: Dr. Steve Blattner, Maine Children's Cancer Program cofounder

" 'To the beach with the dog' has always been a special treat for our family. It all started with our golden retriever, who loved to steal our gloves and dunk them in the ocean during winter walks on the beach. Even after the dog passed on, it remained 'to the beach with the dog'—a chance to be outdoors, to be together as a family, and to romp and have fun in the sand by the ocean."

Idea: **Baking Buried Treasure Cupcakes and Zebra Bars**

From: Jim King and John Stott, Founders of Stonewall Kitchens

Buried Treasure Cupcakes

Bake these yummy treats with your favorite adult (who has an electric mixer!). Makes 12.

INGREDIENTS REQUIRED:

   2 cups sifted cake flour
   2 teaspoons baking powder
   $1/3$ cup butter, softened
   $1/2$ cup peanut butter
   $3/4$ cup dark brown sugar
   $1/4$ cup white sugar
   1 teaspoon vanilla extract
   2 eggs
   $3/4$ cup milk
   berry jam as needed

STEPS
1. Preheat the oven to 350°.
2. Put paper muffin liners in a muffin tin and set aside.
3. Mix the flour and baking powder together in a bowl; set aside.
4. Beat the butter and peanut butter in a mixing bowl until combined. Add both of the sugars; continue to beat until mixture is very fluffy. Add vanilla and one egg and beat until combined. Add the other egg and beat in. Scrape down the sides of the bowl as you go along.
5. With mixer on low, add the flour mixture and milk in small batches (flour, milk, flour, milk, flour), mixing just until blended; do not overmix or you'll have tough cupcakes.
6. Spoon batter into the lined muffin tins, about half full. Then add one teaspoon jam in each. Cover with a bit more batter until three-quarters full.
7. Bake for 25 to 30 minutes. Let cool before digging in.

Zebra Bars

Make this chewy treat with your favorite adult. Makes 36.

INGREDIENTS REQUIRED:

$^2/_3$ cup all-purpose flour

$^1/_4$ teaspoon baking soda

5 tablespoons butter

$^3/_4$ cup peanut butter

1 cup sugar

2 large eggs

1 teaspoon vanilla extract

$^1/_4$ cup berry jam

STEPS

1. Preheat oven to 350°.
2. Lightly smear the insides of an 8- by 8-inch baking pan with butter.
3. Put the flour and baking soda into a small mixing bowl and stir.
4. Put the butter in a 2- to 3-quart saucepan and slowly melt over medium-low heat. Remove the pan from the burner and add peanut butter. Stir until everything is melted and completely smooth.
5. Stir in the sugar. Crack the eggs into the saucepan and beat in with a wooden spoon.
6. Add the flour mixture and stir until blended.
7. Pour the batter into your greased pan. With a spoon, stir the jam and drizzle over the batter in a zigzag pattern.
8. Bake for 35 to 40 minutes. Carefully remove from the oven. Cool on a wire rack. Cut into 36 squares.

Idea:
Building Weather Instruments
From: David Santoro, WGME-Channel 13 Chief Meteorologist

Barometer

A barometer measures the pressure of the air, which changes between storms and fair weather. Although the barometer was invented more than three hundred years ago, it is still used daily by meteorologists around the world.

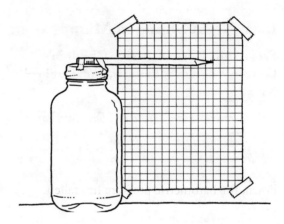

YOU WILL NEED:

Large glass bottle

Balloon

Pencil

Tape

Piece of graph paper

Scissors

Rubber band

STEPS

1. Take the lid off your glass bottle.
2. Cut the balloon with the scissors so that it can be stretched tightly and evenly over the mouth of the bottle. This should make the bottle airtight.
3. Use the rubber band to secure the balloon over the top of the bottle.
4. Lay the pencil on top of the jar and tape one end to the center of the stretched balloon, and again to the edge of the bottle. Tape

down the eraser end so that the writing end sticks out. Your pencil has to be long enough to extend beyond the edge of the jar.

OPERATION

1. Set the jar on a shelf or table indoors.
2. Tape your piece of graph paper to the wall behind the jar and set the jar close enough to it so that the pencil can mark the paper, but can still move freely up and down. Marks on the paper will indicate changes in barometric pressure.

HOW IT WORKS

When the barometric pressure (the pressure of the air) increases, the air outside the bottle will press down on the balloon and the free end of the pencil will move up. When the barometric pressure outside falls below the pressure inside the bottle, the balloon will bulge up and move the free end of the pencil down. In other words, if the pencil points up, the barometric pressure has gone up. It the pencil points down, the barometric pressure has fallen.

Anemometer

An anemometer is used to measure wind speed. This is an unsophisticated version, but it is basically the same instrument used by the National Weather Service and other weather reporting stations.

YOU WILL NEED:

4 paper drinking cups

2 straws

Straight pin or tack

Lid from a glass jar

Crayon or marker

Tape or stapler

Pencil with eraser

CONSTRUCTION

1. Use your crayon or marker to color one of the paper cups so that it is different from the others. Be careful not to crush the cup when you are coloring it.
2. Tape or staple the straws together in the

Anemometer.

middle at a right angle so they form a plus sign.
3. Using the straight pin or tack, make a small hole in the jar lid. You may want your parents' help doing this.
4. Tape a paper cup to each end of both straws. The cups should be on their sides and should all face in the same direction, so that the bottom of one cup faces the top of the next cup.
5. Push the pin or tack through the straws where they are attached (at the center of the plus sign), then through the hole in the jar lid. Finally, stick the pin into the eraser end of the pencil. The straws, with cups attached, should spin freely.

OPERATION

1. Put the writing end of the pencil in the ground.
2. Blow into one of the cups to be sure the straws rotate freely. If they do not, work the straws around the tack or pin until they do.
3. Keep an eye on the colored cup to count the number of times the straws rotate. If you have a clock or watch with a second hand, you can count the number of rotations per minute.

HOW IT WORKS

When the wind blows, it will fill the empty cups with air until enough pressure builds up to make them spin. The faster the cups rotate, the stronger the wind. If the cups are not rotating, the winds are calm.

Idea: Visiting Vinalhaven Island

From: Steve Romanoff, leader of the singing group Schooner Fare

"My kids and I always enjoy visiting the islands off the coast of Maine. One of our favorites is Vinalhaven Island in Penobscot Bay, a 75-minute ferry ride from Rockland. Life slows down on an island, and it's easy to have fun doing very simple things. Kids like to bike around the island roads, exploring the quiet coves and swimming in the old granite quarries. The island people are very friendly, and the place has a warm sense of community. The town has a wonderful public library, a history museum, parks, and restaurants, including a log-cabin bowling alley that serves great pizza. All of this is fifteen miles out to sea. Way cool!"

chapter 9

Hiking

Southern Maine ... 82

Bradbury Mountain State Park,
Pownal ... 82

Douglas Mountain, Sebago ... 82

Fore River Sanctuary, Portland ... 83

Gilsland Farm, Falmouth ... 83

Hacker's Hill, Casco ... 83

Marginal Way, Ogunquit ... 84

Portland Trails, Portland ... 84

Saco Heath Preserve, Saco ... 84

Wells National Estuarine Research
Reserve, Wells ... 84

Wolfe's Neck Woods, Freeport ... 84

Mid-Coast Maine ... 85

Camden Hills State Park, Camden ... 85

Dodge Point Preserve, Newcastle ... 85

Hockmomock Trail/Todd Wildlife
Sanctuary, Bremen ... 85

Josephine Newman Sanctuary,
Georgetown ... 86

Monhegan Island, off Port Clyde ... 86

Morse Mountain/Sewall Beach,
Phippsburg ... 86

Oyster River Bog, Rockland ... 87

Down East Maine ... 87

Acadia National Park,
Mount Desert Island ... 87

Blue Hill, Blue Hill ... 88

Bold Coast Trail, Cutler ... 88

Craig Brook National Fish Hatchery,
East Orland ... 88

Dedham Bald Mountain, Dedham ... 88

Moosehorn National Wildlife Refuge,
Calais ... 89

Petit Manan National Wildlife Refuge,
Steuben ... 89

Central Maine ... 89

French's Mountain, Rome ... 89

Mount Pisgah, Winthrop ... 90

Pine Tree State Arboretum, Augusta ... 90

Singepole Mountain, South Paris ... 90

Streaked Mountain, Buckfield ... 90

Western Maine ... 91

Angel Falls, Township D ... 91

Bald Mountain, Rangeley ... 91

Mount Blue, Weld ... 91

Pleasant Mountain, Denmark ... 92

Sabattus Mountain, Lovell ... 92

Steep Falls Preserve, Newry ... 92

West Kennebago Mountain, Stetsontown
and Upper Cupsuptic Townships ... 93

Northern Maine ... 93

Baxter State Park, Millinocket ... 93

Gulf Hagas Reserve, Bowdoin College
Grant East ... 94

Hedgehog Mountain, Township T15,
R6 ... 94

Mount Kineo, Rockwood ... 94

Moxie Falls, Moxie Gore ... 95

Quaggy Jo Mountain, Presque Isle ... 95

Hiking

Maine offers an amazing variety of opportunities to hike and enjoy the spectacular vistas. This chapter includes a range of hikes for several levels of ability and endurance. Note that we have located each recommended hike by referencing the town and map quadrants from DeLorme Publishing's *Maine Atlas and Gazetteer*.

Safety is an important consideration to plan for before setting out. Be sure to bring the following with you:

- **A map and compass**
- **Water (don't drink untreated water)**
- **Sunscreen**
- **Bug repellent (especially in spring and early summer)**
- **Good hiking shoes**
- **Warm clothing (weather can change suddenly)**
- **A hat**

And do not forget: stay on the trail; be sure to tell someone where you are going and when you plan to return; and carry out everything you carry in—do not litter.

For more information, contact the following agencies:

Maine Bureau of Parks and Lands (Headquarters)
> 22 State House Station, Augusta, ME 04333
> *Call (207) 287-3821 or visit* *www.state.me.us/doc/parks/programs/ db_search/index.html*

Maine Audubon Society
> 118 U.S. Route 1, Falmouth, ME 04105-6009
> *Call (207) 781-2330 or visit* *www.maineaudubon.org*

Southern Maine

Bradbury Mountain State Park
> **Pownal (Map 5, C5)**
> **Trailhead: From Lewiston, head south on Route 136. Turn right onto Route 9 south in Durham. The park's entrance is approximately 4 miles south.**
> **Distance: 6 miles of trails**
> **Difficulty: Slight to moderate**
> **Season: Year-round**
> **Fee: Yes**
> **Bradbury Mountain State Park (207) 688-4712**
> *For more information, visit* *www.state.me.us/doc/parks/programs/ db_search/index.html*

Perhaps the quickest hike to great views of Portland and the ocean, the park's Mountain Trail is just .4 miles round-trip. In the hemlock grove of the longer Tote Road Trail, accessible from the summit, some hikers claim to have seen the ghost of Samuel Bradbury. Several other trails can extend your trek across stone walls and brooks and into balsam groves, a pasture, and hardwood forest.

Douglas Mountain
> **Sebago (Map 4, C4)**
> **Trailhead: Off Dyke Mountain Road (see directions below)**
> **Distance: .5 miles round-trip**
> **Difficulty: Slight**
> **Season: Year-round**
> **Fee: No**

Fifteen minutes of walking through old-growth hemlock and northern hardwood forests brings you to open ledges, and another five minutes brings you to the summit. In summer, wild blueberries and blackberries are a great hiking treat for everyone. Atop the mountain, a 16-foot stone tower affords 280-degree views of Sebago Lake and the White Mountains. On a clear day one can even see the Green Mountains of Vermont. A compass mounted on the tower helps to orient visitors. Those eager for a longer walk can strike out south from the tower along a three-quarter-mile nature trail that loops back to the summit. To return to the base, either retrace your ascent or follow the white-blazed trail to the tower's west.

To find the trailhead: From the village of Sebago Lake, follow Route 114 north 9.5 miles to the junction of Long Hill Road. Follow Long Hill Road 2 miles to Route 107 and turn left after .5 miles onto Dyke Mountain Road (also called Douglas Hill Road). Proceed .3 miles to where an unnamed road leads left to the trailhead. Follow this steep, narrow road .5 miles to the Nature Conservancy sign.

Fore River Sanctuary

Portland (Map 73, E1 or F2)
Trailhead: Enter either from the end of Row Avenue (off Brighton Avenue) or from the parking lot of the Maine Orthopedic Center off Frost Street (off Congress Avenue).
Distance: 2.5 miles of trails
Difficulty: Slight
Season: Year-round, sunrise to sunset
Fee: No
Maine Audubon Society (207) 781-2330 or www.maineaudubon.org
Portland Trails (207) 775-2411 or www.trails.org

In the heart of Portland, blue-blazed trails lead you through meadows and salt marsh to an historic canal towpath that passes by Jewell Falls, whose cascading waters drown out all the city's sounds. Swimming is prohibited.

Gilsland Farm

Falmouth (Map 5, E5)
Trailhead: Farm entrance is off the west side of Route 1, opposite the junction with Route 88.
Distance: 2 miles of trails
Difficulty: Slight
Season: March to November
Fee: No
Maine Audubon Society (207) 781-2330 or www.maineaudubon.org

Well-marked trails wind through salt marsh, woodlands, meadows, and organic gardens. Observation blinds and outlook points allow you to spy wildlife unnoticed. Nearby, the Maine Audubon education center exhibits hands-on displays.

Hacker's Hill

Casco (Map 5, B1)
Trailhead: From Casco, take Route 121 south to Route 11 west to Quaker Ridge Road on left. Gated entrance on left is approximately 1.5 miles south.
Distance: 1 mile round-trip
Difficulty: Moderate
Season: Year-round
Fee: No
High Country Mission (866) 310-8445 or http://mainewebpublications.com/silentpreacherorg/index.html

Hike up a short, steep, paved road to a well-kept local secret. From atop the hill, a clear day affords views of New Hampshire's Presidential Range (including Mount Washington) and six lakes (including Sebago Lake). Hacker's Hill, although privately owned, is accessible to the public due to the voluntary caretaking services of High Country Mission.

Marginal Way

Ogunquit (Map 1, A5)
Trailhead: Oarweed Cove, near Oarweed Restaurant
Distance: 2 miles round-trip
Difficulty: Slight
Season: Year-round
Fee: None
Ogunquit Chamber of Commerce (207) 646-2939 or www.ogunquit.org/

Marginal Way, given to the town by Josiah Chase, is a paved footpath beginning in a corner of Oarweed Cove near the harbor, then running for 1.25 miles to the marvelous expanse of sandy Ogunquit Beach. The bends and inclines along the way are rather gentle as this delightful, exhilarating walk meanders by tangled bayberry and bittersweet bushes, fragrant pink and white sea roses, shaded alcoves formed by wind-twisted trees jutting out onto high granite outcroppings, and humbling views of the mighty Atlantic.

Portland Trails

Trailheads located throughout Portland
Portland Trails (207) 775-2411 or www.trails.org

Created by Portland Trails, an urban conservation organization, this network of multiuse trails within Greater Portland currently numbers 23 trails in various locations throughout the city. Back Cove, Eastern Promenade, Fore River, Martin's Point, and Falmouth Nature Preserve are just a few of the places where these trails are located. Visit the Portland Trails Web site for a map and complete details.

Saco Heath Preserve

Saco (Map 3, B2)
Trailhead: Route 112, 2 miles west of I-95
Distance: 1 mile
Difficulty: Slight
Season: Year-round
Fee: No

Biddeford–Saco Chamber of Commerce (207) 282-1567 or www.biddefordsacochamber.org

A wooded trail opens to a boardwalk over a raised peat bog. All sorts of interesting plants and wildlife are present along this unusual nature trail.

Wells National Estuarine Research Reserve

Wells (Map 3, E1)
Trailhead: Wells National Estuarine Research Reserve visitor center (see directions below)
Distance: 7 miles of trails
Difficulty: Slight
Season: Year-round
Fee: Yes
Wells National Estuarine Research Reserve (207) 646-1555 or www.wellsreserve.org

A network of scenic wildlife trails wind through meadows, marsh, tidal creeks, ponds, woods, and sandy beaches. Maps, information, and children's "discovery packs" are available at the visitor center, which is open daily from May to October and on weekends the rest of the year.

To find the trailheads: From Wells Corner, proceed 1.75 miles north on Route 1. Turn left onto Laudholm Farm Road. Follow signs to Reserve. Trails begin at the visitor center.

Wolfe's Neck Woods

Freeport (Map 6, D1)
Trailhead: Wolfe's Neck Road (see directions below)
Distance: 5 miles of trails
Difficulty: Slight to moderate
Season: Staffed Memorial Day to Labor Day (accessible year-round)
Fee: Yes (Trail maps available in parking area)
Wolfe's Neck State Park (207) 865-4465
For more information, visit www.state.me.us/doc/parks/programs/db_search/index.html

Trails traverse woodlands, bog, tide pools, and meadow as they follow the rocky shore of Casco Bay past Googins Island, where in spring and summer a pair of ospreys can sometimes be seen perched high in their bulky stick nest. Interpretive panels describe natural sights throughout the park. Daily afternoon guided walks are offered in July and August and by appointment for children's groups in spring and fall. Opportunities for picnicking and play abound in the fields by the parking lot.

To find the trailhead: Take Bow Street (across from L.L. Bean in downtown Freeport) 2.5 miles south. Follow the right fork to Flying Point Road and continue for 1 mile to Wolfe's Neck Road on the right. A well-marked entrance is 2.5 miles south.

Mid-Coast Maine

Camden Hills State Park

Camden (Map 14, D4 and D5)
**Trailhead: Park entrance on Route 1,
two miles north of downtown Camden**
**Distance: 30 miles of hiking trails with
access from 5 different trail heads**
Difficulty: Moderate
Season: Year-round
Fee: Yes
*May to mid-October, call (207) 236-3109;
Mid-October to April, call
(207) 236-0848*
*For more information, visit
http://www.state.me.us/doc/parks/
programs/db_search/index.html*

Here in Camden's outdoor playground, well-marked trails on the many hills lead to spectacular surprise views, blueberry barrens, and rocky outcroppings. Among the most popular destinations is Mount Battie. Head up the Nature Trail, an hour-long hike from the parking lot, to the summit, where a cylindrical

stone tower provides an even better view of Penobscot Bay and Camden village below. Information boards identify the islands offshore, which can be seen more clearly through the pay-per-view scopes stationed along the edge.

Dodge Point Preserve

Newcastle (Map 7, B3)
**Trailhead: River Road
(see directions below)**
Distance: 5 to 6 miles of trails
Difficulty: Slight
**Season: Year-round (hunting allowed in
November)**
Fee: No (Maps available)
*Damariscotta River Association
(207) 563-1393*
*For more information, visit
http://www.state.me.us/doc/parks/
programs/db_search/index.html*

Here, at one of the "jewels in the crown" of the state's system of Parks and Preserves, numerous trails and highlight sites skirt the shore of the Damariscotta River. Several of the trails head toward Sand Beach, where you can go for a swim or enjoy a quiet picnic.

To find the trailhead: Signs mark the entrance on the left just 2.6 miles south on River Road, off U.S. Route 1.

Hockmomock Trail/
Todd Wildlife Sanctuary

Bremen (Map 7, B4)
**Trailhead: Keene Neck Road
(see directions below)**
Distance: Approximately 1 to 1.5 miles
Difficulty: Slight
Season: Year-round
Fee: No
*Maine Audobon Society (207) 781-2330 or
www.maineaudubon.org*

Brochures available at the visitor center list 25 special points of interest within the meadows, thickets, forests, and shoreline that the trail traverses, including exposed mussel beds, tide pools, and interesting picnic spots. Enjoy views of Hog Island, home to the Maine Audubon Society's summer ecology camp for teens and adults. Special group tours and an annual summer open house include boat rides to the island.

To find the trailhead: From Route 1 in Waldoboro, follow Route 32 south approximately 5 miles to Keene Neck Road. The trail is located within the Todd Wildlife Sanctuary at the road's end.

Josephine Newman Sanctuary

Georgetown (Map 7, D1)
Trailhead: off Route 127
(see directions below)
Distance: 2 miles of trails
Difficulty: Slight to moderate
Season: Year-round (maps available in parking area)
Fee: No
Maine Audubon Society (207) 781-2330 or www.maineaudubon.org

The trail network includes a half-mile trail with interpretive panels marking reversing falls, marshes, mosses, and glacial features. Other trails wind through coastal woodlands, past mudflat coves, pine forests, marsh, and pasture. Bring binoculars to spot birds and other wildlife.

To find the trailhead: Drive to the junction of U.S. Route 1 and Route 127 in Woolwich, just east of the Woolwich-Bath bridge, and head south on 127 for 9.1 miles to Georgetown. Turn right at the sanctuary sign and follow the entrance road to the parking area.

Monhegan Island

Offshore from Port Clyde (Map 8, D1)
Ferry service to the island is available from Port Clyde, New Harbor, and Boothbay Harbor. Be sure to make reservations ahead.
Port Clyde: Monhegan Boat Lines (207) 372-8848 (year-round)
New Harbor: Hardy Boat Cruises (800) 278-3346 (seasonal)
Boothbay Harbor: Balmy Day Cruises (207) 633-2284 (seasonal)
Distance: 17 miles of trails
Difficulty: Slight to moderate
Season: Year-round
Fee: For ferry passage and trail maps only
For more information, visit www.monhegan.com

There are 18 different trails to choose from on this square-mile island. Day-trippers can loop the island in two to three hours following Burnt Head Trail to Cliff Trail past dramatic headlands and rocky picnic spots. Heading off to Squeaker Cove, connect with the Cathedral Woods Trails through the pines and back to the village. A detour up the Whitehead Trail takes you to the museum. (Overnight guests can follow the full five-hour Cliff Trail route.) Dress for blustery Atlantic winds and take care with uneven footing, strong seas, and rogue waves in some places.

Morse Mountain/Sewall Beach

Phippsburg (Bates College Coastal Research Area), (Map 6, E5)
Trailhead: Off Route 216
Distance: 6 miles (round-trip)
Difficulty: Slight to moderate
Season: Year-round
Fee: No

Walk to sandy Sewall Beach along a maintained gravel road that cuts through beautiful marshes and woods. Enjoy the wildlife, flowers, and berries along the way. After you pass a boat building, a side trail loops off to the right to provide views of ocean, islands, and marsh, as well as a WWII observation post. Follow signs on the main trail to the swimming beach.

To find the trailhead: Take Route 209 (off U.S. Route 1 in downtown Bath) south 12 miles to Route 216. Continue less than one mile. Turn left onto narrow, paved road to parking lot.

Oyster River Bog

Rockland (Map 14, E2 and E3)
Trailhead: Beechwood Street
    (see directions below)
Distance: Approximately 7 miles of
    marked trails (avoid unmarked trails)
Difficulty: Slight to moderate
Season: Year-round
Fee: No (maps available)
Georges River Land Trust
    (207) 596-5166

One of the mid-coast's best-kept secrets, the bog is a 6,000-acre naturalist's paradise of open hardwood and pine forests, peat bogs, vernal pools, waterways, and natural meadows. A narrow, well-marked footpath into the site ensures an unspoiled outdoor adventure into this accessible wilderness. Abundant signs of moose, deer, beaver, frogs, and other wildlife are present near and on the trails. Dress appropriately during hunting season.

To reach the trailhead: From the traffic light in Thomaston, turn onto Beechwood Street and follow for approximately 2.5 miles to a sharp left-hand curve. Park in "Jack Baker Woods" parking lot on your immediate left. Another trailhead is off Route 90 in Rockland, just over the Warren town line.

Down East Maine

Acadia National Park

Mount Desert Island (Map 16, B2 to C4)
Trailhead: Route 3 and Route 233
    (see directions below)
Distance: 125 miles of hiking trails and
    57 miles of carriage roads (suitable for
    bikes and strollers)
Difficulty: Slight to difficult
Season: Year-round
Fee: Yes
Park visitor center (207) 288-3338
For more information, visit
    http://www.nps.gov/acad/

There are numerous trails suitable for children in the park, as well as several children's ecology programs (ages 5 to 12) that involve hiking. The children's programs operate daily and require reservations. On your own you can hike anytime. For at least two of the routes—the Ship Harbor Nature Trail and the Jordan Pond Nature Trail—a self-guiding brochure is available to help you explore the woods, ponds, beaches, and tide pools. For an entirely different experience, cross the sand bar from Bar Harbor to Bar Island at low tide and take a short hike to the island's viewing point. Or you can combine a swim at Sand Beach with a hike to Otter Point along the Ocean Path, passing many scenic points, including Thunder Hole. There are all sorts of opportunities for rock-hopping and exploring. Older children will enjoy the iron ladders on the Beehive Trail, which in its gentler sections loops around The Bowl (a small lake) and down by the ocean.

To get there: From May to October, take Route 3 toward Bar Harbor to the park's visitor center 8 miles southeast of the causeway. From November to April, take Route 233 from downtown Bar Harbor and proceed approximately 3.5 miles to the Acadia National Park headquarters.

Blue Hill

> **Blue Hill (Map 15, A4)**
> **Trailhead: Mountain Road**
> (see directions below)
> **Distance: 2 miles round-trip**
> **Difficulty: Slight to moderate**
> **Season: Year-round**
> **Fee: No**

At 943 feet above sea level, the summit of Blue Hill towers above the rest of the peninsula and has long served as a landmark to mariners. The 360-degree view from its rounded top is even better from the fire tower. Starting in an open meadow, the trail ascends steeply over rocks and wet areas. At the halfway point, it levels off and provides the first glimpse of panoramic views.

To reach the trailhead: Drive from U.S. Route 1 in Orland to Route 15. Head south 11 miles to Mountain Road. Continue .4 miles to the fire tower sign on the left.

Bold Coast Trail

> **Cutler (Map 25, C1 and C2)**
> **Trailhead: Route 191, 4.5 miles northeast**
> **of Cutler center**
> **Distance: 5-mile loop**
> **Difficulty: Moderate (not recommended**
> **for young children)**
> **Season: Year-round**
> **Fee: No**
> *Maine Bureau of Parks and Lands*
> *(207) 287-3821*
> *For more information, visit*
> *www.state.me.us/doc/parks/programs/*
> *db_search/index.html*

Adventuresome families will enjoy traversing the inland bogs and high narrow ledges along a shoreline of dramatic windswept cliffs with fabulous views. Picnic on granite outcroppings overlooking the strong surf. In August, be sure to bring along containers to gather wild blueberries and raspberries. Maps are available at the trailhead parking area.

Craig Brook National Fish Hatchery

> **East Orland (Map 21, D3)**
> **Trailhead: Hatchery Road**
> (see directions below)
> **Distance: Several miles of trails**
> **Difficulty: Slight to moderate**
> **Season: Year-round (visitor center open**
> **May to November)**
> **Fee: No**
> *(207) 469-2803*

Established in 1871, this 135-acre hatchery site is run by the U.S. Fish and Wildlife Service. In addition to hiking trails, the hatchery grounds include swimming areas, picnic tables and grills, a boat ramp, and an Atlantic salmon display pool. Hiking options range from a mile-long nature trail along Craig Brook or a two-mile round-trip walk to Craig Pond (where children can swim and adults can enjoy the scenery), to the more challenging two-hour climb up Great Pond Mountain, which has ample space for picnics at the summit.

To reach the trailhead: Drive six miles east of Bucksport, then turn north off Route 1 onto Hatchery Road. Continue 1.4 miles to the parking lot, where maps are available. Continue one mile north of the parking lot through gated private property. Please be sure to stay on the marked trail.

Dedham Bald Mountain

> **Dedham (Map 23, D4)**
> **Trailhead: Fire Road 61B**
> (see directions below)
> **Distance: 1 mile round-trip**
> **Difficulty: Slight**
> **Season: Year-round**
> **Fee: No**
> *For more information, visit*
> *http://www.adventuresinmaine.com/*
> *hiking/regn_dwnestacad/bald_mtn.htm*

You will enjoy good views all the way to the top on this trail. The flat, wide, and partially wooded summit provides views to Katahdin and Bigelow Mountains, Acadia National Park, and Lake Lucerne, and offers ample space for exploring and picnicking. From the trailhead, you will walk across fields toward a steeper area that travels across granite ledges straight to the summit. At .2 miles, follow white blazes along a route with telephone poles.

To reach the trailhead: Take Upper Dedham Road in Dedham, which is accessed either from U.S. Route 1A near the intersection of Route 46 in East Holden, or from Mill Road, off Route 46 near the Dedham/Bucksport line. From U.S. Route 1A, follow Upper Dedham Road approximately 2.8 miles to Bald Mountain Road on the left. From Mill Road off Route 46, Bald Mountain Road is less than 1 mile on your right. Once you turn onto Bald Mountain Road, drive about 3.6 miles to Fire Road 61B (Johnson Road) on your left.

Moosehorn National Wildlife Refuge

> Calais (Map 36, C5)
> Trailhead: Charlotte Road
>   (see directions below)
> Distance: 50 miles of trails
> Difficulty: Slight
> Season: Year-round
> Fee: No
> *(207) 454-3521*

Get acquainted with a small part of the 22,000-acre refuge and its abundance of wildlife on the site's two self-guided walks just beyond the headquarters building. The wooded nature trail is 1.2 miles long and passes through Dudley's Swamp. The much shorter Woodcock Trail is only one-third of a mile long. It showcases the shrubby habitat of this declining bird species.

To reach the trailhead: Start at the refuge headquarters 2.4 miles down Charlotte Road, which is about 3 miles southwest of Calais off Route 1.

Petit Manan National Wildlife Refuge

> Steuben (Map 17, A3)
> Trailhead: Pigeon Hill Road
>   (see directions below)
> Distance: 4 miles of trail
> Difficulty: Slight
> Season: Year-round
> Fee: No
> *(207) 546-2124*

Although the refuge encompasses scores of offshore bird nesting islands along Maine's coast, it also includes a 2,166-acre peninsula on the mainland, which has two trails. The easier Shore Trail is one mile long, while the three-mile Birch Trail is slightly more difficult. Both offer great views of the ocean and wildlife, and traverse field, marsh, shore, and forestlands. On clear days, the lighthouse on Petit Manan Island can be spotted offshore.

To reach the trailhead: Follow U.S. Route 1 to East Steuben, turn east/south on Pigeon Hill Road and continue six miles to the refuge's parking lot.

Central Maine

French's Mountain

> Rome (Map 20, E3, not marked on map)
> Trailhead: Watson Pond Road
>   (see directions below)
> Distance: 1 mile round-trip
> Difficulty: Slight
> Season: Year-round
> Fee: No

An easy hike to a lovely spot for a family picnic. Head to the summit's open ledges for the area's best views of Great Pond, the village, and Long Pond below.

To reach the trailhead: From Belgrade Lakes Village, follow Route 27 north past Rome Corner (junction of Route 225). Continue on Route 27 for 1.2 miles, then turn left on Watson Pond Road. The trailhead is on the left side of the road 0.7 miles from Route 27.

Mount Pisgah

Winthrop (Map 12, C2)
Trailhead: Fairbanks Road
  (see directions below)
Distance: 2 miles round-trip
Difficulty: Slight
Season: Year-round
Fee: No

Climb the well-worn trail along the power line to the open rock ledge summit and up the fire tower to see great views across Wilson Pond and Androscoggin Lake to the White Mountains, Saddleback, Sugarloaf, Mount Abram, and Mount Blue.

To reach the trailhead: Coming from Winthrop, travel north on Route 41. Turn left on Route 133 toward Wayne. Turn left again 3 miles later onto Fairbanks Road. Proceed 2.5 miles, cross the Wilson Pond narrows, and go another .5 miles to the ranger's cabin. Parking is across the street. The trail leaves from the cabin's back yard.

Pine Tree State Arboretum

Augusta (Map 76, C3)
Trailhead: 153 Hospital Street, across from
  the Augusta Mental Health Institute
Distance: 3.5 miles of trails (plus an
  additional 12-mile loop to the Togus
  Veterans' Hospital on Route 17)
Difficulty: Slight
Season: Year-round
Fee: No
(207) 621-0031

From the Viles Visitor Center, head out on any one of the trails in this 600-acre oasis in the midst of the state capital. Bring a picnic and binoculars to best enjoy the site. Wander through gardens, orchards, and a pine grove where each tree is dedicated to one of Maine's governors.

Singepole Mountain

South Paris (Map 11, D2)
Trailhead: Off Brett Hill Road
  (see directions below)
Distance: 1.5 miles round trip
Difficulty: Slight to moderate
Season: Year-round
Fee: No

Mica-studded ledges and commanding views make this a rewarding and interesting climb. An ever-expanding vista opens up as the trail heads toward the open grass summit, where a 360-degree panorama of western lakes and mountains greets the hiker. Not far from the top, an abandoned mica mine and quarry pond can be found.

To reach the trailhead: Follow Route 117 two miles east from South Paris. Take your second right onto Brett Hill Road. Pass a white farmhouse on the left. As the paved road turns sharply right, continue straight onto a dirt road that heads uphill. The road is joined by the trail (a jeep road) three-quarters of a mile ahead. Park at this intersection in the grassy turnaround.

Streaked Mountain

Location: Buckfield (Map 11, C2)
Trailhead: Streaked Mountain Road
  (see directions below)
Distance: 1 mile round-trip
Difficulty: Slight to moderate
Season: Year-round
Fee: No

Allow ample time for blueberrying or picnicking when you head for the summit of this hill. Views of Mount Washington and the Presidential Range and Oxford County's farms and forests are even better from the radio tower. Rock-hounds will enjoy the summit's ledges where large formations of mica, quartz, and black tourmaline crystals are embedded.

To reach the trailhead: Follow Route 117 four miles northeast of South Paris to where

Streaked Mountain Road turns off to the right (south). Continue on Streaked Mountain Road for about three-quarters of a mile.

Western Maine

Angel Falls

Township D (Map 18, B4)
Trailhead: Bemis Track, off Route 17
  (see directions below)
Distance: 1.25 miles round-trip
Difficulty: Moderate
Season: Year-round
Fee: No

To reach one of New England's highest cascades (90 feet), you will ford running water and crisscross stream bed boulders during even the driest seasons as you make your way up the trail through old hardwood forest that shelters an abundance of interesting mushrooms and fungi. Once you reach Mountain Brook, continue another 15 minutes before rounding the last turn into the cool dampness at the base of the falls. Here you can take a swim in the cold mountain water or picnic on the rocks.

To reach the trailhead: Finding this location is easiest if you're armed with a map. North of Houghton, on the west side of Route 17 at state highway marker 6102, is a dirt road, labeled in DeLorme Publishing's *Maine Atlas and Gazetteer* as Bemis Track. Follow this dirt road northwesterly along Berdeen Stream for approximately 3 miles to a sign and road on your left. This unpaved road takes you past a gravel pit. Park at this junction or closer to the pit. The red-blazed trail leads off to the left.

Bald Mountain

Rangeley (Map 28, E3)
Trailhead: Bald Mountain Road
  (see directions below)
Distance: 2 miles round-trip
Difficulty: Slight to moderate
Season: Year-round
Fee: No

Ascending less than 1,000 feet, this gentle hike leads to spectacular views of Mooselookmeguntic and Upper Richardson Lakes as well as the surrounding mountains. Follow the loop trail through beautiful open stands of hardwoods for a fun supper or lunchtime picnic by the fire tower at the summit. In the mid- to late summer, hunt for wild blueberries along the granite ledges.

To reach the trailhead: Travel from Oquossoc approximately one mile north on Route 4. Take a sharp left onto Bald Mountain Road and follow it .8 mile to the sign on the left.

Mount Blue

Weld (Map 19, C3)
Trailhead: 299 Center Hill Road, off the
  intersection of Routes 142 and 156
Distance: 3 miles round-trip
Difficulty: Moderate
Season: Year-round
Fee: No (Although Mount Blue is in a
  state park, fees are not charged in this
  section of the site)
Mount Blue Sate Park (207) 585-2347 or
  www.state.me.us/doc/parks/programs/
  db_search/index.html

Stop for a picnic halfway up on Center Hill (outhouses are available), or try the one-mile self-guided nature trail loop before heading up to the Mount Blue Trail farther along the road. Steeper and more challenging than the nature trail below, Mount Blue's climb on the east side of Webb Lake rewards you with vistas of the Longfellow Mountains, plus an old fire tower to explore. After you descend, head over to the other section of the state park on the west side of Webb Lake for a swim, or enjoy one of the state park's interpretive nature programs, speakers, or movies.

Pleasant Mountain

Denmark (Map 4, A2)
Trailhead: Off Mountain Road
   (see directions below)
Distance: 3.5 miles round-trip
   (Ledges or Moose Trail)
Difficulty: Slight to moderate
Season: Year-round
Fee: No

Of the mountain's six trails, the Ledges Trail is the most popular and the easiest for children. There is plenty of space on the summit for picnicking and enjoying the panoramic views of lakes, mountains, and forest. There is also an abandoned fire tower. In summer you can add to your feast by picking some wild blueberries on the ledges halfway up the trail.

To reach the trailhead: Follow Route 302 west from Bridgton past Moose Pond. Turn left onto Mountain Road. Turn right at signs for Shawnee Peak Ski Area and continue 3.3 miles to the trailhead and parking.

Sabattus Mountain

Lovell (Map 10, D2)
Trailhead: Sabattus Road
   (see directions below)
Distance: 1.5 miles round-trip
Difficulty: Slight to moderate
Season: Year-round
Fee: No

Well-marked trails and gentle grades make this a great hike for all ages. At the summit the mountain's sheer southwest cliff affords terrific views of Kezar Lake, Kezar Pond, and the White Mountains. A quarter mile farther along the trail is a big boulder with even better views.

To reach the trailhead: Travel north from Fryeburg on Route 5 to Center Lovell. Sabattus Road is .8 mile north of the junction where Route 5A rejoins Route 5. Continue 1.6 miles up Sabattus Road and bear right at the fork. Continue .3 miles to the parking area on the left.

Step Falls Preserve

Newry (Map 18, E2)
Trailhead: Off Route 26
   (see directions below)
Distance: 1 mile round-trip
Difficulty: Slight
Season: Year-round
Fee: No (maps available in parking area)
The Nature Conservancy, Maine Chapter
   (207) 729-5181 or
   http://nature.org/wherewework/
   northamerica/states/maine

After just a 10-minute walk through balsam firs and hardwoods, the roar of the falls can be heard as the icy water tumbles nearly 200 feet down a one-eighth-mile stretch of rocky steps. Come in fall to view the hardwood forest at its most colorful, or in spring if you wish to see the water at its highest. The path follows along the shore of the brook near pools and cascades as it makes its way up to a pleasing view of the mountains of Grafton Notch.

To reach the trailhead: Drive on Route 26 approximately 10 miles northwest of Newry, and watch for the Nature Conservancy sign on the right, next to Wight Brook. (This will come up before you get to Grafton Notch State Park.)

West Kennebago Mountain

Stetsontown (Map 28, C3) and Upper Cupsuptic Townships
Trailhead: Lincoln Pond Road (see directions below)
Distance: 4.5 miles round-trip
Difficulty: Moderate
Season: Year-round
Fee: No

Moving from hardwoods to conifers, you enter a dark and magical forest where boulders are roped by tenacious spruce tree roots, and a host of plant life slowly devours fallen trunks. Cross over small streams and scramble up small boulders to the rustic ranger's cabin, which is still inhabited. (A nearby mountain spring provides the ranger's drinking water.) Follow the path to the fire tower for breathtaking views of lakes and the mountains of Vermont and Quebec. After you descend, follow the gravel road 1.9 miles further for a well-earned swim in the Kennebago River.

To reach the trailhead: Travel west from Rangeley on Route 16, toward Cupsuptic Lake. A dirt road (Morton Cutoff Road) veers right (north) .3 miles north of the Maine Forest Service Cupsuptic Station. Follow this dirt road (bear right, following green arrow signs to Little Kennebago Lake and Big Falls) 3.2 miles to Lincoln Pond Road on the right. On Lincoln Pond Road, continue 5.4 miles (enjoying a stunning view of the mountain along the way), to a sign on the left saying, "Trail to Watchtower."

Northern Maine

Baxter State Park

Spread across several townships north of Millinocket (Map 51, E1)
Trailhead: The southern entrance at Togue Pond Gate is at the intersection of Brook Road and Park Tote Road, T2 R9
Distance: 175 miles of trails
Difficulty: Slight to difficult
Season: Year-round
Fee: Yes (free day use for Maine residents)
Baxter State Park reservation office (207) 723-5140 or www.baxterstateparkauthority.com

At both the north and south ends of the park, Baxter has a number of easy- to moderate-level hikes that are suitable for children, as well as three nature trails, such as the 1.8-mile Daicey Pond Nature Trail. At the end of this route, you can munch on wild raspberries in the summer, rent a canoe at the ranger's station, or hike to Big Niagra Falls for a swim.

If you prefer a longer trail, try the 6-mile round-trip Howe Brooke Trail, which departs from the south end campground. Hikers crisscross boulders and streams on their way up to a series of waterfalls and pools where you can swim in the icy cold water or sunbathe and picnic on the flat boulders.

Visitors should note: Due to its popularity, access to the park may be limited and the gates are sometimes closed. Reservations are encouraged. See the Web site or call the reservations office for further information.

Gulf Hagas Reserve

Bowdoin College Grant East (Map 42, D1; Map 41, C5 and D5)
Trailhead: Off road to Katahdin Iron Works (see directions below)
Distance: 8.6 miles round-trip
Difficulty: Moderate to difficult (not recommended for young children)
Season: Early May to Columbus Day
Fee: Yes

North Maine Woods (207) 965-8135 or visit www.northmainewoods.org/ ki-jo/hagas.html

To purchase The Appalachian Trail Guide to Maine, *visit* http://www.atctrailstore.org/catalog/ index.cfm?compid=1&pcatid=42

Gulf Hagas, the "Grand Canyon of Maine," is considered the most spectacular gorge in the Northeast. It is a high, narrow canyon that channels the waters of the West Branch of the Pleasant River as it drops 400 feet over four miles, creating a breathtaking series of waterfalls. Although not steep, its terrain includes narrow ledges and hundred-foot drop-offs that can be perilous if not approached with full attention. This is a rugged and remote area, so come appropriately equipped.

To reach the trailhead: From Brownville Junction, take Route 11 north approximately 5 miles. Turn left at the sign for Katahdin Iron Works, situated across from a large potato field. This road, which turns from pavement to gravel, passes the iron works at 6.8 miles and comes to a gated bridge crossing where you'll find an update on the logging road conditions. Trail maps are available here. Gulf Hagas, though on public land, is only accessible by private roads managed by Katahdin Iron Works/Mary-Jo, Inc., who charge a toll to use their roads. Once you have paid the toll, continue another 6 to 7 miles to a dirt parking lot. Walk a bit farther up the road to the trail markers on the right.

Hedgehog Mountain

Township T15 R6 (Map 63, A5)
Trailhead: From Winterville, head 4 miles south on Route 11 to the Maine Forest Service picnic and parking area. The trail leaves from the parking lot's southwest corner.
Distance: 1.5 miles round-trip
Difficulty: Slight to moderate
Season: May to Columbus Day
Fee: No

Ascending gently through hardwood forests, the walking trail leads to an open cliff summit that affords clear views of Maine's vast northern wilderness west to Katahdin and Canada.

Mount Kineo

Rockwood (Map 41, A1)
Trailhead: From Greenville, head north approximately 20 miles on Route 15/6 to Rockwood. Proceed to the public landing on the village loop just off the highway. Board the Kineo launch, which operates all day, and cross Moosehead Lake to the base of the mountain.
Distance: 2 to 4 miles, round-trip
Difficulty: Moderate
Season: Year-round
Fee: Yes (boat shuttle service)
Shuttle (207) 534-7725

Two trails head up to the summit of Mount Kineo, the longer and gentler Bridle Trail and the steeper and quicker Indian Trail. The Bridle Trail begins approximately one-third of a mile farther down the southern shore than the Indian Trail. Water is not available on either trail, so be sure to bring plenty of your own. From the mountain top one can see all of Moosehead Lake, Maine's largest, and the modest beginnings of the Kennebec River at the foot of Big Squaw Mountain. Beyond the tower, several trails lead east to spectacular vistas over Kineo's sheer cliffs, which drop 800 feet down to the lake. The trail, which turns right just before the tower, passes by what remains of the cabin used by Maine's first female fire warden.

Moxie Falls

Moxie Gore (Map 40, E3)
Trailhead: Moxie Pond Road
   (see directions below)
Distance: 1.5 miles round-trip
Difficulty: Slight
Season: Year-round
Fee: No

Dropping 100 feet, Moxie Falls is one of New England's highest waterfalls. Follow the trail, steps, and boardwalk to the 40-foot upper falls first, then continue on to where Moxie Stream drops another 90 feet. The trail heads downstream to another great view of the falls.

To reach the trailhead: Drive Route 201 north and turn right just beyond The Forks, before the Kennebec River Bridge. Drive 2 miles east on Moxie Pond (Lake) Road to the Moxie Falls Park sign on the left. Walk .5 miles on the dirt road through the woods to the well-worn footpath on the right. The falls are just a quarter-mile down this trail.

Quaggy Jo Mountain

Presque Isle (Map 65, E1)
Trailhead: Off U.S. Route 1
   (see directions below)
Distance: 2.25 miles round-trip
Difficulty: Slight to moderate
Season: May to Columbus Day
Fee: Yes
Aroostook State Park (207) 768-8341 or visit www.state.me.us/doc/parks/programs/ db_search/index.html

One of Aroostook County's two volcanic rock mountains carved from ancient lava flows, Quaggy Jo takes its name from the Micmac phrase *qua quajo,* meaning twin peaks. It is accessible from trails that leave the camping area in Aroostook State Park. Ascend first by way of the power lines and areas of loose rock to the higher south peak via a trail that starts at campsite 18. Although South Peak is the higher summit, the views of Echo Lake and the park from here are not as striking as those from North Peak. To get there, take the three-quarter-mile trail that leaves from the far side of South Peak's summit and loops back to the parking lot near the camping area. From North Peak, the vista includes Haystack Mountain and Chandler Mountain, as well as the town of Presque Isle.

To reach the trailhead: Drive four miles south of Presque Isle on U.S. Route 1. Turn west at the Aroostook State Park sign and go to the Echo Lake parking area.

chapter 10

Historic Sites and Forts

Southern Maine ... 98

Fort McClary State Historic Site,
  Kittery ... 98
Fort Williams, Cape Elizabeth ... 98
Joshua L. Chamberlain Civil War Museum,
  Brunswick ... 98
Old York, York ... 98
Portland Observatory, Portland ... 99
Portland's Old Port, Portland ... 99
Tate House, Portland ... 99
Victoria Mansion, Portland ... 99
Wadsworth-Longfellow House/Maine
  Historical Society, Portland ... 99
Willowbrook at Newfield ... 100

Mid-Coast Maine ... 100

Colonial Pemaquid/Fort William Henry
  State Historic Site, Pemaquid ... 100
Eagle Island State Historic Site,
  Harpswell ... 100
Fort Edgecomb State Historic Site,
  Edgecomb ... 101
Fort Popham State Historic Site,
  Phippsburg ... 101
Fort Pownall/Fort Point Light,
  Stockton Springs ... 101

Down East Maine ... 101

The Burnham Tavern, Machias ... 101
Fort Knox State Historic Site,
  Prospect ... 102
Raye's Mustard Mill, Eastport ... 102

Western Maine ... 102

Bennett Covered Bridge,
  Wilson Mills ... 102
Norlands Living History Center,
  Livermore Falls ... 102
Perham's of West Paris ... 103
Songo River Lock/*Songo River Queen*,
  Naples ... 103
Wire Bridge, New Portland ... 103

Central Maine ... 103

The Blaine House, Governor's Mansion,
  Augusta ... 103
Maine State House, Augusta ... 103
Old Fort Western, Augusta ... 104
Sabbathday Lake Shaker Community,
  New Gloucester ... 104

Northern Maine ... 104

Double Eagle Park, Presque Isle ... 104
Watson Settlement Bridge, Littleton ... 104

Historic Sites and Forts

Southern Maine

Fort McClary State Historic Site

Route 103, Kittery
(207) 384-5160
Accessible year-round, staffed Memorial
  Day to Labor Day
A fee is required

First erected around 1690, Fort McClary was manned during five wars, from the Revolutionary War to World War I. Today several outbuildings remain, including an 1846 blockhouse as well as granite walls and earthworks. This historic site has a picnic spot and playground. A lily pond across the street and views of busy Portsmouth Harbor add to the fun.

Fort Williams

1000 Shore Road, Cape Elizabeth
(207) 799-2661
Accessible year-round
No fee is required
For more information, visit
  www.portlandheadlight.com

Dating back to 1872, Fort Williams is located in a commanding position near the entrance to Portland Harbor and is home to Portland Head Light. On its 94 acres, you can enjoy beautiful views, trails, a small beach, picnic tables, and ocean breezes great for flying kites.

Joshua L. Chamberlain Civil War Museum

226 Maine Street, Brunswick
(207) 729-6606
Open spring to fall
A fee is required
For more information, visit
  www.curtislibrary.com/chamberlain.htm

Joshua Lawrence Chamberlain was a Civil War hero, four-term Maine governor, and president of Bowdoin College. His former home was renovated into a museum that commemorates the war hero's historical accomplishments.

The home is sparsely furnished to maintain its authenticity. On display in its public rooms you'll find such interesting artifacts as a pair of Chamberlain's boots (one of which was patched after he was shot in the instep during a battle at Gettysburg), his Civil War sword, white gloves, insignia from the Twentieth Maine volunteers, and the epaulets from his uniform.

Old York

Lindsay Road and Route 1A, York
(207) 363-4974
Open from mid-June to Columbus Day
  weekend
A fee is required
For more information, visit www.oldyork.org

Old York's seven historic buildings, displays, hands-on exhibits, and interactive demonstrations and programs offer glimpses into life in southern Maine from the mid-1600s onward. A wide variety of special children's activities take place all summer long, including candle making, stitchery, storytelling, scavenger hunts, weaving, scrimshaw, history camp, and even interactive theatrical "jail break" tours involving tales of mysterious escapes, notorious criminals, redemption, crime, and punishment. The break is staged at night in the Old Gaol (jail). Once the King's Prison for the entire Province of Maine, the gaol today features dungeons, cells, and jailer's quarters constructed in the early 1700s, as well as instruments of torture used in the sixteenth century. Displays inside the gaol include hands-on and interactive exhibits as well as an outdoor pillory.

Portland Observatory

138 Congress Street (Munjoy Hill), Portland
(207) 774-5561
Open from Memorial Day to Columbus Day
A fee is required
For more information, visit www.portlandlandmarks.org

An octagonal wooden signal tower built in the early 1800s, Portland Observatory is one of the city's most historic sites. Guided tours to the top of the 86-foot observatory provide panoramic views of the harbor and a chance to imagine what it was like to scan the horizon for ships and use signal flags to alert the town of returning vessels that were still hours away from the dock.

Portland's Old Port

305 Commercial Street (Convention & Visitors Bureau)
(207) 774-5561
Tours available from July 5 to Columbus Day
A fee is required
For more information, visit www.portlandmaine.com

Take a 1.5-hour guided walking tour through the historic center of Portland to learn about the life and architecture of the city in the mid-nineteenth century.

Tate House

1270 Westbrook Street, Portland
(207) 774-9781
Open June 15 to September 30
A fee is required
For more information, visit www.tatehouse.org

The only pre-Revolutionary home in Greater Portland, this historic house was built in 1755 for George Tate, a senior mast agent for the British Royal Navy. The Tate House is now owned and operated by the National Society of the Colonial Dames of America. Tour the historic house, view the raised-bed herb garden, and enjoy an informative talk on the history of the era.

Victoria Mansion

109 Danforth Street, Portland
(207) 772-4841
Open May to October and in December
A fee is required
For more information, visit www.victoriamansion.org

This landmark Portland house was built between 1858 and 1860 for Ruggles Morse, a wealthy Mainer who made his fortune in the hotel industry in New Orleans. The Victorian Mansion is considered the finest surviving Italian villa style house in America today. "Christmas at Victoria Mansion," when the house is elaborately decorated for the holidays, is a popular event.

Wadsworth-Longfellow House/ Maine Historical Society

489 Congress Street, Portland
(207) 774-1822
Open June to October
A fee is required
For more information, visit www.mainehistory.org

Dating back to 1785, the Wadsworth-Longfellow House was the first brick house built in Portland. Currently a National Historic Landmark, it was the boyhood home of poet Henry Wadsworth Longfellow. A graduate of Bowdoin College in Brunswick and a professor at Bowdoin and Harvard, Longfellow was best known for his poems, including *Hiawatha* and *Evangeline: A Tale of Acadie.*

Longfellow's grandfather, General Peleg Wadsworth, built the Wadsworth-Longfellow house. The poet's sister bequeathed the house to the Maine Historical Society in 1901. The house contains eighteenth-century furniture and paintings as well as family memorabilia. There are twelve rooms open to the public.

In addition to the Wadsworth-Longfellow House, the Maine Historical Society maintains a research library (where you can research your genealogy, among other things) and the Center for Maine History Museum.

Willowbrook at Newfield

Main Street, Newfield
(207) 793-2784
Open from mid-May to late September
A fee is required
For more information, visit
www.willowbrookmuseum.org

Willowbrook is a nineteenth-century village with 37 buildings listed on the National Register of Historic Places. Exhibits show how the Industrial Revolution influenced a Victorian-era country village. Observe the carriage house, homesteads, firehouse, shoe shop, creamery, and even a restored 1894 carousel and organ. Picnic on site, dine at the restaurant, or shop at the country store.

Mid-Coast Maine

Colonial Pemaquid/Fort William Henry State Historic Site

Off Route 130, New Harbor
(207) 677-2423
The season runs from Memorial Day to Labor Day but the site is accessible all year
A fee is required
For more information, visit
www.state.me.us/doc/parks/programs/
historic.html (use search link)

A seventeenth-century fort on Pemaquid Harbor and a museum displaying native and early colonial artifacts make this location unique. Summer activities include interpretive tours, fishing off the state pier, and picnicking, all a stone's throw away from sandy Pemaquid Beach Park. Special group tours for children are also available in early spring and late fall by reservation.

Eagle Island State Historic Site

Three miles offshore of Harpswell, Casco Bay (access by boat only)
(207) 624-6080
Open June 1 to Labor Day
A fee is required
For more information, visit
www.state.me.us/doc/parks/programs/
historic.html (use search link)
For information on boat tours to the island, visit www.eagleislandtours.com

Bring a picnic for a full or half-day excursion to the island summer home of North Pole Explorer Admiral Robert E. Peary and his family. This home has spectacular views. It is perched on the north end of the island and was designed to give the impression of being aboard a ship. Tour the house and its exploration memorabilia, explore the entire island, stroll in the gardens, hike the trails, or fish off the pier.

To get to the island you can book a boat

tour, or, if you bring your own boat, you can drop your group at the dock at the north end of the island and a ranger will tender you to shore from moorings they make available.

Fort Edgecomb State Historic Site

Eddy Road, Edgecomb
(207) 882-7777
Open Memorial Day to Labor Day
A fee is required
For more information, visit
www.state.me.us/doc/parks/programs/
historic.html (use search link)

Reputed to be the best example of a nineteenth-century fort in Maine, the two-story octagonal blockhouse of Fort Edgecomb sits on a high point overlooking the Sheepscot River. Peer through the musket ports to catch a glimpse of seals or osprey. Picnic or fish from three acres of riverfront. Printed schedules of monthly military reenactments are mailed upon request.

Fort Popham State Historic Site

Route 209, Phippsburg
(207) 287-4975
Open Memorial Day to Labor Day
A fee is required
For more information, visit
www.state.me.us/doc/parks/programs/
historic.html (use search link)

Fort Popham is a semicircular granite structure that rises 30 feet above the Kennebec River. You'll find ample space for climbing and exploration and rocky areas for fishing. Picnic on its seven acres overlooking the river or on the sandy shore of nearby Popham Beach State Park. Explore the adjacent grounds of the 1607 Popham Colony or climb the path up Sabino Hill to Fort Baldwin, a World War I–era site with panoramic views.

Fort Pownall/Fort Point Light

Fort Point Road, Stockton Springs
(207) 287-4975
Open Memorial Day to Labor Day
A fee is required
For more information, visit
www.state.me.us/doc/parks/programs/
historic.html (use search link)

Located within a 154-acre state park on Cape Jellison's eastern tip, the site contains earthworks of nineteenth-century Fort Point Light and eighteenth-century Fort Pownall, which guarded the Penobscot River and was the site of two Revolutionary War–era battles. Walk the trails, fish from the pier, picnic, or watch the sea birds and boats.

Down East Maine

The Burnham Tavern

2 Free Street, Machias
(207) 255-4432
Open mid-June to Labor Day
A fee is required

The Burnham Tavern is the oldest building in eastern Maine (built in 1770), and the only one with roots to the Revolutionary War. The tavern displays artifacts and memorabilia from that period, including paintings, furnishings, and photographs. Civil War relics are also featured.

Fort Knox State Historic Site

Off Route 174 at the Waldo–Hancock Bridge, Prospect
(207) 469-7719
The season runs from Memorial Day to Labor Day; accessible year-round
A fee is required
For more information, visit www.state.me.us/doc/parks/programs/historic.html (use search link)

This is Maine's largest historic fort, built of granite in the mid 1800s and garrisoned during the Civil War and Spanish and American War. It features 64 cannon mounts, four batteries, two complete cannons, underground stairways, brick archways, and other passages to explore. Guided walks available during the summer as well as live performances on weekend evenings. Performance schedules are available by calling the Friends of Fort Knox at (207) 223-0087.

Raye's Mustard Mill

83 Washington Street, Route 190, Eastport
(207) 853-4451
Open year-round (seven days a week from May to December)
No fee is required
For more information, visit www.rayesmustard.com

Watch mustard being made in one of the few remaining stone mills still operating in the western world. A remnant of early technology, this nineteenth-century mustard mill utilizes technology that remained virtually unchanged from the Middle Ages to World War I. During the summer, tours are scheduled regularly. In other months tours are available by appointment or by chance. A gift shop (with mustard and other Maine-made foods) is also on the premises.

Western Maine

Bennett Covered Bridge

Route 16, three miles south of Wilson Mills
Accessible year-round
No fee is required

Set in the picturesque western Maine hamlet of Wilson Mills, this 92-foot-long covered bridge is one of only a handful left in Maine. Built in the 1890s, it spans the Magalloway River beneath Aziscohos Mountain.

Norlands Living History Center

290 Norlands Road, Livermore Falls
(207) 897-4366
Public tours are available from June to Labor Day for children over five; special family festivals and programs take place throughout the year
A fee is required
For more information, visit www.norlands.org

Situated on the 430-acre Washburn Estate, the Living History Center enables you to experience and observe what life was like in a small rural Maine village in the 1800s. Set on a hill overlooking fields and forests, the center consists of five buildings: a school, library, church, house, and barn. Weekly summer programs for children include Native American storytelling and crafts. Four different family live-in programs are also available each year for parents and children ages 8 to 17. Live-in sessions run for three days and nights and immerse families in the daily life of either an eighteenth- or nineteenth-century farm family through role-playing, instruction, storytelling, and research. School and home-school programs are also available.

Perham's of West Paris

194 Bethel Road (Route 26), West Paris
(207) 674-2341
Open year-round
No fee is required

Built at the Trap Corner crossroads in 1919, this store/museum/advice center is a local historic landmark. Known as "rock-hound heaven," it is a place where you can admire or purchase the gems on the shelf or get all the advice and tools you will need for a do-it-yourself family outing in the mineral-rich mines of the nearby Oxford Hills, where it is "finders keepers" for everyone that visits. Free maps of Perham's own quarries, all within a ten-mile radius of the store, are also available.

Songo River Lock/*Songo River Queen*

Route 302, Naples (next to Sebago Lake State Park)
(207) 693-6861 (*Songo River Queen*)
Steamboat Rides run a limited schedule in June, full schedule July 1 to Labor Day
A fee is required

Built in 1830, the Songo River water lock is the oldest in the state. One of 27 locks built between Portland and Long Lake, it is the only one in operation today. To travel back to a time when steamboats plied this waterway, board the *Songo River Queen* (a replica of a Mississippi paddlewheel boat) in Naples Village. Twice-daily narrated cruises leave for Long Lake, traveling through the lock.

Wire Bridge

Wire Bridge Road off Route 146, New Portland
(207) 628-4441 (town office)
Open year-round
No fee is required
For more information, visit:
    www.state.me.us/mdot/maint_op/
    covered/wirebrg.htm

Built between 1864 and 1866, this 198-foot-long steel edifice, dramatically suspended over the Carrabassett River, is on the National Historic Register. You can stroll across this Maine Historic Civil Engineering Landmark by walking beneath the 25-foot shingled towers at either end.

Central Maine

The Blaine House, Governor's Mansion

192 State Street, Augusta
(207) 287-2301
No fee is required
Open year-round, Tuesday through Thursday, 2:00 to 4:00 P.M.

The official residence of Maine governors, this 1833 house was once the home of prominent political leader James G. Blaine. Blaine served as Secretary of State for two Presidents, Speaker of the U.S. House of Representatives, and U.S. Senator. In 1919, the Blaine family donated the building to the State of Maine.

Maine State House

State Street, Augusta
(207) 287-1400 (Clerk of the Legislature)
Open daily, year-round
No fee is required
For more information visit:
    www.state.me.us/legis/senate/about/
    generalinfo/visitinginfo.htm

Observe history in the making at Maine's Capitol Building. When the state legislature is in session (check ahead), both the house and senate chambers are open to the public. You can also stroll past the governor's office and the attorney general's office. Historical exhibits, including the Hall of Flags, are also on display. Tour guides are on site most mornings.

Old Fort Western

16 Cony Street, Augusta
(207) 626-2385
Call for hours of operation and special
   events
A fee is required
For more information, visit
   www.oldfortwestern.org

Costumed interpreters and hands-on demonstrations from butter churning to musket drills allow summer visitors to travel back in time at this eighteenth-century fort. Said to be the nation's oldest stockade fort, it housed Benedict Arnold and his troops in 1775. Weeklong afternoon apprenticeship programs are available for children ages 8 to 15 each summer. Special public events such as reenactments are also scheduled during the summer.

Sabbathday Lake Shaker Community

707 Shaker Road (Route 26),
   New Gloucester
(207) 926-4597
The season runs from Memorial Day to
   Columbus Day
A fee is required
For more information, visit
   www.shaker.lib.me.us

At America's last inhabited Shaker Community, the few remaining members of this eighteenth-century religious sect maintain a living museum and welcome visitors to their Sunday Services. Guided tours for the public and school groups are available. (Not recommended for children younger than 8.)

Northern Maine

Double Eagle Park

Spragueville Road, off U.S. Route 1, 3.5
   miles south of downtown Presque Isle
(207) 768-8341 (nearby state park)
Accessible year-round
A fee is required

The launch site of the first transatlantic balloon flight in 1978, this park features a replica of the *Double Eagle II* helium balloon in which a three-man crew made the passage from Presque Isle to France in less than seven days. Double Eagle Park is located close to Aroostook State Park on the shores of Echo Lake.

Watson Settlement Bridge

Carson Road, off U.S. Route 1,
   2.5 miles south of Littleton center
(207) 538-9862 (Littleton Town Office)
The bridge is accessible year-round
No fee is required

Built in the early 1900s and open to vehicle traffic until 1985, this is Maine's most northerly covered bridge and one of nine still standing in the state. Its wooden trusses straddle the Meduxnekeag River.

chapter 11

Islands

Southern Maine ... 106

Eagle Island ... 106
Great Chebeague Island ... 106
Great Diamond Island ... 107
Mackworth Island ... 107
Peaks Island ... 107

Mid-Coast Maine ... 108

Damariscove Island ... 108
Islesboro ... 108
Matinicus ... 108
Monhegan Island ... 109
North Haven ... 109
Seguin Island ... 109
Vinalhaven ... 110

Down East Maine ... 110

Campobello ... 110
Frenchboro ... 110
Isle au Haut ... 111
Swans Island ... 111

Islands

The Maine coast hugs a multitude of bays, harbors, and inlets totaling an impressive 3,500 miles—the same coastal distance from New Hampshire all the way to Florida. This scenic coastline is sprinkled with numerous islands of all shapes, sizes, and character. Many are privately owned, and most are available only by private boat, but there are a few islands serviced by public ferry transportation, and they are definitely worth the trip. Hiking, picnicking, exploring marine life, and drinking in the beautiful vistas top the list of island activities. Call ahead to find out the current ferry schedule and to determine which activities your desired island permits.

Southern Maine

Eagle Island

HOW TO GET THERE:

Dolphin Marina, South Harpswell (207) 833-6000; from mid-June through Labor Day
Eagle Tours, Yarmouth (207) 744-6498; from mid-June to Labor Day
Atlantic Seal Cruises (207) 865-6612 (There is no public ferry to the island)
For more information, visit the Friends of Peary's Eagle Island Web site at http://home.gwi.net/~eagle

Now a state historic site, this 17-acre island was the home of Robert E. Peary, the first North Pole explorer. His house, which sits on the cliffs of the northernmost point, was designed to feel like the prow of a boat. Peary's home, now open from June 15 through Labor Day, provides breathtaking views of the ocean. The island is also home to many nesting birds, including some ferociously hungry sea gulls. A few moorings are available, and a tender will bring you to the dock. Bring a picnic. Outhouses are available.

Great Chebeague Island

HOW TO GET THERE:

Casco Bay Lines, State Pier, Portland (207) 774-7871 or www.cascobaylines.com; year-round
Chebeague Transportation Company Water Taxi, Chebeague Island (207) 846-3700; year-round

Great Chebeague was historically a popular camping site for Native American tribes, and certain artifacts can still be found on the island. Today the island hosts a year-round community as well as a larger summer population. Measuring four miles long and two miles wide, Great Chebeague is the largest island in Casco Bay. Although there are numerous roads, several other islands offer more scenic biking routes, though a good route runs from the ferry dock to Chandler's Cove, which boasts a quarter-mile of white sand beach. During low tide, visitors can walk from Great Chebeague to Little Chebeague. Swimming is good at both Deer Point and Hamilton Beach. The rocks at Sunset Landing and the small beach near Division Point are great for climbing. The island does not provide many eateries, so bring a picnic.

Great Diamond Island

HOW TO GET THERE:

Casco Bay Lines, State Pier, Portland (207) 774-7871 or www.cascobaylines.com; year-round

Great Diamond is connected to Little Diamond Island by a sand spit, and both islands are privately owned. Fort McKinley, an important defense point of Portland in WWII, is located on the east side of Great Diamond and over the last several years has been restored and converted to a private community. A restaurant is open here in the summer, located just at the end of the dock ramp. It is a fun place for a meal, and you can walk on the small beach next door. Visitors can reach the island by private boat or ferry, just a 30-minute ride across Casco Bay.

Mackworth Island

HOW TO GET THERE:

Accessible by car from Route 1 in Falmouth, at the tip of Mackworth Point
Western Region office of the Maine Bureau of Public Lands: (207) 778-8231

Governor Percival Baxter donated Mackworth Island for the Baxter School for the Deaf, which continues to own and maintain this 100-acre island jutting out into Casco Bay. A wonderful path lines the perimeter of the 1.25-mile island, offering incredible views of Casco Bay and giving access to small pocket beaches. The island is known for its great birding and fishing (the striper and bluefish are usually good in late May and early June). The sandbar on the south side of the island extends several hundred yards during low tide, creating a fun walk, literally out into the bay. Remember to bring warm layers—the island tends to be windy and cool. A bridge connects the island to the mainland in Falmouth, and limited parking is available for visitors. The island closes at sunset. A detailed brochure is available from the Maine Bureau of Public Lands.

Peaks Island

HOW TO GET THERE:

Casco Bay Lines, State Pier, Portland (207) 774-7871 or www.cascobaylines.com; year-round

Although Peaks Island is technically considered a part of Portland, it feels like it is a world away. After a fun 18-minute boat ride, visitors to this two-square-mile island can enjoy many activities such as biking, sea kayaking, hiking, bird watching, and swimming. It is possible to bike most of the island's five-mile circumference in just 30 minutes. (Bike rentals are available, including tandem bikes and child seats.) It is relaxing and fun to walk through the wooded terrain and look at, but not pick, the beautiful wildflowers. Kids love playing in the coves and beach areas. Sandy Bar Beach, on the southern end of the island, is great for playing and swimming. It is also possible to rent kayaks on-island. There is a bird sanctuary that hosts nesting grebes and sea ducks. In the summer, the Fifth Maine Regiment Community Center, just a 10-minute walk from the ferry dock, is open for visitors who want to expand their knowledge about the Civil War era. On the northeast side of the island, a fortification from a WWII naval artillery emplacement called Battery Steele is a great place to picnic. The residents on Peaks are generally friendly and most will be happy to give directions to any of the above sites, or you can ask directions from the Peaks Island police or the people who work at Hannigan's Market, near the dock where the ferries load and unload.

Mid-Coast Maine

Damariscove Island

HOW TO GET THERE:

Accessible by private boat operators.
*For more information about transportation
and the island, call the Boothbay Harbor
Region Chamber of Commerce at
(207) 633-2353*

Even before the Jamestown and Plymouth colonies were established, Damariscove was being visited regularly by European fishermen, beginning in 1605. Rich in history, Damariscove is the source of many infamous ghost tales that kids love to hear, and you can read about them in Chip Griffin's book, *Coming of Age on Damariscove Island* (available from the Boothbay Region Historical Society). Ecologists are fascinated by the island's two hundred acres, which are completely treeless. It is currently owned by the Nature Conservancy. The wildflowers on the island create a purple, white, and yellow sea that is gorgeous to gaze upon while hiking the trails. The northern half of the island is closed to the public from March 15 through August 15, during the nesting season for gulls and eider ducks, but the southern half stays open, and walking paths are maintained. One of the outermost islands in the Boothbay region, Damariscove offers a wonderful gravel beach, a pond, and a deep harbor for splashing around. On the south side is a small protected cove with a fishing camp, a stone wharf, and an old life-saving station that was abandoned in the 1940s and is now privately owned. There is no public ferry out to the island, but a public mooring is available.

Islesboro

HOW TO GET THERE:

Maine State Ferry Service, Lincolnville (207) 789-5611; call for schedule or visit www.state.me.us/mdot/opt/ ferry/ferry.htm
Telford Aviation, Knox County Regional Airport, Owls Head (207) 596-5557; year-round

Islesboro is Penobscot Bay's most popular island for biking. There are a few challenging spots (the roads are narrow, with no shoulders), but generally the biking is relaxing and scenic. The 11-mile island is nearly separated in two where the land draws inward in the middle. The town park and picnic area at the south tip of the island are wonderfully scenic. The Sailor's Memorial Museum is worth a visit, too, because you can climb the nearby 28-foot lighthouse.

Matinicus

HOW TO GET THERE:

Telford Aviation, Knox County Regional Airport, Owls Head (207) 596-5557; year-round
Maine State Ferry Service, Rockland (207) 596-2202; call for schedule or visit www.state.me.us/mdot/opt/ ferry/ferry.htm

Twenty miles off of Rockland, Matinicus boasts only dirt roads and a dirt airstrip. Life here is rustic in every sense; many of the year-round residents do not have running water or electricity in their homes. Many rare birds, such as puffins and razorbill auks, make this small island their nesting ground. There are two sandy beaches, Markey Beach and South Sandy Beach, as well as a mile of shoreline trails. Wild roses bloom everywhere in mid-July, dramatically increasing the island's beauty. West Point offers a wonderful view. Rental cottages and moorings are very limited.

Ferry service to Matinicus is irregular, with four trips per month June through August, and three each in May and September. It may be best to take your own boat to the island.

Monhegan Island

HOW TO GET THERE:

Monhegan-Thomaston Boat Line, Port Clyde (207) 372-8848; year-round
Balmy Days Cruises, Boothbay Harbor (207) 633-2284; seasonal
For more information, visit
www.monhegan.com

Ten miles from the mainland, Monhegan Island supports a year-round population of no more than 75 people. With only 20 percent of the island inhabited, the rest of the island is wild and incredibly beautiful. Seventeen miles of frequently challenging trails weave through the woods and along the 150-foot cliffs of the exposed southeast coast. (Get a trail map on the island before starting out.) Almost all views seen from Monhegan are magnificent, but those from both Black Head and White Head are particularly notable. Lobster Cove is a great place for spying birds and an old shipwreck. Although you can swim at Swim Beach, near the dock, there is no lifeguard. There is a contemporary artists' colony on the island, and numerous artists have open studio hours for visitors. The Historical Museum in the lighthouse keeper's building is open from July through September. The view from the lighthouse hill is well worth the steep climb, especially at sunset. If you arrive by private boat, you can drop off passengers at the dock, but no tie-ups are allowed. Moorings are hard to come by, so plan to set anchor. The residents of Monhegan are very serious about preserving their island, so they forbid biking and camping, and smoking is banned outside the village.

North Haven

HOW TO GET THERE:

Maine State Ferry Service, Rockland (207) 596-2202; call for schedule or visit www.state.me.us/mdot/opt/ferry/ferry.htm
Telford Aviation, Knox County Regional Airport, Owls Head (207) 596-5557; year-round

The gigantic summer homes on the island give North Haven an elegant tone. There are fewer tourists and public facilities on North Haven than on neighboring islands. This eight-mile-long and six-mile-wide island is a bit hilly, but still fun for biking. Indian Point, on the eastern end of the island, is a scenic biking destination. The ocean-side meadow on the point has a picturesque shade tree and an incredible view. Also on the eastern edge of the island, Mullen's Head Park is great for swimming and offers accommodation for picnics, with numerous tables available. Pulpit Beach is another good public swimming area. The island has several small shops, many selling boating paraphernalia. Sunsets over the Camden Hills are spectacular from many different island vantage points.

Seguin Island

HOW TO GET THERE:

Private trips run during the summer; contact the Maine Maritime Museum in Bath at (207) 443-1316
For more information about the island, contact the Friends of Seguin Island, P.O. Box 866, Bath, ME 04530; call (207) 443-4808, or visit www.seguinisland.org

In 1794, George Washington ordered the first lighthouse to be built on Seguin. Situated right off the mouth of the Kennebec River three miles from the mainland, the island is a very scenic spot. It is a good climb from the beach to get to the promontory where the

53-foot-tall lighthouse stands, but the view is well worth the effort. The island itself is expansive and fun for exploring. Visitors should be very careful about the steep cliffs. A few moorings are available for private boaters, but you will need your own dinghy to get to shore. There are no public facilities here.

Vinalhaven

HOW TO GET THERE:

Maine State Ferry Service, Rockland (207) 596-2202; call for schedule or visit www.state.me.us/mdot/opt/ferry/ferry.htm

Telford Aviation, Knox County Regional Airport, Owls Head (207) 596-5557; year-round

The all-around most popular island in Penobscot Bay, Vinalhaven is great for a day trip or short vacation. Although the island is eight miles long and five and a half miles wide, most of the interesting spots are clustered together within three miles of the ferry terminal. There are two wonderful nature preserves within walking distance: Ambrust Hill and Lanes Island (which is attached to Vinalhaven by a bridge). Both boast hiking trails, picnic tables, and incredible ocean views. On the west side of the island, the Basin is a large tidal pool that spans several acres and is surrounded by wooded scenic trails. Near the town park, Booth's Quarry is a great place to swim in clean spring water. Arey Neck, on Vinalhaven's east side, provides fabulous views of Isle au Haut. Biking is great all over the island, especially to Brown's Head Light at the island's northeast corner. Tiptoe Mountain is really a big hill for easy hiking, with great views of Camden. Vinalhaven's Historical Society Museum displays a restored horse-drawn galamander, a huge wagon that was once used for moving blocks of granite from local quarries.

Down East Maine

Campobello

HOW TO GET THERE:

Accessible by bridge from Lubec, Maine, or by car ferry from the New Brunswick mainland, in Canada
For more information, visit www.campobello.com

This Canadian island is the site of the former family summer home of President Franklin D. Roosevelt. The estate is now an international park, dually governed by Canada and the United States. It consists of 2,800 acres of beaches, cleared fields, forests, rocky shoreline, and wetlands. There are scenic trails great for walking and several picnic areas with charcoal grills. The walk along the eastern beaches is wonderful, and the likelihood of spotting a few whales during the fall is great. The wonderful East Quoddy Light is located at the northeast tip of the island and well worth the walk; however, make note of the tide schedules, as it is quite easy to get stranded for hours if you don't time your walk right. During the summer, FDR's family cottage, the beautiful gardens, and two greenhouses are open to the public.

Frenchboro

HOW TO GET THERE:

Maine State Ferry Service, Bass Harbor, (207) 594-8181; call for schedule or visit www.state.me.us/mdot/opt/ferry/ferry.htm

With fewer than 40 year-round residents, the Frenchboro community has dedicated the past decade to attracting more locals to inhabit the island. For those familiar with the wonderful qualities of Frenchboro, one of just fourteen year-round Maine island communities, it is hard to imagine so few people wanting to live there. Eight miles south of Mt. Desert Island,

Frenchboro's four square miles are mainly undeveloped forest. Beautiful trails, of varying difficulty, lead in all directions to the various coves and beaches. For example, you can walk to the head of the harbor and continue south along the dirt road, then branch off on a footpath through the woods to Little Beach, arriving in about 10 or 15 minutes. There you can gather beach peas, look for orchids in the nearby bog, or sit on a driftwood log while you picnic, watching lobster boats work offshore.

The Frenchboro Historical Society is open all summer, and on the second Saturday in August, rain or shine, there is a food-laden Lobster Festival that includes local art, crafts, face painting, and kids' games.

Isle Au Haut

HOW TO GET THERE:

Isle au Haut Ferry Service, Stonington (207) 367-6516; year-round
Telford Aviation, Knox County Regional Airport, Owls Head (207) 596-5557; year-round
For more information, visit www.isleauhaut.com

This 6,000-acre island was named by French navigator Samuel Champlain in 1604. The name translates to "high island" in English. Half of the island is a part of Acadia National Park, which maintains a campground with five lean-to shelters at Duck Harbor. The campground also offers fire rings, picnic tables, pit toilets, and water hand-pumps, and is open May 15 through October 15. There are 18 breathtaking miles of hiking trails on the island. The trails, which are often wet and rough, pass along rocky shoreline, wooded land, marshes, bogs, and a mile-long freshwater lake. The view is spectacular from Duck Harbor Mountain, as well as from Western Harbor and Duck Harbor itself. From June to September, visitors can elect to hike with knowledgeable park rangers. The park wisely discourages biking. The infamous Captain Kidd is rumored to have buried treasure on Isle au Haut. No one has ever discovered it, though kids still love to search for it.

Swans Island

HOW TO GET THERE:

Maine State Ferry Service, Bass Harbor (207) 244-3254; call for schedule or visit www.state.me.us/mdot/opt/ferry/ferry.htm
For more information, visit www.swansisland.com

Within Swans Island's 7,000 acres are 12 miles of paved roads that are great for biking. The town provides a public launching ramp and tender float in Mackerel Cove. There are two interesting museums—the Museum of Island History and the new Lobster and Marine Museum—as well as two lighthouses, one at Burnt Coat Harbor and the other at Hockamock Head. You can swim at Carrying Place Beach and Fine Sand Beach, but the water is very cold. Freshwater swimming is also possible at Quarry's Pond, but swimmers must be careful of hidden rocks. There is one general store on the island, which provides picnic fare for a fun day out in the woods, harbors, and coves.

chapter 12

Lighthouses

Southern Maine...114

Cape Neddick Light...114
Cape Elizabeth Light...114
Portland Head Light...115
Spring Point Ledge Light...115

Mid-Coast Maine...115

Seguin Island Light...115
Burnt Island Light...115
Pemaquid Point Light...116
Monhegan Island Light...116
Marshall Point Light...116
Owls Head Light...117
Rockland Breakwater Light...117
Grindle Point Light...117
Browns Head Light...117
Fort Point Light...118

Down East Maine...118

Isle au Haut Light...118
Dyce Head Light...118
Bass Harbor Head Light...119
Burnt Coat Harbor Light...119
West Quoddy Head Light...119

Lighthouses

The coast of Maine is home to 67 lighthouses, some among the very first constructed in this country. They offer beautiful vistas and the lure of adventure and history. During the 1980s the last lighthouses were automated. Most are now privately owned, with the Coast Guard retaining rights to manage those which have actively operating light and fog signals.

Not all Maine lighthouses are accessible or open to the public. We describe nineteen you can visit either by car, ferry, or private boat. A good place to learn more about lighthouses is the Shore Village Museum in Rockland (see Chapter 13). It has one of the largest collections of lighthouse and Coast Guard material in the nation. For lighthouse souvenirs, visit the Lighthouse Depot, which bills itself as the world's largest lighthouse gift store. It is located on U.S. Route 1 in Wells.

Southern Maine

Cape Neddick Light

Offshore from Cape Neddick, at the end of Nubble Road, York
York Parks and Recreation
(207) 363-1040
For more information, visit
www.lighthouse.cc/capeneddick

Otherwise known as Nubble Light, Cape Neddick was built in 1879. One of the youngest Maine lights, Cape Neddick is also one of the most celebrated. It is both difficult and dangerous to cross the sandbar between the light and its parking lot; visitors are encouraged to enjoy the view from the parking lot. The light is beautifully lit during the holiday season. The light still guides ships at sea; every six seconds, a red light flashes. Its beacon can be seen for 13 miles and is accompanied by a foghorn.

Cape Elizabeth Light

Two Lights State Park, off Route 77, Cape Elizabeth
The state park is open from April to November; the lighthouse is not open to the public
Accessible by car (state park only)
Two Lights State Park (207) 799-5871
For more information, visit
www.lighthouse.cc/capeelizabeth

The Cape Elizabeth Light was originally part of a pair known as the Two Lights, built in 1829. Despite public outcry, the government ordered that all twin lights be converted to single beacons in 1924. The present light is one of the most powerful on the New England coast. It flashes every 30 seconds and is visible for 27 miles. The lighthouses are now privately owned, but visitors can enjoy viewing them from Two Lights State Park. The park also offers a picnic area, trails, fishing, and the remnants of a World War II coastal defense station. Nearby, at the end of Two Lights Road, you can get a great sandwich at the Lobster Shack.

Portland Head Light

**Fort Williams Park, 1000 Shore Road,
Cape Elizabeth**
Grounds open year-round
Accessible by car
**Greater Portland Chamber of Commerce
(207) 772-5800**
*For more information, visit
www.portlandheadlight.com*

Portland Head Light has the distinction of being one of the most photographed lighthouses in the world. The oldest light in Maine, it was established in 1791 under George Washington's administration. The light has taken many hits over the years, including the great September storm of 1869, which swept away the old cast-iron fog bell and caused the destruction of at least 20 ships. The light achieved immortality through Henry Wadsworth Longfellow's poetry. In fact, visitors can check out some of Longfellow's most famous lines on a plaque on the side of the lighthouse.

Spring Point Ledge Light

**Fort Preble State Park, Fort Road,
South Portland**
**Located on the grounds of the Portland
Harbor Museum; call for tour dates**
Accessible by car
**Portland Harbor Museum
(207) 799-6337**
*For more information, visit
www.lighthouse.cc/springpoint*

One of only three caisson-style lights in Maine, the Spring Point Ledge Light looks something like a sparkplug. In the 1950s the Army Corps of Engineers connected the light to shore by building a breakwater with 50,000 tons of local granite. Visitors to the light can also tour the ruins of Fort Preble. The Spring Point light has both red and white beacons, each visible for about 12 miles.

Mid-Coast Maine

Seguin Island Light

**3 miles off the mouth of the Kennebec
River; nearest town is Georgetown**
**Grounds open year-round; tower open
for occasional tours**
**Ferry tours available from Maine
Maritime Museum in Bath
(see Chapter 13)**
**Friends of Seguin Island, Inc.
(207) 443-4808**
*For more information, visit
www.lighthouse.cc/seguin*

Established during George Washington's presidency in 1795, Seguin Island Light still aids seafarers. In fact, it is one of only two lights in New England with a first-order lens (the other is in Boston Harbor). A first-order lens is the largest lighthouse beacon. Although the actual lighthouse tower is somewhat small, at 53 feet, it is the highest in Maine, for it is built on high land. The first island light in Maine, Seguin Island Light has a mysterious past, complete with rumors of buried treasure and ghosts!

Burnt Island Light

At the entrance to Boothbay Harbor
Grounds open seasonally
**Tour boat available from Fisherman's
Wharf from mid-May to mid-October**
**Call (207) 633-7200 for schedule or
call the Marine Resources Aquarium
at (207) 633-9559**
**Boothbay Harbor Region Chamber of
Commerce (207) 633-2353**
*For more information, visit
www.lighthouse.cc/burntisland*

The Marine Resources Aquarium offers a unique experience at its Burnt Island Light Educational Facility. The aquarium has set up a conservation education program on five-acre Burnt Island, offering the chance to explore rocky and sandy beaches, marshes, meadows, and forests through a self-guided nature tour. The lightkeeper's house, built in 1821, is now a living history museum. In the late 1880s, the Lighthouse Service realized that Burnt Island Light was guiding ships directly onto the Cuckolds, two treacherous ledges outside of Boothbay Harbor. The light was altered so ships could pass the ledges safely. The light still guides ships today, with a red and white beam that is visible 12 to 15 miles away.

Pemaquid Point Light

End of Route 130, Bristol
Grounds and museum in keeper's house
   open year-round
Accessible by car
The Fisherman's Museum
   (207) 677-2494
For more information, visit
   www.lighthouse.cc/pemaquid

This light provides one of the most picturesque scenes in Maine. Built at the end of a long stretch of rocky ledge constantly pounded by the surf, this is undoubtedly one of the most photographed and visited lights in the state. Since the tides can be extremely dangerous here, visitors should take extreme care while exploring the ledges. One of the most enticing parts of Pemaquid Light is the chance to see whales playing in the deep water nearby. Early lightkeepers established the tradition of farming on the grounds, so several barns dot the landscape as well. Pemaquid Light stands 38 feet tall, with a white light that flashes every six seconds. Visible for 14 miles, the beacon still helps guide area mariners.

Monhegan Island Light

Monhegan Island
Open seasonally
Ferry access year-round from Port Clyde;
   call (207) 372-8848
Seasonal ferries from mid-June to mid-
   September from Boothbay Harbor;
   (207) 633-2284
Monhegan Historical and Cultural
   Museum Association (207) 596-7003
For more information, visit
   www.lighthouse.cc/monhegan

The site of the first fishing settlement in Maine, Monhegan Island seemed like an ideal place for a lighthouse. In 1824 construction began on the light. A foghorn was built on neighboring Manana Island. Over the years, several types of foghorns and beacons have been used. The tower now has a flashing white beam, visible for more than 20 miles. Until 1982, the Coast Guard manned the light, but it is now automated. The Monhegan Museum now occupies the old keeper's house; it specializes in geology, fishing, and the natural history of Monhegan Island. The light is also the home of some of the Betty Noyce Collection, an impressive collection of art donated by the late Maine philanthropist Betty Noyce.

Marshall Point Light

Off Route 131 in Port Clyde, at the tip of
   the St. George peninsula
Grounds and museum in keeper's house
   open year-round
Accessible by car
Marshall Point Lighthouse Museum
   (207) 372-6450
For more information, visit
   www.lighthouse.cc/marshall

Marshall Point Light, established in 1823, was an important beacon for local fishermen and for mariners involved in the lumber trade. When the keeper's house fell into disrepair in the 1980s, the St. George Historical Society restored the building, and in 1990 established a museum there. Located on the first floor, the museum focuses on lighthouse keepers and the local fishing industry. The upper story of the house is a private residence.

Owls Head Light

End of Lighthouse Road, Owls Head
Grounds open year-round
Accessible by car
Owls Head Town Office (207) 594-7434
For more information, visit
www.lighthouse.cc/owls

Built in 1826, the Owls Head Light still assists modern seafarers. In fact, the Owls Head tower is visible 16 miles offshore. The light has had several types of fog signals over the years; the first was a bell with machinery powered by the tides. Today the fog signal is electronic. It is possible to climb around the trails near the light, but be careful of the sheer cliffs nearby. The tower itself is closed to the public, and a Coast Guardsman lives in the former keeper's house. Visitors may climb a wooden staircase up to the tower to have a look around.

Rockland Breakwater Light

End of Samoset Road, Rockland
Grounds open year-round; lighthouse
not open to the public
Accessible by car
Rockland-Thomaston Area Chamber of
Commerce (207) 596-0376
For more information, visit
www.lighthouse.cc/rocklandbreakwater

Only 20 minutes away from the Owls Head Light, the Rockland Breakwater Light is located at the end of an almost mile-long breakwater constructed from huge granite blocks. In its early days, it consisted only of two small red lights. Later, as the Army Corps of Engineers extended the breakwater to its present distance, it became more important for the facility to have a fog signal and a bigger light. The present beacon is visible 17 miles offshore.

Grindle Point Light

North side of the entrance to Gilkey
Harbor, Islesboro
Museum open year-round; tower open in
the summer by appointment
Ferry available from Lincolnville Beach
to Grindle Point; call (207) 789-5611
for schedule or visit
www.state.me.us/mdot/opt/ferry/
ferry.htm
Islesboro Town Office (207) 734-2253
For more information, visit
www.lighthouse.cc/grindle

The Grindle Point Light was built in 1851, but the light was deactivated in 1934. When the town of Islesboro took over the grounds in 1935, it created a Sailors' Memorial Museum in the old keeper's quarters. In 1987, townspeople convinced the Coast Guard to move the beacon back to the original tower. Presently, Grindle Point has a green beacon that flashes every four seconds and is visible for seven miles. In addition to its characteristic square lighthouse, the island also offers wonderful biking, swimming at Dark Harbor, and a public beach at Pendleton Point.

Browns Head Light

Entrance to Fox Island Thorofare,
Vinalhaven Island
Grounds open year-round
Ferry service available from Rockland to
Vinalhaven; for schedule, call
(207) 596-2203 or visit
www.state.me.us/mdot/opt/ferry/
ferry.htm
Vinalhaven Town Office (207) 863-4471
For more information, visit
www.lighthouse.cc/brownshead

The 20-foot-high Browns Head Light and accompanying keeper's house were built in 1832.

In later years, the crude quarters were renovated and a 28-foot brick tower replaced the previous one. The station housed a fog bell for many years. When the station was automated in 1987, the town of Vinalhaven agreed to maintain the light. (Read more about Vinalhaven in Chapter 11.)

Fort Point Light

Fort Point State Park, Cape Jellison, off U.S. Route 1 in Stockton Springs
Grounds open year-round
Accessible by car
Fort Point State Park (207) 941-4014
For more information, visit
www.lighthouse.cc/fortpoint

The Fort Point Light watches over the entrance to the Penobscot River and was built in 1836 by order of President Andrew Jackson. The present square, white light tower was built in 1857. Surprisingly, the original fog bell of the light remains on the grounds. In 1988 the Coast Guard automated Fort Point Light, the last one to be automated in the United States. In the same year, the Coast Guard transferred ownership of the site to the Maine Bureau of Parks and Lands.

Down East

Isle Au Haut Light

Robinson Point on Isle Au Haut, south of Deer Isle in East Penobscot Bay
The grounds are open to the public; the lighthouse is not
Ferry access from Stonington; call Isle au Haut Boat Company (207) 367-6516 or visit http://isleauhaut.com
The Keeper's House (207) 367-2261
For more information, visit
www.lighthouse.cc/isleauhaut

One of the most enticing parts about the Isle au Haut light (built in 1907) is The Keeper's House, the renovated lightkeeper's quarters that now serves as a bed and breakfast offering a unique opportunity to spend the night at an historic light station. In addition, the island offers great hikes, bike rides, and amazing scenery. Access to the island is easiest in the summer. The island does not allow cars, and The Keeper's House has no electricity.

Dyce Head Light

Battle Avenue (off Route 166), Castine
Grounds open year-round; lighthouse not open to the public
Accessible by car
Castine Town Office (207) 326-4502
For more information, visit
www.lighthouse.cc/dicehead

Construction on the Dyce Head Light began in 1829, and it has subsequently been rebuilt two times. The light sits at the entrance of the Penobscot River, where it has seen a lot of action over the years. In the late 1930s, as shipping in the Penobscot region slowed, the light was discontinued. Today the light is a private residence. However, it is possible to take beautiful photos from the shore, or follow the public path for a close-up view of the light.

Bass Harbor Head Light

Off Route 102A in Tremont, Mount Desert Island
Grounds open year-round; lighthouse not open to public
Accessible by car
Acadia National Park (207) 288-3338
For more information, visit www.lighthouse.cc/bassharbor

Bass Harbor Light attracts many visitors who come to admire its beauty and take photographs. The light is located around the corner from Bear Island, on the southern tip of Mount Desert Island, and is now the residence for the Coast Guard's Officer in Charge of the Aids to Navigation Team, Southwest Harbor. (Visitors are asked to respect the privacy of the occupants.) Established in 1858, the light still assists navigation with an automated red light that flashes every four seconds, and is visible 13 miles away.

Burnt Coat Harbor Light

Swans Island, south of Mount Desert Island
Open year-round
Access by boat only; contact Maine State Ferry Service in Bass Harbor (207) 244-3254 or visit www.state.me.us/mdot/opt/ferry/ferry.htm
For more information, visit www.lighthouse.cc/burntcoatharbor

Burnt Coat gets its unusual name from a chart maker's mistake. A French chart named the island *Brule Cote* (French for *Burnt Hill*), but the chart maker mistook *Cote* for *Coat*. The light was discontinued in 1977 when an automated light was built on the grounds. After many complaints from mariners, however, the lighthouse was reestablished the next year. The lighthouse is about four miles from the ferry landing, at the tip of Hockamock Head.

West Quoddy Head Light

Quoddy Head State Park, South Lubec Road, Lubec
State park open from May to October
Accessible by car
West Quoddy Head Light Keepers Association (207) 733-4646
For more information, visit www.lighthouse.cc/westquoddy

The easternmost point in the United States, West Quoddy Head is the first place in the country to see the sun rise. The light was built in 1808. In 1869, it was outfitted with a steam whistle that sounded like a locomotive's whistle. Overlooking the Bay of Fundy, West Quoddy is one of the most famous lights in Maine, perhaps because of its distinctive red-and-white-striped tower. The light still aids seafarers with its white beam, which is visible 18 miles away.

Museums

Southern Maine ... 122

The Auto Museum at Wells ... 122

The Center for Maine History, Portland ... 122

The Children's Museum of Maine, Portland ... 122

Kittery Naval Shipyard Museum, Kittery ... 123

The Museum of African Tribal Art, Portland ... 123

The Perry-MacMillan Arctic Museum and Arctic Studies Center, Brunswick ... 123

Portland Harbor Museum, South Portland ... 123

Portland Museum of Art, Portland ... 124

Willowbrook Museum, Newfield ... 124

Mid-Coast Maine ... 124

The Farnsworth Art Museum, Rockland ... 124

Lincoln County Museum and Old Jail, Wiscasset ... 124

Maine Maritime Museum, Bath ... 125

Maine Watercraft Museum, Thomaston ... 125

The Musical Wonder House, Wiscasset ... 125

Penobscot Marine Museum, Searsport ... 125

The Shore Village Museum, Rockland ... 125

Down East Maine ... 126

The Abbe Museum, Bar Harbor ... 126

Natural History Museum of the College of the Atlantic, Bar Harbor ... 126

The Wendell Gilley Museum, Southwest Harbor ... 126

The Wilson Museum, Castine ... 127

Central Maine ... 127

Children's Discovery Museum, Augusta ... 127

Maine State Museum, Augusta ... 127

Norlands Living History Museum, Livermore ... 127

State Capitol Building, Augusta ... 127

Western Maine ... 128

Nowetah's American Indian Museum, New Portland ... 128

The Stanley Museum, Kingfield ... 128

Western Maine Children's Museum, Carrabassett Valley ... 128

Wilhelm Reich Museum and the Orgone Energy Observatory, Rangeley ... 128

Northern Maine ... 129

Ashland Logging Museum, Ashland ... 129

Cole Land Transportation Museum, Bangor ... 129

Hudson Museum, Traditional and Contemporary Cultures, Orono ... 129

Lumbermen's Museum, Patten ... 129

Maine Discovery Museum, Bangor ... 129

Maine Forest and Logging Museum, Bradley ... 129

Moosehead Marine Museum, Greenville ... 130

Nylander Museum, Caribou ... 130

Museums

Maine has an amazingly wide selection of interesting museums. Some, such as the Children's Museum of Maine, offer the chance for even the smallest children to get their hands in the action. Others give their visitors a look at the Maine of years past—the Norlands Living History Museum, for example. Best of all, the museums in this chapter will excite children (and adults) of all ages. The choices that unfold here offer everything from summer art lessons to whale watches to Civil War reenactments. Each one celebrates and shares Maine's history in a unique way. You can also check the Web at www.mainemuseums.org for more information.

Southern Maine

The Auto Museum at Wells

U.S. Route 1, Wells
(207) 646-9064
Open Memorial Day through
Columbus Day

You will find a well-rounded display of more than 70 classic, special interest, and commercial vehicles here, including Stanley, Rolls Royce, Pierce Arrow, and lots more. In addition, there is a display of operating nickelodeons, picture machines, and violin-playing mills sure to be a hit with kids. Take a peek in the gift shop, which offers models, books, and auto-related items.

The Center for Maine History

Maine Historical Society, 489 Congress
Street, Portland
(207) 774-1822
The museum is open year-round; the
Wadsworth-Longfellow House is open
June to October
For more information, visit
www.mainehistory.org

The Center for Maine History offers changing exhibitions on a wide variety of topics in Maine history. Of special note is an original signed copy of the Declaration of Independence. Special children's tours and activities are offered throughout the year as well as tours of the Wadsworth-Longfellow House, which is filled with many original furnishings and offers a charming and intimate glimpse into the life of a fascinating family. Take time to enjoy the Longfellow Garden behind the house, a green oasis in the middle of downtown Portland.

The Children's Museum of Maine

142 Free Street, Portland
(207) 828-1234
Open year-round
For more information, visit
www.childrensmuseumofme.org

The Children's Museum has a wonderful range of activities for children, including Toddler Park, a play station designed for children up to three years old. For older children, the museum has computer and science exhibits. Every one of the 25 exhibits in the Museum is hands-on and safe. A particularly unusual part of the museum is the Camera Obscura—one of only three open to the public in the whole country, which offers an eagle's-eye view of the city skyline.

Kittery Naval Shipyard Museum

Roger Road Extension, Kittery
(207) 439-3080
Open Monday through Friday during the summer months, by appointment during the rest of the year

The Kittery Naval Shipyard Museum preserves the history of the seacoast area around Kittery, Maine's oldest incorporated town. The oldest naval shipyard in the United States, Kittery displays ship models and artifacts from the nineteenth-century, including tools, uniforms, and memorabilia from past launchings. The most interesting exhibits focus on the shipyard's present mission to overhaul and rebuild submarines. Further, the museum displays artifacts from World War II–era German submarines.

The Museum of African Tribal Art

122 Spring Street, Portland
(207) 871-7188
Open year-round
For more information, visit
http://www.africantribalartmuseum.org/index1.htm

The Museum of African Tribal Art is the only museum in New England devoted exclusively to Sub-Saharan African Tribal Art, representing more than 1,000 years of history. It is dedicated to collecting, preserving, teaching, and increasing public appreciation of African tribal art and culture. The museum offers family-oriented activities and exhibits.

The Perry-MacMillan Arctic Museum and Arctic Studies Center

9500 College Station, Hubbard Hall, Bowdoin College, Brunswick
(207) 725-3416
Open year-round
For more information, visit
http://academic.bowdoin.edu/arcticmuseum/

The only museum in the country dedicated exclusively to Arctic studies, this facility remains virtually unknown to most Mainers. The museum is named after two Bowdoin College graduates, Robert E. Peary, the first explorer to reach the North Pole (1909), and his protégé, Donald B. MacMillan. The displays include their gear, photographs, and artwork, as well as other artifacts donated by the MacMillan and Peary families.

Portland Harbor Museum

Spring Point, on the campus of Southern Maine Technical College on Fort Road, South Portland
(207) 799-6337
Open year-round
For more information, visit
www.portlandharbormuseum.org

The museum is located on the grounds of historic Fort Preble, overlooking beautiful Casco Bay. Enjoy a maritime museum, a working lighthouse, a nineteenth-century fort, and vistas of Casco Bay, all on one campus. The permanent exhibit of nineteenth-century wooden shipbuilding includes sections of the South Portland–built clipper ship *Snow Squall*.

Portland Museum of Art

7 Congress Square, Portland
(207) 775-6148
Call for hours
For more information, visit
www.portlandmuseum.org

In addition to housing an impressive Winslow Homer exhibit in the award-winning C. S. Payson Building, the museum also offers ARTREK, summer multimedia art programs for different age groups. This remarkable program fills up quickly, so call early to register. In addition, on the first Friday of every month the museum hosts Free Friday Family Festivals, in which family-oriented activities, music, films, and tours are linked to a museum exhibit.

Willowbrook Museum

Elm Street, Newfield
(207) 793-2784
Open in summer months
For more information, visit
www.willowbrookmuseum.org

The Willowbrook Museum is a restored nineteenth-century village with 37 buildings and horse-drawn vehicles. The museum displays various restored furniture and period tools from both home and farm. One of the most exciting parts of the living village is the 1894 Armitage-Herschell carousel. Willowbrook offers its visitors a unique opportunity to travel back in time.

Mid-Coast Maine

The Farnsworth Art Museum

352 Main Street, Rockland
(207) 596-6457
Open year-round
For more information, visit
www.farnsworthmuseum.org

One of the best things about the Farnsworth Art Museum is that it offers art classes and workshops for a wide range of ages. The classes change seasonally. The museum also houses the Wyeth Center, which boasts the country's most extensive collection of works by Andrew and Jamie Wyeth. The Wyeth Center is located in a beautifully renovated New England–style church. Focusing on Maine's role in American art, the Farnsworth offers one of the finest regional art collections in the country.

Lincoln County Museum and Old Jail

Federal Street, Wiscasset
Open July and August
(207) 882-6817

When construction began on the Lincoln County Jail in 1811, people regarded its design as state of the art. Carved out of granite slabs, the dim cells were considered more humane than the typical open-air jails of the time. The cells range from a small isolation room to airy rooms for women and debtors. Graffiti on the walls are all that remain from the sailors who spent a considerable amount of time in the jail. Deemed obsolete by 1913, the jail was closed. Its final task was to house confiscated contraband alcohol during Prohibition. Another point of interest is the jailer's house, which contains early models of shackles and handcuffs used in the jail.

Maine Maritime Museum

243 Washington Street, Bath
(207) 443-1316
Open year-round
For more information, visit
    www.bathmaine.com

With its unique historic shipyard, educational programs for adults and children, and changing gallery exhibits, the Maine Maritime Museum preserves and shares Maine's exciting nautical history. The museum offers the chance to see both a shipyard and an apprentice shop, but even more exciting are the seasonal narrated cruises on the Kennebec River. The newest addition, the *Chippewa*, a ferryboat from 1923, gives visitors a chance to tour the river in style, and perhaps even catch a glimpse of a bald eagle or osprey. Another cruise offers access to an archaeological dig not open to the general public. Call for reservations.

Maine Watercraft Museum

4 Knox Street Landing, Thomaston
(207) 354-0444
Open year-round
For more information, visit
    www.midcoast.com/~oldboats/

The Watercraft Museum's goal is to preserve, restore, and—most important—use wooden boats from pre-1960 Maine. The museum offers a collection of about 130 small craft; it is even possible to rent an antique boat. With grounds full of shipbuilding history, this museum makes it clear how Thomaston earned its nickname as "the town that went to sea." An unusual feature of the Watercraft Museum is that it is possible to arrive by car or by boat; call for directions by water.

The Musical Wonder House

18 High Street, Wiscasset
(207) 882-7163 or (207) 882-6373
Open late May through October
For more information, visit
    www.musicalwonderhouse.com

An 1852 Sea Captain's Mansion is the backdrop for this impressive collection of mechanical musical instruments that provide an opportunity to experience the sights and sounds of the Victorian era. These restored antique musical boxes, player pianos, and many other mechanical musical treasures should not be missed if your children have an interest in music. A gift shop is also on the premises.

Penobscot Marine Museum

Church Street at Route 1, Searsport
(207) 548-2529
Open Memorial Day through
    mid-October
For more information, visit
    www.penobscotmarinemuseum.org

The Penobscot Marine Museum brings to life the nineteenth-century world of seafaring families from Penobscot Bay. The museum consists of twelve historic buildings, each with a different focus, such as a former sea captain's home and a restored schoolhouse. Although not all the buildings are open to the public, their exteriors leave quite an impression of nineteenth-century life. One of the nice parts of the museum is its gift shop, which has an extra-large children's section.

The Shore Village Museum

104 Park Drive, Rockland
(207) 594-0311
Open by appointment throughout the year
For more information, visit
    www.lighthouse.cc/shorevillage/

This museum—dubbed Maine's lighthouse museum—has one of the largest collections of unique U.S. Coast Guard artifacts, including working foghorns, search-and-rescue gear, buoys, bells, and boats. Also, families of Civil War veterans have donated war memorabilia, including uniforms, weapons, and army records, mostly representing the Fourth Maine Regiment. Another interesting feature is the Llewella Mills Doll Collection, 34 contemporary dolls wearing costumes from 1399 to the 1890s.

Down East Maine

The Abbe Museum

Two locations:
- **26 Mount Desert Street, Route 3, Bar Harbor, open year-round**
- **Sieur de Monts Spring, Acadia National Park, open from Memorial Day weekend to mid-October**
- **(207) 288-3519**

For more information, visit www.abbemuseum.org

Founded in 1927 by Dr. Robert Abbe, the museum provides the opportunity to explore Maine's Native American history. The Museum has rotating exhibits, workshops taught by native artists, and a fine collection of over 1,800 Wabanaki baskets. In 2001 the museum opened a much larger second location in the former YMCA building in downtown Bar Harbor. The most memorable part of the new location is the Circle of the Four Directions, which brings the natural world inside. The Abbe Museum has established itself as a leader in collecting, preserving, and interpreting Maine's history. Many of the museum's programs seem better suited for teenagers than younger children. Call for details and registration information.

Natural History Museum of the College of the Atlantic

105 Eden Street, Bar Harbor
(207) 288-5015
Open year-round
For more information, visit www.coamuseum.org

The Museum's main goal is to instruct its visitors about the ecology and natural history of coastal Maine, focusing on how past and present human activity affects the natural environment. The Natural History Museum specializes in native plants and animals of Mount Desert Island and the Gulf of Maine. The museum also offers an impressive Summer Field Studies for Children program and a Summer Family Week session. Call for details about these exceptional programs.

The Wendell Gilley Museum

Route 102 (Main Street) and Herrick Road, Southwest Harbor
(207) 244-7555
Open year-round; call for hours during winter months

The Wendell Gilley Museum showcases the work of a world-renowned bird carver. This Southwest Harbor native was one of the few recognized pioneers of this indigenous American art form. In addition to the permanent Gilley collection, the museum features changing exhibits by outstanding historical and contemporary wildlife artists. Woodcarving demonstrations are given daily. Workshops from one day to ten weeks in duration are offered throughout the year. A summer session is especially designed for children ages nine and up.

The Wilson Museum

Perkins Street, Castine
(207) 326-6545 (curator)
Open late May to the end of September

Over the span of his lifetime, Castine resident John Wilson built an extensive collection of anthropological artifacts from all over the world. In 1921, the Wilson Museum was established to house his collection, which includes crafts and tools from Venezuela, Peru, and Ethiopia, and spears and weapons from Java and the Philippines. Another exhibit is dedicated to antique rifles dating from the 1580s to the 1880s. The museum also has a replica of a kitchen from 1805 and an operating blacksmith forge.

Central Maine

Children's Discovery Museum

265 Water Street, Augusta
(207) 622-2209
Open year-round
For more information, visit
www.members.mint.net/cdm

The Children's Discovery Museum opened its doors a few years ago to rave reviews. Run by volunteers, the museum boasts workshops for both children and families, such as Family Science Night. During the summer, the museum runs popular summer camp programs for all ages on themes such as Fairy Tale Science or American Girls. The museum emphasizes a hands-on approach and has opened a recycling center. Although it offers activities for a range of ages, its best activities are for children up to fifth grade.

Maine State Museum

Station 83, State House Complex,
Augusta
(207) 287-2301
Open year-round

With special emphasis on natural history, the Maine State Museum has a wide variety of attractions. Visitors are greeted by the LION, an 1846 steam locomotive; the LION used to haul logs, but now it rests in the front lobby of the museum. The displays include stuffed animals and birds posed in natural scenes, live fish, and gems and minerals of Maine. The Museum also offers a look at Maine's native people with its exhibition, "12,000 Years in Maine." Further, the Maine State Museum has special programs for children that run year-round; call for details.

Norlands Living History Museum

290 Norlands Road, Livermore
(207) 897-4366
Open year-round
For more information, visit
www.norlands.org

A year-round working farm and living history museum, Norlands has been painstakingly restored to preserve the heritage and culture of nineteenth-century rural life in Maine. There is an opportunity to participate in seasonal activities such as Jingle Bell Rides, Maple Syrup Days, and Civil War reenactments. Tours present a very personal perspective of the post–Civil War days in rural Maine.

State Capitol Building

State Street, Augusta
(207) 287-1400 Clerks office
(207) 287-5790 Legislative information
Open year-round.

Construction of the native granite State Capitol building in 1829 was under the direction of renowned architect Charles Bulfinch who designed many other notable New England buildings, including Faneuil Hall in Boston. Bulfinch also assisted in the design of the United States Capitol in Washington, D.C. The Maine State Capitol building houses a variety of artifacts, including portraits of former Maine governors. The Hall of Flags is an exhibit of Maine's battle flags. There is also a gallery where kids can watch the legislature in session.

Western Maine

Nowetah's American Indian Museum

2 Colegrove Road (Route 27), New Portland
(207) 628-4981
Open year-round

Nowetah Wirick, a descendant of the Abenaki and Paugussett Indians, and her husband Roger Wirick, a Cherokee, built this museum in 1969 and have owned and operated it ever since. While they display Indian art and artifacts from many areas, they have a separate room devoted to Maine Indian baskets and bark containers. The museum gift shop offers genuine American Indian arts and crafts.

The Stanley Museum

40 School Street, Kingfield
(207) 265-2729
Open year-round (Call for hours)
For more information, visit
www.stanleymuseum.org/

The Stanley brothers of Kingfield invented the Stanley Steamer, a car used at the turn of the twentieth century. The autos had steam engines and were more similar to steam locomotives than they are to today's automobiles. A Stanley Steamer set a land-speed record in 1906, when it reached an impressive 127 miles per hour. The Stanley Brothers donated the building to the town of Kingfield. The town used it for a school before it was turned into the museum. The museum exhibits the Stanley brothers' automobiles and a photo display by their sister, Chansonetta Stanley Emmons.

Western Maine Children's Museum

Carrabassett Valley
(207) 235-2211
Open year-round
For more information, visit
www.mainemuseums.org/htm/115.htm

This nonprofit museum's focus is on providing an interactive atmosphere for both children and adults that encourages learning and fun. An infant/toddler play space is available, and group tours are accommodated. Call for information on what workshops and programs are being offered.

Wilhelm Reich Museum and the Orgone Energy Observatory

Dodge Pond Road, Rangeley
(207) 864-3443
Open year-round
For more information, visit
www.wilhelmreichmuseum.org/

Located in the home and workplace of Wilhelm Reich, a renowned physician-scientist, this museum is set on 175 acres of fields, woodlands and hiking trails. Reich's final wish was to create an educational science center. The museum displays several inventions and pieces of equipment Reich used in his experiments. In addition, the museum houses a special discovery room for children. The museum's main family attractions are the seasonal outdoor events, such as the Children's Festival, Apple Cider Making, the Family Winter Carnival, and a Kite Workshop.

Northern Maine

Ashland Logging Museum

Garfield Road, Ashland
(207) 435-6039
Open in summer months

Ashland Logging Museum is located in the midst of an astounding 3.8 million acres of forest in Aroostook County in northern Maine. This museum brings its visitors back to a time of north woods prosperity with its blacksmith's shop and machine shed, both full of exhibits and artifacts of the Maine lumbering industry.

Cole Land Transportation Museum

405 Perry Road, Bangor
(207) 990-3600
Open seasonally, May to November

This museum displays more than 200 vehicles, ranging from a locomotive to logging sleds and trucks, snowplows, fire trucks, vintage cars, and wagons and sleighs.

Hudson Museum, Traditional and Contemporary Cultures

University of Maine
5746 Maine Center for the Arts, Orono
(207) 581-1901
Closed Mondays and holidays
For more information, visit
www.ume.maine.edu/~hudsonm/

Exhibits of traditional and contemporary cultures open the doors to greater understanding of people around the world. Call for information on children's programs and special events.

Lumbermen's Museum

Shin Pond Road, Route 159, Patten
(207) 528-2650
Open Memorial Day to Columbus Day
For more information, visit
www.lumbermensmuseum.org

The Lumbermen's Museum consists of ten buildings, one of which is a log cabin reconstructed from the loggers' cabins of the 1860s. The museum seeks to preserve the logging culture, which began to decline in the 1960s. Founded in 1962, the museum houses north woods artifacts, specifically early log haulers, a working sawmill, and innumerable tools and reconstructions of various buildings found in logging camps.

Maine Discovery Museum

74 Main Street, Bangor
(207) 262-7200
Open year-round
For more information, visit
www.mainediscoverymuseum.org

Opened in 2001, the Maine Discovery Museum is the largest interactive museum for kids north of Boston. With exhibits on nature, music, geography, and more, it offers kids the opportunity to not only learn but participate. Among the many attractions are a beaver lodge replica and a huge kaleidoscope in which children can play. Group visits and birthday parties are both welcome.

Maine Forest and Logging Museum

Leonard's Mills, off Route 178, Bradley
(207) 581-2871
Open year-round
For more information, visit
www.leonardsmills.com

This museum takes visitors back to the eighteenth century, complete with a sawmill, a blacksmith's shop, and a reconstructed log cabin, among other things. Most of the time the experience is self-guided, with signs to assist visitors. For a few days a year, however, volunteers arrive to fill the camp and "live" like the loggers did long ago. During the winter months many of the buildings close, but when the snow flies, the vintage horse-drawn sleds come out. Call ahead for snow conditions.

Moosehead Marine Museum

North Main Street, Greenville
(207) 695-2716
Weekends from Memorial Day to June, daily from July to September
For more information, visit www.katahdin cruises.com/museum.html

Focusing on the northern Maine lakes, the Moosehead Marine Museum has an extensive collection of steamboat memorabilia and early photographs of the Moosehead area. The star of the show, though, is the *Katahdin*, a restored steamship. The *Katahdin* takes tours past Moose Island and Burnt Jacket Point. Once a week, it makes longer journeys to Kineo Mountain, where visitors have the opportunity to get out and explore. Call for details and reservations.

Nylander Museum

657 Main Street, Caribou
(207) 493-4209
Open limited hours, Memorial Day to Labor Day
School groups by appointment year-round
For more information, visit www.nylandermuseum.org

This museum was dedicated in 1939 and houses the geological, marine life, and natural history collections of Olof Nylander. It includes examples of taxidermy, preserved specimens for classification, raised relief maps and models, and several touch tables for children. Outside, there is a garden area featuring native medicinal plants and the recently developed Collins Pond Path—a trail through a wetlands area.

chapter 14

One of a Kind

Learn the State of Maine Motto
   and Song . . . 132

Learn the State of Maine Counties
   Song . . . 132

See Maine's Largest Trees . . . 132

Take a Ghostly Tour, York . . . 133

See Spouting Rock, Kennebunkport . . . 133

Go on a Candy Factory Tour,
   Westbrook . . . 133

Enter the Beach to Beacon 1K Young
   People's Run, Cape Elizabeth . . . 134

Take in a Portland Sea Dogs Professional
   Baseball Game, Portland . . . 134

Attend a Portland Pirates Professional
   Hockey Game, Portland . . . 134

Discover Maine's Only Desert,
   Freeport . . . 134

Check out the World's Largest Rotating
   Globe, Yarmouth . . . 134

Discover the Ancient Shell Heaps,
   Newcastle . . . 135

Find Special Sheet Music at Bagaduce
   Lending Library, Blue Hill . . . 135

Survey the Stars in Orono and
   Portland . . . 135

Tour the Maine State Building,
   Poland Spring . . . 135

Strike it Rich: Pan for Gold in the Swift
   River, between Byron and Roxbury . . . 136

Visit the "Field of Dreams," Unity . . . 136

Take in Maine's Grand Canyon,
   Gulf Hagas, Moosehead Region . . . 136

One of a Kind

Learn the State of Maine Motto and Song

MAINE MOTTO: *DIRIGO*

Pronunciation: "*Deer*-i-go" or "Dir-*eye*-go"

Derivation: Latin

Meaning: "I direct," or "I lead"

MAINE SONG: *State of Maine Song*, BY ROGER VINTON SNOW

To hear the tune, visit **http://www.state.me.us/sos/kids/ allabout/symbols/song.htm** and click on the speaker.

Grand State of Maine,
proudly we sing
To tell your glories to the land,
To shout your praises till the echoes ring.
Should fate unkind
Send us to roam,
The scent of the fragrant pines,
The tang of the salty sea
Will call us home.

CHORUS:
Oh, Pine Tree State,
Your woods, fields, and hills,
Your lakes, streams, and rockbound coast
Will ever fill our hearts with thrills,
And tho' we seek far and wide
Our search will be in vain,
To find a fairer spot on earth
Than Maine! Maine! Maine!

Learn the State of Maine Counties Song

TO THE TUNE OF "YANKEE DOODLE DANDY"

There are 16 counties in our state:
Cumberland and Franklin,
Piscataquis and Somerset,
Aroostook, Androscoggin.
Sagadahoc and Kennebec,
Lincoln, Knox, and Hancock,
Waldo, Washington, and York,
Oxford and Penobscot.

See Maine's Largest Trees

Visit Maine's Register of Big Trees at **http://www.state.me.us/doc/foliage/kids/ bigtree.html** to learn more or to nominate a potential champ.

CORK ELM, KITTERY

Where to find it: 2 to 4 Wentworth Street, near Gate One of the Portsmouth Naval shipyard.

This tree is 86 feet tall!

SCARLET OAK, PORTLAND

Where to find it: Deering Oaks Park, Park Avenue

This tree is 46 feet tall!

KOUSA DOGWOOD, PORTLAND

Where to find it: On the property of the Sacred Heart Church, corner of Mellon and Sherman Streets

This tree is 30 feet tall!

AMERICAN ELM, YARMOUTH

Where to find it: Corner of Route 88 and Yankee Drive

This tree, known as "Herbie," is the largest elm in New England at 93 feet and a circumference of 229 inches!

SHINGLE OAK, YARMOUTH

Where to find it: In front of Merrill Memorial Library on Main Street

This tree is 52 feet tall!

EUROPEAN LINDEN, PHIPPSBURG

Where to find it: The Phippsburg Center Congregational Church on Parker Road

This tree is 104 feet tall!

YELLOWWOOD, AUGUSTA

Where to find it: Corner of Columbia and State Streets

This tree is 51 feet tall!

WHITE PINE, MORRILL

Where to find it: Heading south from the center of Morrill on Route 131, it will be on the right. If you reach the Hartsthorn Road, you've gone too far.

Confirmed as one of the largest in the nation, this tree is 132 feet tall!

HONEY LOCUST, LIVERMORE FALLS

Where to find it: Livermore Falls Cemetery, 2 Main Street

This tree is 58 feet tall!

YELLOW BIRCH, DEER ISLE

Where to find it: Reach Road Farm, Reach Road, 2 to 3 miles from Route 15, on the right.

This tree is the largest birch tree in the nation, measuring 76 feet from crown to base, with a circumference of 252 inches!

Take a Ghostly Tour

Ghostly Tours
250 York Street (Route 1A), York
(207) 363-0000 (seasonal phone)

Journey with a guide amidst the shadows of the unknown in Old York Village to hear authentic ghost stories, witch tales, and folklore. This candlelight evening tour includes several interesting twists and turns. Call ahead for ticket information.

See Spouting Rock

Ocean Avenue, Kennebunkport
For more information, call the Chamber of Commerce (207) 967-0857

Drive Ocean Avenue past St. Ann's Episcopal Church. Spouting Rock is just past the church on the right. A natural formation, the spray of sea water occurs each time waves enter two ragged cliffs known as Blowing Cave and explode upward.

Go on a Candy Factory Tour

Haven's Candies
87 County Road, Westbrook
(207) 772-1557 or (800) 639-6309
For more information, visit
www.havenscandies.com

Visit Haven's Candies, which has been in operation for more than 80 years. Young and old enjoy the guided or self-directed tours. On the day you visit, they may be making fudge, turtles, peanut brittle, chocolate lobsters, saltwater taffy, salted cashews, creams, or one of hundreds of other handcrafted delights—all sold in the store.

Enter the Beach to Beacon IK Young People's Run

> **When: The first Saturday in August**
> **Where: Fort Williams Park, Shore Road, Cape Elizabeth**
> **How to Register: Peoples Heritage Bank, P.O. Box 9540 Portland, Maine 04112 or call (888) 480-6940**

The Beach to Beacon 10K Road Race is the largest and most exciting foot race in the State of Maine. Olympians and world-class runners compete along with masters, joggers, and walkers. The 1K Young People's Run, for children 12 and under, takes place after the 10K at scenic Fort Williams Park.

Take in a Portland Sea Dogs Professional Baseball Game

> **The Portland Sea Dogs**
> **Hadlock Field, 271 Park Avenue, Portland**
> *For more information, visit*
> *www.portlandseadogs.com*

Hadlock Field is conveniently located just off Exit 6A of Interstate 295 and is a great place to watch the Sea Dogs, a farm team of the Boston Red Sox. From the lighthouse that pops up with every home run to visits with Slugger, the team mascot, Sea Dogs fans enjoy exciting baseball in this 6,860-seat stadium. Hadlock Field has won accolades for its design, which brings fans close to the action.

Attend a Portland Pirates Professional Hockey Game

> **The Portland Pirates**
> **Cumberland County Civic Center, 1 Civic Center Square, Portland**
> **(207) 775-3458 or (207) 828-4665**
> *For more information, visit*
> *www.portlandpirates.com*

The Cumberland County Civic Center is located in the heart of downtown Portland, within walking distance of the waterfront, restaurants, and ample parking. The Portland Pirates are part of the American Hockey League and an affiliate of the National Hockey League's Washington Capitals. The Pirates play their home games at the Civic Center from October to April each year.

Discover Maine's Only Desert

> **95 Desert Road, Freeport**
> **(207) 865-6962**
> *For more information, visit*
> *www.desertofmaine.com*

Just a few miles from L.L. Bean and the center of Freeport, you'll find this 50-acre oasis of dunes and "desert." The sand was deposited by glaciers that once covered Maine and melted 11,000 years ago. You can explore this fascinating phenomenon by a narrated coach tour or walk the trails yourself. Be sure to take in the sand art from artists at work—or create your own! Open seasonally.

Check Out the World's Biggest Rotating Globe

> **DeLorme Map Store, Yarmouth**
> **Just off Route 1 at the Freeport Line, Yarmouth**
> **(207) 846-7100 or (800) 642-0970**
> *For more information, visit*
> *www.delorme.com*

Named Eartha, the DeLorme globe is the world's largest rotating globe! Completed on

July 23, 1998, Eartha is the largest printed image of the Earth ever created and was developed and designed using computer technology. It represents one of the largest computer mapping databases in the world. At a scale of 1:1,000,000, one inch on Eartha equals nearly sixteen miles on the Earth. The globe's surface consists of 792 panels, each 8 degrees latitude by 10 degrees longitude. Eartha weighs approximately 5,600 pounds and has a surface area of more than 5,300 square feet.

Discover the Ancient Shell Heaps

Glidden's Point, Damariscotta River Association's Salt Bay Preserve, Mills Road, Newcastle
Damariscotta River Association: (207) 563-1393

Known locally as the "Glidden Middens," this is an ancient site on the banks of the Damariscotta River where Native Americans held large gatherings (feasts). Listed on the National Register of Historic Places, this fascinating place is protected, and removal of the 2,400-year-old shells is unlawful.

To find the shell heaps, walk the Salt Bay Heritage Trail. The trailhead is located across the street from Lincoln County Publishing, which allows free parking if you park as far from the building as possible.

Find Special Sheet Music at Bagaduce Lending Library

Bagaduce Lending Library
3 Music Library Lane, Blue Hill
(207) 374-5454
For more information, visit
http://bagaducemusic.org

The Bagaduce Lending Library collects, preserves, and lends printed music to more than 20 countries worldwide, specializing in choral, instrumental, vocal, and keyboard music, both classical and popular. Check out their special

State of Maine Collection, where they showcase native Maine composers and arrangers. The Library also provides music education programs.

Survey the Stars in Orono and Portland

Where can you star gaze? Your back yard, a hilltop, the beach—or you can visit one of two planetariums in Maine. Graham Morissette, a Maine Children's Cancer Program patient, thought the stars in Maine were magical, especially the shooting stars. The clear nights, absence of city lights, and a geography that allows many broad vistas, all enhance this experience.

Southworth Planetarium
University of Southern Maine Science Building
96 Falmouth Street, Portland
(207) 780-4249
For more information, visit
www.usm.maine.edu/planet

Maynard F. Jordan Planetarium and Observatory
University of Maine, Wingate Hall, Orono
(207) 581-1341
For more information, visit
www.umainesky.com

Tour the Maine State Building

Poland Spring
Poland Spring Preservation Society
(207) 998-4219 (Beverly Tripp)

Originally built for the Columbian Exposition at the Chicago World's Fair in 1893, this historic building was later moved by special freight to Danville Junction, then the pieces were hauled by horse and wagon to the Poland Spring resort belonging to Hiram Ricker. Today it serves as a history museum for the town of Poland Spring. For photos and a history of the building, visit *http://www.baharris.org/historicpolandspring/MaineStateBldg/MSB.htm*

Strike it Rich: Pan for Gold in the Swift River

Here is a chance to find real gold flakes (and gold nuggets, too, if you're lucky)! Try panning for gold in the Swift River where it runs close beside Route 17 between Roxbury and Byron (just north of Rumford on the way to Rangeley). *NOTE: Access the river only in areas where it abuts Route 17. Do not cross private property.*

> **Perham's of Maine**
> **194 Bethel Road (Route 26),**
> **West Paris**
> **(207) 674-2341**

Perham's of Maine will sell you the equipment you'll need to pan for gold. They can also help with instructions. Your children can experience the adventure of finding real treasures in nature.

Visit the "Field of Dreams"

> **On the shores of Lake Winnecook (Unity Pond), off Route 202, Unity**

Here is a great place for kids and their families to enjoy a wide array of sporting events and enjoy Maine's great outdoors at the same time. Established by the Bert G. and Coral B. Clifford Charitable Foundation, this "Field of Dreams," as it is called, is dedicated to fun.

Among the activities you can experience:

- Score the winning goal in soccer.
- Catch the biggest frog in the lake.
- Watch the Spirit of Unity steam train go by at noon.
- Play Home Run Derby with the family.
- Find the bald eagles' nest.

- Become the family's tennis champ.
- Throw a ringer in horseshoes.
- Finish off with a picnic lunch on the shores of Lake Winnecook.

Take in Maine's Grand Canyon

> **Gulf Hagas**
> **Moosehead Region, West Branch Pleasant River, Bowdoin College Grant East**
> **Map 42, D1 in DeLorme Publishing's** *Maine Atlas and Gazetteer*

The Appalachian Trail follows the rim of this incredible three-mile canyon, nicknamed the "Grand Canyon of the East." It includes dramatic vertical rock formations, chutes, pools, and five waterfalls. The falls are particularly spectacular during the spring runoff.

From Brownville Junction, follow Route 11 north about 5 miles. Turn left at the sign for Katahdin Iron Works onto a paved road which quickly becomes dirt. Follow about 6 miles to a rope gate at the remains of the Katahdin Iron Works. Gulf Hagas, though on public land, is only accessible by private roads managed by Katahdin Iron Works/Mary-Jo Inc., which charges a toll for their use. Once you've paid the toll, continue another 6 to 7 miles to a dirt parking lot. From here you must hike in to the Gulf, and some fording of streams may be required. A map is a good idea; the *Appalachian Trail Guide to Maine* can be purchased at *http://www.atctrailstore.org/catalog/index.cfm?compid=1&pcatid=42*

chapter 15

Parks, Preserves, and Sanctuaries

Southern Maine ...138

Bradbury Mountain State Park, Pownal ...138

Crescent Beach State Park, Cape Elizabeth ...138

East Point Sanctuary, Biddeford Pool ...138

Ferry Beach State Park, Saco ...139

Fore River Sanctuary, Portland ...139

Popham Beach State Park, Phippsburg ...139

Reid State Park, Georgetown ...139

Sebago Lake State Park, Casco ...139

Two Lights State Park, Cape Elizabeth ...140

Wolfe's Neck Woods State Park, Freeport ...140

Mid-Coast Maine ...140

Camden Hills State Park, Camden ...140

Damariscotta Lake State Park, Jefferson ...140

Josephine Newman Sanctuary, Georgetown ...141

Lake St. George State Park, Liberty ...141

Moose Point State Park, Searsport ...141

Rockport Marine Park, Rockport ...141

Swan Lake State Park, Swanville ...141

Warren Island State Park, near Islesboro in Penobscot Bay ...142

Down East Maine ...142

Acadia National Park, Mt. Desert Island ...142

Birdsacre Sanctuary at Stanwood Homestead Museum, Ellsworth ...142

Blagden Preserve, Mt. Desert Island ...142

Cobscook Bay State Park, Edmunds Township ...143

Cutler Coast Preserve, Cutler ...143

Holbrook Island Sanctuary, Brooksville ...143

Lamoine Beach State Park, Lamoine ...143

Quoddy Head State Park, Lubec ...144

Roque Bluffs State Park, Roque Bluffs ...144

Roosevelt Campobello International Park, off Lubec ...144

Shackford Head State Park, Eastport ...144

Central Maine ...144

Peacock Beach State Park, Richmond ...144

Pine Tree State Arboretum, Augusta ...145

Range Ponds State Park, Poland Spring ...145

Western Maine ...145

Bigelow Preserve, Farmington ...145

Grafton Notch State Park, Newry ...145

Mount Blue State Park, Weld ...146

Rangeley Lake State Park, Rangeley ...146

Step Falls, Newry ...146

Smalls Falls, Township E, near Madrid ...146

Northern Maine ...146

Allagash Wilderness Waterway, Clayton Lake ...146

Aroostook State Park, Presque Isle ...147

Baxter State Park, Millinocket ...147

Lily Bay State Park, Beaver Cove, Greenville ...147

Mattawamkeag Wilderness Park, Mattawamkeag ...147

Peaks-Kenney State Park, Dover-Foxcroft ...148

White Mountain National Forest, Bethel ...148

Parks, Preserves, and Sanctuaries

Maine offers spectacular natural beauty and innate charm, whether you visit a state park or just pull off the highway and wander. The state's diverse environment and activities can please all nature-loving families. From the beauty of the coast to the splendor of the mountains, Maine has plenty to see and do.

The Bureau of Parks and Lands is readily accessible for visitors. The Audubon Society is also a helpful place to call. In fact, one of the benefits of going to the parks, preserves, and sanctuaries in season is the knowledgeable and helpful staff. Many of the parks have nature programs, or at least information stations, where your nature questions can be answered.

For more information, contact the following agencies.

Maine Bureau of Parks and Lands (headquarters)
22 State House Station
Augusta, ME 04333
Call (207) 287-3821, or visit
www.state.me.us/doc/parks/programs/
db_search/index.html

Maine Audubon Society
118 U.S. Route 1
Falmouth, ME 04105-6009
Call (207) 781-2330, or visit
www.maineaudubon.org

Southern Maine

Bradbury Mountain State Park
528 Hallowell Road, Route 9, Pownal
(207) 688-4712
Open year-round

Only six miles from downtown Freeport, this 600-acre park is great for daytime adventures. There are a wonderful ball field and playground near the picnic area. Horseback riding and mountain biking are permitted on six and a half miles of the eight miles of hiking trails and groomed cross-country trails. From the top of Bradbury Mountain's 484-foot peak, one can see views of Casco Bay and the White Mountains. The mountain is also a great location for spotting eagles, migrating ospreys, and red-tailed hawks.

Crescent Beach State Park
Route 77, Cape Elizabeth
(207) 799-5871
Open Memorial Day through
Columbus Day

This 243-acre park has a mile of fine sand and stone beaches. Both swimming and fishing are popular at this restful area. The park offers bath houses, 130 picnic sites, grills, a playground, and a snack bar. Crescent Beach is perfect for a fun, yet relaxing, day in the sun.

East Point Sanctuary
Lester E. Orcutt Boulevard,
Biddeford Pool
Central Maine Audubon (207) 781-2330
Open year-round
For more information, visit
www.maineaudubon.org

Secluded at the tip of the Biddeford Pool peninsula, this Audubon-run sanctuary is considered one of the best birding spots in southern Maine. Visitors can view alcids, gannets, red-throated loons, sea ducks, and terns. There is also a chance of seeing some harbor seals. The 30-acre preserve also provides incredible ocean views. Depending on the time of year, fun boat rides are available out to two islands within the sanctuary: 15-acre Stage

Island, and 30-acre Wood Island. (There is a short trail leading to a discontinued lighthouse on Wood Island, but watch out for poison ivy.) No pets or bikes are allowed in the preserve.

Ferry Beach State Park

95 Bay View Road, Saco
(207) 283-0067 in season
(207) 624-6080 off-season
Open Memorial Day through September 30; day use only
For more information, visit
www.state.me.us/doc/prkslnds/ferry.htm

This 117-acre park has been deemed one of the best beaches for families. Several miles of white sand beaches between the Saco River and Pine Point are enjoyable, and so are the hardwood forest, swamps, and beach dunes within the park. Plants seen on the sand and dunes are bayberry, beach pea, heather, sweet fern, and poison ivy. The sand itself is made up of glacial outwash from 10,000 years ago. The park provides swimming, changing rooms, a picnic area, nature trails, and guided nature programs.

Fore River Sanctuary

Row Avenue, Portland
Maine Audubon: (207) 781-2330
Open year-round
For more information, visit
www.trails.org/index.html

Right inside the city of Portland lies this Audubon-run sanctuary. The 76-acre preserve consists of a small salt marsh, hemlock ravines, pine uplands, groves of red oaks, 2.5 miles of nature trails, and a view of Portland's only waterfall. Deer, mink, and otter frequent the preserve, as well as hawks, migrating warblers, and shore and wading birds. Brochures and programs are available at the site. The sanctuary is a great change of pace after a day of Portland's city activities.

Popham Beach State Park

10 Perkins Farm Lane, Phippsburg
(207) 389-1335
Open April 15 through October 30

This 529-acre park fronts one of Maine's rare sandy beaches. At low tide, fun tidal pools can be found among the large rock outcroppings along the shoreline. Popham provides a great place for swimming, fishing, and picnicking, and its beautiful sunsets are also a big attraction. Bath houses, freshwater showers, and charcoal grills are available.

Reid State Park

375 Seguinland Road, off Route 127,
Georgetown
(207) 371-2303
Open year-round

With 766 acres, a mile-and-a-half stretch of beach, a saltwater pond, and numerous wooded trails, it is no wonder this state park receives 150,000 visitors every year. Ocean fishing is good here when the striped bass are running. Swimming in the warm pond is refreshing, and cross-country skiing or snowshoeing in the woods is wonderfully peaceful. The trails do tend to get buggy during the summer, but climbing on the rocky shore is always fun. A snack bar, picnic area, charcoal grills and fireplaces, bath house, and showers are all available for public use.

Sebago Lake State Park

11 Park Access Road, off Route 302,
Casco
(207) 693-6231 Labor Day through
June 19; (207) 693-6613 June 20
through Labor Day
Open April 15 through October 15
(weather permitting)

Sebago Lake takes the honor of being the most popular Maine state park, as well as being deemed a recreational mecca. The 46-square-mile lake is wonderful for salmon and trout fishing, boating, and swimming. Although the day-use and camping areas are separated, both have extensive beaches. The day-use area is equipped with picnic tables, grills, and a boat ramp. There is a lifeguard on duty. There are 250 campsites, both lakeside and in the woods, with new bath houses and hot showers. There are several great short hiking trails. Informative summer programs include guided nature walks, talks, and amphitheater programs. The park permits cross-country skiing, snowshoeing, and snowmobiling in winter. This 1,300-acre park appears to have it all.

Two Lights State Park

Two Lights Road, off Route 77,
  Cape Elizabeth
(207) 799-5871
Open year-round

This rocky headland is great for climbing and is a perfect vantage point for viewing the entrance to Casco Bay and watching lobstermen haul traps. The historic twin lighthouses nearby were originally called Two Lights, but are now referred to as Cape Elizabeth Light. Within the park's 40 acres are picnic tables, grills, a small playground, walking paths, and a shelter spot. There are also remnants of a coastal defense installation from WWII.

Wolfe's Neck Woods State Park

425 Wolfe's Neck Road, Freeport
(207) 865-4465 April–October
(207) 624-6080 November–March
Open Memorial Day through Labor Day

This grassroots-sponsored park is dedicated to outdoor recreation and education, and there are frequent guided programs here for the public. Interpretive signs flank the five miles of hiking trails that run along the Harraseeket River and the rocky shore of Casco Bay. Searching for crabs and other sea life is fun.

You can spot nesting osprey in the early summer. The rest of the 233-acre park is made up of marsh and forest. There are several picnic sites with charcoal grills and restrooms. Cross-country skiing is permitted during the winter.

Mid-Coast Maine

Camden Hills State Park

280 Belfast Road (U.S. Route 1), Camden
(207) 236-3109 in season
(207) 236-0849 off-season
Open May 15 through October 15
For more information, visit www.state .me.us/sosnew/kids/allabout/visit /state_parks.htm

This beautiful wooded area spans 5,500 acres of mountains and coastline. With five miles of challenging biking trails and twenty-five miles of fairly easy hiking trails, Camden Hills is a great place for any family. From the peak of Mount Battie, hikers have an incredible view of several lakes, wooded hills, Camden Harbor, and the islands of Penobscot Bay. Maiden Cliff also presents breathtaking views. Although the campsites and showers are closed during the winter, cross-country skiing, snowshoeing, and winter hiking are still available. Located just outside the picturesque town of Camden, Camden Hills State Park is a relaxing and desirable spot for any visitor.

Damariscotta Lake State Park

8 State Park Road, off Route 32,
  Jefferson
(207) 549-7600 in season
(207) 941-4014 off-season
Open Memorial Day through Labor Day

Although this park is only 17 acres, it is in absolutely breathtaking surroundings. Amenities include a sand beach (with lifeguard), a group-use shelter, picnic tables, and grills. If natural beauty is what you are searching for, you'll find it here.

Josephine Newman Sanctuary

Route 127, Georgetown
Maine Audubon: (207) 781-2330
Open year-round
For more information, visit
www.maineaudubon.org/eoth.htm

This 119-acre preserve is surrounded by salt marshes on two sides and includes two miles of walking trails, a former beaver pond, a rivulet brook, rocky shoreline, and tidal mud flats around the head of Robinhood Cove. The forests are decorated with red oaks, white pines, red spruce, and hemlocks. The bird life varies greatly, and coyotes, snowshoe hares, mink, and whitetail deer have all been spotted in the park.

Lake St. George State Park

Route 3, Liberty
(207) 589-4255
Open May 15 through September 30

The clean, spring-fed waters of Lake St. George are fabulous for swimming, boating, and fishing. The lake is stocked with brook trout and salmon, while bass and white perch are native to the area. Rowboats and canoes can be rented, and a boat launch is available for public use. Thirty-eight lakefront campsites are equipped with showers and toilets, and picnic sites stud the grassy lake shore near the access gate. Aside from the lake, the 360-acre park also includes ten miles of trails for hiking, mountain biking, snowmobiling, and cross-country skiing.

Moose Point State Park

310 West Main Street (U.S. Route 1),
Searsport
(207) 548-2882 in season
(207) 941-4014 off-season
Open Memorial Day through September
30; day use only

With 183 acres, this picturesque park has incredible views of Penobscot Bay. The terrain varies widely, from an evergreen grove to tidal pools. There are easy hiking trails and picnic tables. Kids love playing in the pools as well as the grove, making this park a perfect spot to spend an afternoon.

Rockport Marine Park

Off Pascal Avenue, Rockport
Harbormaster (207) 236-0676

This town-maintained park displays some interesting artifacts from the old days when Rockport was a limestone-processing center, including an old lime kiln. On one side of the park is a working boatyard. The park has been a favorite among locals and visitors alike for decades. There are picnic tables on the flat grassy land overlooking the town floats that provide public access to Rockport Harbor. A large statue of Andre the Seal celebrates the memory of his past frequent visits.

Swan Lake State Park

100 West Park Lane, off Frankfort Road,
Swanville
(207) 525-4404 in season
(207) 941-4014 off-season
Open Memorial Day through Labor Day

This 67-acre state park is one of Maine's newest. Here you'll find a sandy beach and swimming area as well as a great playground and picnic area with barbecue pits. A shelter is available for gatherings in the park, and a lifeguard is on duty.

Warren Island State Park

Near Islesboro in Penobscot Bay
(207) 236-3109 in season
(207) 236-0849 off-season
Open Memorial Day through September 15

This small, 70-acre island state park has the benefit of being sheltered by surrounding larger islands. There is no public ferry access directly to Warren Island, but there is public docking and mooring on the lee side of the island for those who bring their own boat. Otherwise, visitors can cross on the State Ferry from Lincolnville to Islesboro, then canoe or kayak to Warren Island. The island has ten well spread-out campsites, two Adirondack shelters, picnic sites, and fresh water. Two miles of trails circle the rustic spruce-clad island, where whitetail deer and red squirrels are common. The mackerel and striped bass fishing can be great, and the sand beach on the south side of the island is wonderful.

Down East Maine

Acadia National Park

Mount Desert Island
Hulls Cove Visitor Center:
(207) 288-3338
Open year-round
For more information, visit
www.nps.gov/acad/home.htm

Acadia has consistently been Maine's most all-around popular park. This 35,000-acre national park offers a wide range of activities due to its diverse natural environments. From May through October, guides are available to lead informational walks, hikes, cruises, and slide shows. Also during the summer, kids 8 and up are able to participate in Acadia's Junior Ranger program, as well as several other ranger-led programs specifically geared for children. Although all of Acadia is worth exploring, some of the more notable locations are on the eastern side of the park—Cadillac Mountain, Thunder Hole, and the Beehive are all visitor favorites. Sea kayaking out to the neighboring islands, such as Little and Great Cranberry, is also wonderful. Even though some roads and services are closed during the off-season, Acadia still presents many fun activities during the winter, such as winter camping, cross-country skiing, snowmobiling, ice skating, and ice fishing.

Birdsacre Sanctuary at Stanwood Homestead Museum

289 High Street (Route 3), Ellsworth
(207) 667-8460
Grounds open year-round; Museum open mid-June through mid-October

Located adjacent to the Stanwood Homestead Museum (once the home of pioneer ornithologist Cordelia Stanwood), this 130-acre sanctuary is great for bird watching and offers picnic facilities and nature trails. Rehabilitation facilities for ducks, songbirds, hawks, and owls are also on-site. The trails can be used for cross-country skiing in winter months.

Blagden Preserve

Off Indian Point Road,
Mount Desert Island

All 110 acres of this secluded preserve represent the natural beauty of the northwest corner of Mt. Desert Island. Mainly consisting of wooded walking paths, the preserve also features 300 yards of gorgeous shoreline and views of Blue Hill Bay. Often visitors spy seals sunning on the rocks. The Indian Point area was one of the very few places on the island to escape the devastating fire of 1947. Informative guides and maps are available at the caretaker's house.

Cobscook Bay State Park

Off Route 1, off Lower Edmunds Road, Edmunds Township
Park office in Dennysville: (207) 726-4412
Open May 15 through October 15

In the Abenaki language, *Cobscook* means "boiling tides," which is an accurate description of the swirling tidal currents that sweep through Cobscook Bay. Tides can reach as much as 24 feet in the bay, so caution is important. Sea fishing for flounder and mackerel is usually good and sea kayaking is not only popular, but also manageable for beginners *in certain areas with explicit directions from park staff.* The 888-acre park also has seven miles of wonderful hiking and biking trails, of which five are groomed for cross-country skiing in the winter. The park offers campsites, hot showers, and a picnic area. Interesting wildlife, such as deer, moose, seals, loons, eagles, and black ducks (in the winter) can be seen in this unique park.

Cutler Coast Preserve

Route 191, Cutler
Maine Bureau of Parks and Lands
(207) 827-5936
Open year-round

Located both west and east of Route 191, the Cutler Coast Preserve boasts five miles of dramatic ocean shore and cliffs. Within its 2,115 acres, trails mainly follow the coast, but also lead to well-dispersed hike-in campsites. (These are primitive facilities—tent sites and pit toilets only.) The preserve consists mostly of grassland, spruce woods, and heath. There are two main hiking loops, one running for 5.8 miles and the other for 9.8 miles. Several log ladders connect the trails to cobble beaches below the cliffs. Fishing and boating are good, and there are several small boat launches within the preserve. Visitors might see eagles, falcons, or owls within the park, as well as eider ducks, porpoises, seals, and whales offshore.

Holbrook Island Sanctuary

172 Indian Bar Road, off Back Road, Cape Rosier, Brooksville
(207) 326-4012
Open year-round; day use only
For more information, visit www.state.me.us/cgibin/doc/parks/ find_one_name.pl?park_id=9

According to the wishes of Anita Harris, the donor of this 1,230-acre preserve, the Holbrook Island Sanctuary has not been modernized. The park is traversed by a few old roads, but mainly by paths and animal trails. The varied landscape consists of scenic forests, rocky and beach shoreline, mud flats, wetlands, ponds, meadows, and steep hills carved from the volcanic bedrock. In meadows and wetlands, gorgeous wildflowers bloom from early spring through the late fall. Many animals frequent the sanctuary, such as beavers, bobcats, coyotes, deer, foxes, otters, and porcupines. The birding is particularly good during both spring and fall migration; blue herons and ospreys nest near the pond and estuary, while bald eagles and peregrine falcons are also sometimes seen. For activities, the park provides hiking, cross-country skiing, canoeing, and kayaking. A boat launch and picnic tables are available. Also, there is an extensive nature walk series, with diverse topics ranging from plant and animal life to historical human inhabitants.

Lamoine Beach State Park

23 State Park Road, off Route 184, Lamoine
(207) 667-4778 in season
(207) 941-4014 off-season
Open May 15 through October 15

Located on Frenchman Bay, this small 55-acre park has few visitors but is a real gem. Here you'll find a 61-site campground, picnic area, boat launch, saltwater fishing pier, children's playground, hot showers, and toilets. Swimming in the bay can be chilly, but you can always stay onshore and simply enjoy the panoramic views of Mount Desert Island.

Quoddy Head State Park

South Lubec Road, off Route 189, Lubec
(207) 733-0911 in season
(207) 941-4014 off-season
Open May 15 through October 15

This 481-acre state park is the most eastern point of the United States and the site of the beautiful West Quoddy Head Lighthouse. It has wonderful trails along volcanic rock bluffs 80 feet above the ocean, providing a fantastic view. The park also contains thick evergreen forests that are great for bird watching. Boardwalks carry hikers over delicate peat bogs where you can spot rare plant life.

Roque Bluffs State Park

145 Schoppee Point Road, Roque Bluffs
(207) 255-3475 in season
(207) 941-4014 off-season
Open May 15 through September 30

Both fresh- and saltwater swimming are available at Roque Bluffs State Park, where dunes separate the ocean from the 66-acre pond. There is a pebble beach in this 274-acre park, as well as a picnic area with grills, a changing area with toilets, and a children's playground.

Roosevelt Campobello International Park

Campobello Island, New Brunswick,
accessible from Lubec
(506) 752-2922
Open Saturday prior to Memorial Day
through Columbus Day

At one time, this Canadian island was the family summer home of President Franklin D. Roosevelt. The Roosevelt family compound is now preserved as part of an international park, dually governed by Canada and the United

States. The park consists of 2,800 acres of beaches, cleared fields, forests, rocky shoreline, and wetlands, which encompass about one-third of the island. There are scenic trails great for walking and several picnic areas with charcoal grills. The walk along the eastern beaches is wonderful, and in the fall there is a good likelihood of spotting a few whales offshore. At the international park, FDR's family cottage, the beautiful gardens, and two greenhouses are open to the public.

Campobello also offers many other interesting sights, such as the wonderful East Quoddy Head Lighthouse at the northeast tip of the island and the Herring Cove Provincial Park adjacent to the international park.

Shackford Head State Park

Deep Cove Road, west of Route 190,
Eastport
(207) 941-4014
Open year-round, always unsupervised

This park offers 90 acres of undeveloped peninsula with beaches, protected coves, and two fossil beds. Hiking trails through the woods to the rocky headland only take about 20 minutes to complete. Five Civil War–era ships were towed here and burned in the early 1900s, making old war ship artifacts a possible find. The park provides wonderful views of Cobscook Bay and Broad Cove.

Central Maine

Peacock Beach State Park

Route 201, Richmond
(207) 582-2813 in season
(207) 624-6080 off-season
Open Memorial Day through Labor Day;
day use only

Only 12 short miles away from Maine's state capital, Peacock Beach on Pleasant Pond is a great place for family picnics. The park's 100 acres include a beach, picnic area, and life-guard-protected swimming area.

Pine Tree State Arboretum

153 Hospital Street (Route 9), Augusta
(207) 621-0031
Open year-round

On 224 wooded acres right in the state capital are five miles of trails for hiking and cross-country skiing. The arboretum's plant collections include perennial gardens and many species of trees. Outdoor education programs are offered in spring and fall.

Range Ponds State Park

31 State Park Road, off Route 122,
Poland Spring
(207) 998-4104 in season
(207) 624-6080 off-season
Open May 15 through October 15; day use only

A great ball field, picnic area, and lifeguard-protected swimming area compose this 750-acre park. The combined activities make a great afternoon for the family.

Western Maine

Bigelow Preserve

Accessed from Stratton, Routes 16 and 27, Farmington
(207) 778-8231
Open year-round

With 35,000 acres, frontage on a large, un-spoiled lake, 17 miles on the Appalachian Trail, and one of the ten peaks above 4,000 feet in Maine, Bigelow is a popular spot in the spring, summer, fall, and winter. Although temperatures in the winter are consistently sub-zero, a lodge near the Round Barn camp-sites is open to alpine skiers and snowmobilers in the preserve. Bigelow entertains a host of other activities, including hiking, biking, swimming, canoeing, fishing, picnicking, and camping. Campsites are basic, with no running water facilities. The preserve is wonderful for spotting bears, beavers, coyotes, moose, and sixty different species of birds. Flagstaff Lake and Bigelow Mountain are the two main attractions within the preserve.

Grafton Notch State Park

Route 26, Newry
(207) 824-2912 in season
(207) 624-6080 off-season
Open May 15 through October 15

This overwhelmingly scenic park of 3,112 acres offers hiking trails that range widely in difficulty and provide fantastic views of the White Mountains. There are also geologically impressive caves, a wooded nature preserve, incredible waterfalls, and three breathtaking gorges. It is easy to visit all three gorges, (Screw Auger Falls Gorge, Mother Walker Falls Gorge, and Moose Cave Gorge) in just a few hours. All kids, especially younger ones, need close supervision in this part of the park because the trails closely approach steep drop-offs. Screw Auger Falls Gorge is the most accessible, and its plunging water creates shallow pools in which kids love to play. However, it is better to picnic at Mother Walker Falls Gorge because traffic from the road cannot be heard from there. Picnic areas include tables and grills. During the winter, a local club maintains all the snowmobiling trails. A fall sojourn in the park will reward visitors with gorgeous foliage.

Mount Blue State Park

299 Center Hill Road, Weld
(Park Office)
(207) 585-2261 in season
(800) 332-1501 off-season
Open year-round

There are two sections to the 5,000 acres that make up Mount Blue State Park. The smaller park (Webb Beach) is located on the southwest shore of Webb Lake and includes a sand beach, a boat launch, and boat rentals. The larger park (Center Hill Area) is located east of Route 142 and is noted for its fantastic views. Mount Blue, rising 1,800 feet, is a monadnock—a mass of hard, volcanic rock that has resisted all natural forces of erosion while surrounding softer rock has eroded away over time. The trail to the abandoned fire tower at the summit of Mount Blue provides a popular and fairly easy day hike.

Rangeley Lake State Park

South Shore Drive, Rangeley
(207) 864-3858 in season
(207) 624-6080 off-season
Open May 15 through September 15

Trout and landlocked salmon fishing are usually good within the park's 691 acres. Moose watching is also popular here. Spruce-fir woods, a mile of Moose Country Corridor Trail, and a mile of lake make this park one of the most beautiful spots in Maine. There are 50 campsites with showers, 40 spread-out picnic spots, a boat launch, and a kid's play area in the park.

Step Falls

Route 26, Newry

Right in the Grafton Notch area, this natural water park has several pools and waterfalls. Unfortunately, there are no road signs, but visitors can pinpoint the location in DeLorme Publishing's *Maine Atlas and Gazetteer*. Visi-tors hike along a half-mile marked path before reaching the magnificent falls. Although the spot can be difficult to find for visitors unfamiliar with the area, it is well worth the effort. Look for it about half a mile east of the boundary of Grafton Notch State Park.

Smalls Falls

Route 4, Township E, near Madrid

This popular roadside picnic area pinpoints where Mill Stream joins the Sandy River. There are several waterfalls and a swimming area here, as well as short, easy trails up to the top of the cliffs. Although the falls are beautiful all year, it can be quite cool here in the spring and fall, so dress accordingly.

Northern Maine

Allagash Wilderness Waterway

Clayton Lake
For information, contact the Maine Bureau of Parks and Lands, Northern Region Headquarters: (207) 941-4014

This waterway, winding along 92 miles of wooded shoreline, is a canoeing paradise. Numerous campsites along the river offer peaceful resting spots after long, enjoyable days on the water. Canoeing is particularly good at gorgeous Round Pond and down through the Allagash Falls, where the river provides fun natural obstacles. For those who desire a guide, several professional outfitters offer trips lasting from overnight to a week. There are plenty of moose and otter on the adjacent shoreline, as well as an array of local birds. Although the protected corridor along the waterway is lined with trees and home to plenty of wildlife, the rest of the surrounding forest is still commercial timberland.

Aroostook State Park

**87 State Park Road, off Spragueville
  Road, Presque Isle
(207) 768-8341
Open Memorial Day through Labor Day**

Aroostook State Park's current 700-acre (soon to be 800-acre) spread is typically representative of natural environments in northern Maine. Impressive twin-peaked Quaggy Jo Mountain dominates the landscape, offering its best view from the northern peak. The park also offers numerous trails for nature walks, groomed cross-country skiing and snowmobiling, as well as a beautiful beach for launching and docking boats. Canoes, paddleboats, and life jackets can be rented, and a lifeguard is available. Campsites and picnic areas are fully equipped with tables, charcoal grills, bath houses, and a new shower house.

Baxter State Park

**64 Balsam Drive, Millinocket
  (reservation office)
Reservation office: (207) 723-5140
Open May 15 through October 15;
  October 16 through December 1;
  April 1 through May 14, day use only
December 1 through March 31, winter
  camping in selected areas**
*For more information, visit
  www.baxterstateparkauthority.com*

Baxter State Park offers approximately 200 miles of trails, 46 mountain peaks and ridges, 10 campgrounds, and several streams and ponds. On famous Mount Katahdin, Baxter Peak is officially the highest peak in Maine (5,267 feet above sea level) and the first place in the United States to receive sunlight. Baxter accommodates hikers of all abilities, but visitors should inquire about the difficulty level of all trails; for example, the Knife's Edge trail is so named for a reason. Aside from hiking, the park has wonderful fishing and canoeing, as well as designated campgrounds equipped with tent space and/or bunkhouses with fireplaces and running water. Due to its popularity, the park does fill up during late summer and the gates are sometimes closed. Reservations are encouraged. September is a great time to see the spectacular foliage. Visitors should note that the gravel roads inside the park are narrow, winding, and primitive. See the Web site or call the reservations office for further information.

Lily Bay State Park

**Beaver Cove, near Greenville
(207) 695-2700 in season
(207) 941-4014 off-season
Open May 1 through October 15**

Located on the eastern shore of Moosehead Lake (Maine's largest), Lily Bay State Park offers great salmon and togue (lake trout) fishing year-round. Sailing and canoeing are also popular, supported by two boat launch sites. The 925-acre park is physically separated for overnight and day use by a 1.6-mile hiking trail. At the day-use area you'll find a sandy beach, a grassy picnic area, and a playground. The 91 campsites, divided into two areas, are mostly lakeside. Hunting is permitted in season, and snowmobiling in the winter is notably good. Snowshoeing and cross-country skiing are also possible in the winter.

Mattawamkeag Wilderness Park

**Mattawamkeag
(207) 736-4881 in season
(888) 724-2465 off-season
Open Memorial Day through October 15**

This town-owned park has been called one of Maine's best-kept secrets because of its remoteness and peacefulness. This 1,200-acre park includes a sandy beach along a rapidly moving river and 12 miles of hiking trails. Fly fishing and whitewater rafting are just two of the fun activities to pursue here. The river is naturally stocked with salmon, and there are several designated fly-fishing sites. Adventurous visitors can canoe or kayak down the Class V rapids during the spring, but they are easier for families when the water is low during late summer. There are 52 regular campsites (seven with electricity), nine Adirondack shelters, picnic sites, and one hike-in site.

Peaks-Kenney State Park

Off Route 153, Dover-Foxcroft
(207) 564-2003 in season
(207) 941-4014 off-season
Open May 15 through September 30

Tucked around the south shore of Sebec Lake, this 839-acre park has a sandy beach and lifeguard-protected swimming area, as well as nine miles of hiking trails through mature hardwood forest. There are hiking and amphitheater programs geared for adults and kids throughout the season. Although there is no boat launch facility within the park itself, there is a public ramp near the access road. Canoe rentals are available. The togue and salmon fishing is great. The park offers 56 campsites.

White Mountain National Forest

South and west of Bethel
Evans Notch Forest Service Center, 18
Mayville Road, Bethel: (207) 824-2134
For more information, visit
www.fs.fed.us/r9/white/

Part of the White Mountain National Forest (47,000 acres) lies in western Maine. Here one can find 160 hiking trails, 60 miles of snowmobiling trails, five campgrounds, picnic areas, and roadside stops surrounded by lush, green forest and gorgeous rivers. Most of the hills are easy to climb, with the exception of a few tough peaks. The views are incredible, and visitors can often spot moose and other wildlife. Check their informative Web site before starting out.

chapter 16

Picking Fruit

Strawberries ... 150
Season begins in late June

Raspberries ... 152
Season begins in the middle of July

Wild Blueberries ... 153
Season begins in late July

Highbush Blueberries ... 154
Season begins in late July

Apples, Cider, and Fall Family Fun ... 155
Season begins in late August

Picking Fruit

The Maine Department of Agriculture maintains listings of many, but not all, Maine farms and farm stands, including ones that offer the chance to pick your own. Call (207) 287-3491 or visit their Web site at www.mainefoodandfarms.com.

You can freeze the extra fruit (strawberries, raspberries, and blueberries) you have picked. Just double bag the whole, unblemished berries in heavy freezer bags and freeze. We recommend that you rinse the berries after thawing, just before you are ready to use them.

Strawberries

The season begins in late June. Be sure to call ahead to check on availability of fruit, hours of operation, and whether or not you need to bring your own containers. You may also want to ask whether there are any age restrictions for very young children. Strawberries do not continue to ripen after they have been picked, so encourage young harvesters to gather only the fully red berries.

Southern Maine

BAR MILLS

Snell's Family Farm
John E. Snell Sr.
1000 River Road (Route 112), Bar Mills
207-929-6166

BRUNSWICK

Juniper Edge Farm
Jeanne E. Johnson
Harpswell Road (Route 123),
    Brunswick
(207) 725-6414

BUXTON

Estes Farm
Carl & Lorraine Estes
114 Waterman Road, Buxton
(207) 929-4801

CAPE ELIZABETH

Maxwell's Farm
Ken & Elsie Maxwell
Off Route 77, near Two Lights,
    Cape Elizabeth
(207) 799-3383

GORHAM

Patten's Farm
Donald Patten
County Road, Gorham
(207) 839-4667

Wagner's Strawberries
Nelson Wagner
222 Libby Avenue, Gorham
(207) 839-3629

WELLS

Spiller Farm
Bill & Anna Spiller
Route 9A, Wells Branch Road, Wells
(207) 985-2575 or 985-3383

Mid-Coast Maine

BOWDOINHAM

**Fenimore's Strawberry &
    Vegetable Farm**
Donald & Pat Fenimore
West Bowdoin Road, Bowdoinham
(207) 353-2360

Prout's Vegetables
Dave & Polly Prout
Brown Point Road, Bowdoinham
(207) 666-5604

DRESDEN

Green Point Farms
Robert Gleason
Route 128, Dresden
(207) 737-2218

Popp Farm
David Popp
Off Route 128, Dresden
(207) 737-4351

THORNDIKE

Schartner Farms
Herbert & Phyllis Schartner
Route 220, Thorndike
(207) 568-3668

UNION

What-a-View Farm
Lanny & Linda Dean
Coggin Hill Road, off Route 117, Union
(207) 785-4866

Down East Maine

ORLAND

Silveridge Farm
Bob & Earlene Chasse
Silver Lake Road, Bucksport, and U.S.
    Route 1, Orland
(207) 469-7836

PEMBROKE

Crow's Brook Farm
Roger & Suzanne Riquier
Little Falls Road, Pembroke
(207) 726-3971

SEDGEWICK

C and G Growers
Claire Gray
Routes 175 & 176, Sedgewick
(207) 326-9311

Central Maine

AUBURN

Farmer Whiting's
William E. Whiting & Sons
822 Summer Street, Auburn
(207) 782-4356

CLINTON

Richardson's Strawberry Farm
Rich & Judy Richardson
Hinckley-Canaan Road, Clinton
(207) 453-2093

GREENE

Ridgeside Farm
Eric Sideman and Barbara Eldridge
Anson Road, Greene
(207) 946-3717

KENTS HILL

Kents Hill Orchard
The Apple Shed
Henry & Corinne Drake
1625 Main Street (Route 17),
    Kents Hill
(207) 685-3522

POLAND

Verrill's Vegetable Stand
Sue & Steve Verrill
270 Bailey Hill Road, Poland
(207) 998-2301

POLAND SPRING

Chipman Farm
Douglas Chipman
62 Range Hill Road, off Route 26,
    Poland Spring
(207) 998-3450

SABATTUS

Jillson's Farm/Sugarhouse
Edward & Patricia Jillson
Old Lisbon Road, Sabattus
(207) 375-4886

WAYNE

Stevenson's Strawberry Farm
Ford Stevenson
Berry Road, Wayne
(207) 685-3532

WEST GARDINER

Goodwin Strawberry Farm
Steve Goodwin
Neck Road, West Gardiner
(207) 724-3231

WEST TURNER/HEBRON

Dot Rupert's Strawberry Farm
Bill & Dot Rupert
Fern Street, West Turner/Hebron
(207) 966-2721

Western Maine

CORNVILLE

Hughes Strawberry Farm
Kathy & Paul Hughes
James Road, Cornville
(207) 474-8969

DENMARK

Bucknell Farm
Frank & Roger Bucknell
Route 160, Denmark
(207) 452-2241

PORTER

Buzzy's Greenhouse
Arnold & Ramona Knowles
Cross Road, Porter
(207) 625-4454

WEST FARMINGTON

Farm-to-You Roadside Market
David Pike
Routes 2 & 4, West Farmington
(207) 778-2187

Northern Maine

CARIBOU

Goughan Farms
Mark & Gloria Goughan
Fort Fairfield Road, Caribou
(207) 498-6565

EAST CORINTH

Adams Strawberry Acres
Joseph & Carol Adams
Route 15, East Corinth
(207) 285-3324

Tate's Strawberry Farm
Ken & Bev Tate
136 Puddleduck Road
(Route 43), East Corinth
(207) 285-3410

KENDUSKEAG

Tate's Greenhouse and Strawberries
Harold & Eleanor Tate
Town House Road, Kenduskeag
(207) 884-7601

VAN BUREN

Thibeault Strawberry Farm
Normand & Yvonne Thibeault
Marquis Road, Van Buren
(207) 868-2225

Raspberries

The season begins in the middle of July. Be sure to call ahead to check on availability of fruit, hours of operation, and whether you need to bring your own containers. You might want to make the Raspberry Lemon Yogurt Muffins in Chapter 5 with some of the berries you pick!

Southern Maine

BIDDEFORD

Whistling Wings Farm
Don & Julie Harper
427 West Street, Biddeford
(207) 282-1146

SANFORD

Greenlee Farm
John Greenlee
Grammar Road, Sanford
(207) 324-4827

WELLS

Spiller Farm
Bill & Anna Spiller
Route 9A, Wells Branch Road, Wells
(207) 985-2575 or 985-3383

Mid-Coast Maine

BOWDOINHAM

Hilltop Raspberry Farm
Richard Dunbar
Post Road, Bowdoinham
(207) 737-4988

The Ledges
J. M. Bouldin
Route 138, Bowdoinham
(207) 666-8827

THORNDIKE

Schartner Farms
Herbert & Phyllis Schartner
Route 220, Thorndike
(207) 568-3668

Central Maine

AUBURN

Lothrop Berry Farms
Linwood & Joyce Lothrop
574 South Main Street, Auburn
(207) 782-1711

CLINTON

Richardson's Strawberry Farm
Rich & Judy Richardson
Hinckley-Canaan Road (Route 23),
    Clinton
(207) 453-2093

LITCHFIELD

Blue Shale Berry Farm
Tom & Ellen Wood
Plains Road, Litchfield
(207) 268-4489

LIVERMORE

Wells Farm
Richard & Lucille Wells
Robinson Road, Livermore
(207) 897-3572

SABATTUS

Willow Pond Farm
Charles & Jill Agnew
Route 9, Sabattus
(207) 375-6662

Western Maine

BUCKFIELD

Maple Crest Farm
Kendall & Marilee Cooper
Paris Hill Road, Buckfield
(207) 336-2466

Northern Maine

EAST CORINTH

Adams Strawberry Acres
Joseph & Carol Adams
Route 15, East Corinth
(207) 285-3324

Wild Blueberries

The season begins in late July. Be sure to call ahead to check on availability of fruit, hours of operation, and whether you need to bring your own containers. You may also want to ask whether there are any age restrictions for very young children. Check out the great blueberry recipes in Chapter 5, and be sure to visit the Wild Blueberry Association Web site at www.wildblueberry.com for lots of great blueberry tips!

Southern Maine

CUMBERLAND CENTER

Pleasant Valley Acres
Betty Weir
547 Pleasant Valley Road, Cumberland
    Center
(207) 829-5588

SPRINGVALE

Rivard Farm
Gerard Rivard
Blanchard Road, Springvale
(207) 324-5566

Mid-Coast Maine

STOCKTON SPRINGS

Staple Homestead
Basil & Mary Staples
County Road, Stockton Springs
(207) 567-3393 or 567-3703

Down East Maine

BEDDINGTON

Beddington Ridge Farm
Ron & Carol Varin
Route 193, Beddington
(207) 638-2664

SEDGEWICK

Bay View Farm
Robert Colburn
Ridge Road, Sedgewick
(207) 359-2719

SOUTHWEST HARBOR

Ben's Berry Patch
B. C. Worcester Jr.
Love Pond Road, Southwest Harbor
(207) 244-3944

Central Maine

AUBURN

Lothrop Berry Farms
Linwood & Joyce Lothrop
574 South Main Street, Auburn
(207) 782-1711

SOUTH CHINA

Wagner's Maple Syrup House
Carol & Philip Wagner
Route 32, South China
(207) 445-2214

Western Maine

BROWNFIELD

The Blake Farm
Terry Blake
Brownfield
(207) 935-2041

NEW SHARON

Grace's Gourmet Foods
Grace M. Firth
Back side of Cape Cod Hill, New Sharon
(207) 778-3904

OXFORD

Henrickson Farms
Roy Henrickson
Allen Hill Road, Oxford
(207) 539-4890

RANGELEY

Blueberry Hill Farm
Don Palmer
Dallas Hill Road, Rangeley
(207) 864-5647

Highbush Blueberries

The season begins in late July. Be sure to call ahead to check on availability of fruit, hours of operation, and whether you need to bring your own containers. You may also want to ask whether there are any age restrictions for very young children.

Southern Maine

ACTON

Blueberry Hill Farm
Kevin Ham
Milton Mills Road, Acton
(207) 457-1151

BRUNSWICK

Lipovsky Gardens
Louis & Mary Lipovsky
369 Casco Road, Brunswick
(207) 725-7897

BUXTON

Estes Farm
Carl & Lorraine Estes
114 Waterman Road, Buxton
(207) 929-4801

Maine-ly Fun!

Central Maine

KENTS HILL

Steep Hill Farm
George & Brenda Joseph
Clyde Wells Road, Kents Hill
(207) 685-4155

Apples, Cider, and Fall Family Fun

The season begins in late August and extends into October. Many orchards offer other fun things to do while you are visiting, such as pumpkin picking. Check the Maine apple growers list at http://pmo.umext.maine.edu/apple/growerlist.htm. Be sure to call ahead to check on availability of fruit, hours of operation, and whether you need to bring your own containers. And don't forget to take a peek at the apple recipes in Chapter 5!

Southern Maine

ACTON

Romac Orchard
H Road, Acton
(207) 636-3247

ALFRED

Gile Orchards
Routes 202 & 4, Alfred
(207) 324-2944

BAR MILLS

Snell's Family Farm
John E. Snell Sr.
Route 112, 1000 River Road, Bar Mills
207-929-6166

LIMINGTON

Brackett Orchards
Route 11, Limington
(207) 637-2377

Dole Orchards
Route 11, Limington
(207) 793-4409

LYMAN

Lakeview Orchard
Brock Road (off Routes 202 & 4), Lyman
(207) 324-5598

RAYMOND

Meadow Brook Farm
Route 85, Raymond
(207) 627-7009

SPRINGVALE

McDougal Orchards
Hanson's Ridge Road, Springvale
(207) 324-5154

STANDISH

Randall Orchards
Randall Road, off Route 25, Standish
(207) 642-3500

WELLS

Spiller Farm
1123 Branch Road, Wells
(207) 985-2575

Mid-Coast Maine

BOWDOIN

Rocky Ridge Orchard
Route 210, Bowdoin
(207) 666-3658

HOPE

Apple Barn at Hope Orchards
Route 105, Hope
(207) 763-4090

JEFFERSON

County Fair Farm
Route 32, Jefferson
(207) 549-3536

SEARSMONT

Bear Wall Orchard
Higgins Road, North Searsmont
(207) 342-5471

WHITEFIELD

Bailey's Orchard
Hunts Meadow Road (off Route 17)
Whitefield
(207) 549-7680

WINTERPORT

Hillcrest Orchards
560 Main Road South (Route 1A)
Winterport
(207) 223-4416

Central Maine

AUBURN

Apple Ridge Farm
Perkins Ridge Road, Auburn
(207) 777-1696

Wallingford's Fruit House
1240 Perkins Ridge Road, Auburn
(207) 784-7958

EAST WINTHROP

Whit's Apples
Case Road (off Route 202)
East Winthrop
(207) 395-4436

KENTS HILL

Kents Hill Orchard
The Apple Shed
1625 Main Street (Route 17)
Kents Hill
(207) 685-3522

MANCHESTER

Lakeside Orchards
Readfield Road (Route 17), Manchester
(207) 344-2479

MONMOUTH

Chick Orchards, Inc.
155 Norris Hill Road (right next to
winery), Monmouth
(207) 993-4452

More High Farm
Off Route 202 (⅛ mile at top of hill)
Monmouth
(207) 933-3778

VASSALBORO

Lemieux's Orchard
Priest Hill Road, North Vassalboro
(207) 923-3519

POLAND

Goss Farm
158 Megquier Hill Road, Poland
(207) 998-2565

Western Maine

SOUTH HIRAM

Apple Acres Farm
Durgintown Road, South Hiram
(207) 647-4725

WATERFORD

Fillebrown Orchards
Plummer Hill Road, Waterford
(207) 583-4779

Northern Maine

BREWER

Harris Orchard
Wiswell Road, Brewer
(207) 989-3435

DIXMONT

Maine-ly Apples
Route 7, Dixmont
(207) 234-2043

chapter 17

Fun Places to Visit

Amusement Parks and Arcades ...158

Aquaboggan Water Park, Saco ...158

Blackbeard's USA, Bangor ...158

Fun-O-Rama, York Beach ...158

Funtown/Splashtown USA, Saco ...158

Odyssey Park, Trenton ...158

Palace Playland, Old Orchard Beach ...158

Village Park Family Entertainment Center, Old Orchard Beach ...159

York's Wild Kingdom Amusement Park, York Beach ...159

The Animal World ...159

Acadia Zoo, Trenton ...159

Kelmscott Farm, Lincolnville ...159

Maine Wildlife Park, Gray ...159

Morris Farm, Wiscasset ...160

Smiling Hill Farm, Westbrook ...160

Telemark Inn and Llama Farm, Bethel ...160

Wolfe's Neck Farm, Freeport ...160

York's Wild Kingdom Zoo, York Beach ...160

Ocean Life ...160

Beals Island Shellfish Hatchery, Beals Island ...160

Craig Brook National Fish Hatchery, East Orland ...161

Marine Resources Aquarium, West Boothbay Harbor ...161

Mt. Desert Oceanarium, Bar Harbor ...161

Mt. Desert Oceanarium, Southwest Harbor ...161

Fun Places to Visit

Amusement Parks and Arcades

Aquaboggan Water Park

U.S. Route 1, Saco
(207) 282-3112
Open late June to Labor Day
For more information, visit
www.mainewaterpark.com

Water slides, water rides, pools, and play areas offer a variety of ways to cool off and have fun. Height restrictions apply for some activities. Arcades, go-carts, a snack bar, and gift shops are also on-site.

Blackbeard's USA

339 Odlin Road, Bangor
(207) 945-0233
Open early May to October
For more information, visit
www.blackbeardusa.com

Play outside all afternoon at the batting cages, with remote-controlled boats on the pond, at the 18- and 36-hole mini-golf courses, up and down the climbing wall, and round and round the go-cart track. (Height/age restrictions apply for riding the go-carts.)

Fun-O-Rama

13 Beach Street, York
(207) 363-4421
Open May to October
For more information, visit
www.fun-o-rama.net

More than 300 games and amusements can be found inside this arcade, located on the sandy ocean beach.

Funtown/Splashtown USA

U.S. Route 1, Saco
(207) 284-5139
Open weekends in May and June, some weekdays in June, every day July to Labor Day
For more information, visit
www.funtownsplashtownusa.com

Take a ride on the banks, twists, and drops of the 100-foot-high wooden roller coaster at Maine's largest water and amusement park. Get wet enjoying the water slides and pools and then dry off on more than 30 rides for small children and families. You can also relax playing 18 holes of mini-golf and enjoying the arcades, batting cages, gift shops, and eateries.

Odyssey Park

Bar Harbor Road (Route 3), Trenton
(207) 667-5841
Open Memorial Day to Labor Day

Fun activities for all ages include a Hole-in-One driving range, bumper boats on a big pond, Laser Tag, go-cart tracks, and an arcade. Height restrictions apply on certain rides.

Palace Playland

1 Old Orchard Street, Old Orchard Beach
(207) 934-2001
Open weekends late May to mid-June, every day from mid-June to early September
For more information, visit
www.palaceplayland.com

Soar into the air on New England's largest gondola, the Sun Wheel, to view the seven miles of ocean beach surrounding this amusement park. Enjoy free admission into this park, which offers plenty of rides and games for adults and children, history buffs, and thrill seekers. There are also weekly fireworks displays.

Village Park Family Entertainment Center

4 Old Orchard Street, Old Orchard Beach
(207) 934-7666
Open Memorial Day to Labor Day

Carnival fun is featured here along with food stands and gift shops. Enjoy the batting cages, arcade, kiddie bounce, and skill games. This park is situated across from a seven-mile sandy ocean beach.

York's Wild Kingdom Amusement Park

23 Railroad Avenue, York Beach
(800) 456-4911
Open Memorial Day to Labor Day
For more information, visit
www.yorkzoo.com

Located on York's scenic sandy beach, this park offers all kinds of old-fashioned fun. Enjoy the family rides, midway games, funhouses, arcade, batting cages, paddle boats, haunted house, gift shops, and concession stands.

The Animal World

Acadia Zoo

Bar Harbor Road (Route 3), Trenton
(207) 667-3244
Open May to November

Wildlife of the world (including Maine) are on display here, along with the state's only indoor rain forest exhibit and a special petting area for domestic animals. You'll also find a

gift shop and concession stand. Camels and moose, porcupines and gibbons, foxes and leopards are among the 45 species exhibited at this 15-acre site.

Kelmscott Farm

Van Cycle Road, off Route 52, Lincolnville
(207) 763-4088
Open year-round
For more information, visit
www.kelmscott.org

Peer over the fences and into the stalls to view more than 150 animals representing 20 rare breeds of livestock, including sheep, ponies, horses, pigs, cattle, goats, and poultry. Kelmscott Farm is a nonprofit organization dedicated to their conservation. Enjoy the educational tours, materials, frequent demonstrations, and special events as you learn all about these historic—and increasingly rare—breeds. You'll also find a gift shop and traditional herb garden at this scenic hillside farm.

Maine Wildlife Park

Route 26, Gray
(207) 657-4977 or (207) 287-4471 (for hearing impaired)
Open mid-April to Veterans Day
For more information, visit
www.state.me.us/ifw/wildlifepark.htm

See and learn about Maine's native wildlife at this state facility designed to offer refuge and veterinary care to orphaned and injured animals. Learn how you can help protect the moose, lynx, black bears, mountain lions, bobcats, great horned owls, otters, kestrels, and wood turtles that share our great outdoors. Nature trails, picnic spots, educational exhibits, shops, and group tours offer something for everyone.

Morris Farm

156 Gardiner Road (Route 27), Wiscasset
(207) 882-4080
Open year-round
For more information, visit
www.morrisfarm.org

This 50-acre organic farm of cow pastures and hay fields includes a pond, waterfall, streams, a vegetable garden, poultry, American Guinea Hogs, and a small woodlot. Come explore its rolling, open fields. Bring a picnic and take off on a self-guided farm tour. Special hands-on events include school programs, summer programs, and adult workshops.

Smiling Hill Farm

Route 22, on the Westbrook/Scarborough Town Line
(800) 743-7463 or (207) 775-4818
Open year-round
For more information, visit
www.smilinghill.com

Visit more than 200 traditional and rare farm animals at the Barnyard Petting Farm, including many new arrivals at the Maternity Barn. Look for chicks at the Hatching House. Pick a pumpkin in the fall, enjoy cross-country ski trails and sleigh rides in the winter, learn how maple syrup is made in the spring, and visit the Dairy and Farm Market year-round.

Telemark Inn and Llama Farm

591 Kings Highway, Bethel
(207) 836-2703
Open year-round
For more information, visit
www.telemarkinn.com

School and camp groups and families will begin to see the world through the eyes of animals as they go llama trekking through the woods, ride an ox cart, watch sled and ski dogs, learn to horseback ride, and meet Nandi, the pet cow. Day activities are available for school groups, camps, and others by reservation only.

Wolfe's Neck Farm

Wolfe's Neck Road, Freeport
(207) 865-4469
Open year-round
For more information, visit
www.wolfesneckfarm.org

Come any time of year to this working farm to visit the cows, pigs, and sheep in their barns, pastures, and pens. Special seasonal programs include a spring calf watch, when visitors can actually see cows give birth. In the fall, enjoy pumpkin hayrides. Picnic tables and hiking trails also on-site.

York's Wild Kingdom Zoo

23 Railroad Avenue, York Beach
(800) 456-4911
Open Memorial Day to Labor Day
For more information, visit
www.yorkzoo.com

See hundreds of exotic animals from around the world. Enjoy demonstrations, animal rides, wildlife theater, and educational talks. Take the "Wings over Maine" walk through the aviary, and visit the bear and monkey exhibits and the Australia collection. There is also a petting zoo for all ages.

Ocean Life

Beals Island Shellfish Hatchery

25 Perio Point, Beals Island,
off Jonesport
(207) 497-5769
The season runs from May to September

Learn about aquaculture in Maine at this site where working clams and algae tanks are on view. Discover even more about the Gulf of Maine at the Education Center, which houses a touch tank and visual displays.

Craig Brook
National Fish Hatchery

Hatchery Road, East Orland
(207) 469-2803
Open year-round
For more information, visit
   www.hollyeats.com/BealsHatchery.htm

Established in 1871, this 135-acre hatchery site is run by the U.S. Fish & Wildlife Service. In addition to an Atlantic salmon display pool, the hatchery grounds include swimming areas, picnic tables and grills, a boat ramp, and hiking trails.

Marine Resources Aquarium

At the end of McKown Point Road,
   West Boothbay Harbor
(207) 633-9559
Open from Memorial Day to
   Columbus Day
For more information, visit
   www.maine.gov/dmr/rm/aquarium/
   index.html

Maine's marine life is on display at this state-owned facility located on the rocky shore. Encounter all sorts of interesting creatures in the Touch Tank or peer down through the water to get a close-up look and pet the sharks and skates. Enjoy daily educational presentations and informative exhibits. Bring along a picnic and have lunch at the picnic tables overlooking the outer harbor.

Mt. Desert Oceanarium—
Bar Harbor

Route 3, Thomas Bay, Bar Harbor
(207) 288-5005
Open from mid-May to mid-October

Lobsters, seals, and a seaside marsh are the focus of the hands-on displays, tours, and demonstrations here. See live seals at the seal pavilion. Board the lobster boat display at the Lobster Museum. Take a marsh tour or step

inside a real lobster hatchery. Picnic by the gazebo or visit the gift shop.

Mt. Desert Oceanarium—
Southwest Harbor

Clark Point Road, Southwest Harbor
(207) 244-7330
Open from mid-May to late October

Here you can listen to whale sounds in the whale exhibit and hold live sea animals at the Touch Tank. Watch native sea life in the Living Room's 20 tanks. If you're interested in natural history, boatbuilding, or fishing, you can learn all about Maine's ocean heritage from the many interactive and informational exhibits at the Marine Aquarium and Fishing Museum. When you are done, visit the book and gift shop.

chapter 18

Skiing and Snowboarding

Alpine Skiing and Snowboarding ... 164

Bigrock, Mars Hill ... 164
Big Squaw Mountain Resort, Greenville ... 164
Black Mountain, Rumford ... 164
Camden Snow Bowl, Camden ... 164
Eaton Mountain, Skowhegan ... 164
Lonesome Pine Trails, Fort Kent ... 165
Lost Valley, Auburn ... 165
Mt. Abram Ski Resort, Locke Mills ... 165
Mt. Jefferson Ski Area, Lee ... 165
New Hermon Mountain, Prospect ... 165
Saddleback, Rangeley ... 165
Shawnee Peak, Bridgton ... 165
Sugarloaf/USA, Carrabassett Valley ... 166
Sunday River, Bethel ... 166
Titcomb Mountain Ski Area, West Farmington ... 166

Nordic Ski Centers ... 166

Acadia Winter Trails Association/ Friends of Acadia, Bar Harbor ... 166
Beech Ridge Farm XC Ski Center, Scarborough ... 166
The Bethel Inn Touring Center, Bethel ... 167
Bill Koch Youth Ski League, Auburn ... 167
Black Mountain, Rumford ... 167
The Birches Ski Touring Center, Rockwood ... 167
Carter's XC Ski Centers, Oxford ... 167
Harris Farm XC Ski Center, Dayton ... 167
L.L. Bean Outdoor Discovery Program, Freeport ... 167
Lost Valley Touring Center, Auburn ... 167
Rangeley Lakes Cross-Country Ski Trails, Rangeley ... 168
Ski-A-Bit, West Buxton ... 168
Smiling Hill Farm, Westbrook ... 168
Sugarloaf/USA Outdoor Center, Carrabassett Valley ... 168
Sunday River Cross-Country Ski Center, Bethel ... 168
Titcomb Mountain Cross-Country Trails, West Farmington ... 168

Skiing and Snowboarding

Alpine Skiing and Snowboarding

There are a lot of skiing and snowboarding opportunities in Maine. For the latest conditions, call Ski Maine Ski Conditions at (207) 773-SNOW, and check out the Ski Maine Association Web site at www.skimaine.com.

Bigrock

37 Graves Road, Mars Hill
(207) 425-6711
For more information, visit www.bigrockmaine.com

Bigrock has 980 feet of vertical drop, 14 trails, 4 lifts (one double chair, three poma lifts, and one handle tow), as well as snowmaking for a third of the mountain. Rentals are available, and there is a ski school on the premises.

Big Squaw Mountain Resort

Route 15/Rockwood Road, Greenville
(207) 695-1000
For more information, visit www.bigsquawmountain.com

With a vertical drop of 1,750 feet and 18 trails, Big Squaw offers four lifts (one triple chair, one double chair, one T-bar, and one pony lift), snowmaking, a ski school, rentals, and terrain for all abilities.

Black Mountain

Glover Road, Rumford
(207) 364-8977

Black Mountain is a full-service mountain with 12 trails and two T-bar lifts, well suited for families with young children. It offers alpine, cross-country skiing, and snowboarding lesson programs for children during the week. The snow tubing park, one of the biggest in Maine, is lit for evening use, as are six of the alpine trails. Black Mountain is equipped for snowmaking.

Camden Snow Bowl

Hosmer Pond Road, Camden
(207) 236-3438
For more information, visit www.camdensnowbowl.com

Beautiful ocean vistas await those who ski here at 1,300-foot Ragged Mountain. Ten trails are served by a double chair lift and two T-bars and supported with snowmaking and lights. Also on the premises is Maine's only public toboggan chute, site of the annual National Toboggan Championships.

Eaton Mountain

86 Lambert Road, Skowhegan
(207) 474-2666
For more information, visit www.eatonmountain.com

Eaton Mountain is a family-run mountain with one chair lift and 18 trails for skiers of all abilities. They also offer a snow tubing park with rope-tow lift, night skiing, ski instruction for all levels, rentals, and excellent snowmaking.

Lonesome Pine Trails

2 Forest Avenue, Fort Kent
(207) 834-5202

Lonesome Pine Trails offers 13 trails and two lifts (one T-bar and one J-bar) plus a half-pipe and glade skiing. Rentals and lessons are available.

Lost Valley

Lost Valley Road, Auburn
(207) 784-1561
For more information, visit
www.lostvalleyski.com

Lost Valley offers two chair lifts and a T-bar service, on 15 well-groomed trails of various degrees of difficulty. The children's ski school starts the first full week in January and lasts six weeks. The Mighty Mike program is offered to children ages 4 to 6, and the junior Ski/Ride instruction program is offered at all levels, for ages 7 and up.

Mt. Abram Ski Resort

Howe Hill Road, Locke Mills
(207) 875-5002
For more information, visit
www.skimtabram.com

Mt. Abram is a family-oriented mountain offering 1,030 vertical feet, five lifts, and 35 trails, with separate areas and lifts for novices. They also offer high-capacity snowmaking, night skiing, and expert ski schools. A wide variety of skiing and snowboarding instruction programs begin at age 4 for skiing and age 7 for snowboarding.

Mt. Jefferson Ski Area

Route 6, Lee
(207) 738-2377

Mt. Jefferson Ski Area offers 12 trails and three lifts (two T-bars and a rope tow), plus rentals, lessons, a half-pipe, and a snowboard terrain park.

New Hermon Mountain

126 George Road, Prospect
(207) 848-5192

New Herman Mountain is a family-run mountain with 18 trails and two lifts (one double chair and one T-bar) for all abilities. Also offered are a ski school, snack bar, equipment rentals, night skiing, and snowboarding instruction.

Saddleback

Saddleback Road, Rangeley
(207) 864-5671
(207) 864-3380 (snow report)
For more information, visit
www.saddlebackskiarea.com

Saddleback has five lifts, two double chair lifts, and three T-bars, along with 40 alpine ski trails—almost equally distributed among beginner, intermediate, and expert terrain—on 1,830 vertical feet of mountain. An excellent ski school is offered for all ages and abilities.

Shawnee Peak

Route 302, Bridgton
(207) 647-8444
For more information, visit
www.shawneepeak.com

Shawnee Peak's diverse terrain, on 1,300 vertical feet, offers a variety of challenges for all abilities. There are beautiful learning trails, glades, and professionally designed snowboard features and terrain parks. In all, 38 trails are serviced by five lifts (double, triple, and quad chairs, plus a rope tow). Night skiing is available every night but Sunday. Excellent children's programs are offered, starting at age four.

Sugarloaf/USA

Route 27, 5092 Sugarloaf Access Road, Carrabassett Valley
(800) THE-LOAF
For more information, visit
www.sugarloaf.com

Sugarloaf, with 2,820 vertical feet, is ranked number-one overall best mountain in the East. It offers the only lift-serviced above-tree skiing in the East, and boasts a total of 15 lifts, including two high-speed super quads, and 126 trails with 92-percent snowmaking coverage. Excellent children's instruction programs start at age three. Sugarloaf is also one of America's top snowboarding resorts, ranking number one in North America terrain parks, with the biggest half-pipe in the USA.

Sunday River

Sunday River Road, Bethel
(800) 543-2SKI
For more information, visit
www.sundayriver.com

Sunday River offers 126 trails and glades, and the most open terrain in Maine, descending from eight interconnected mountains. The 2,340 vertical feet are serviced by 18 lifts, including four high-speed quads. The half-pipe is considered one of the best in New England. Excellent programs in skiing and snowboarding are available, starting at age three.

Titcomb Mountain Ski Area

**180 Ski Slope Road,
West Farmington**
(207) 778-9031
For more information, visit
www.titcombmountain.com

While Titcomb is a small mountain, with 10 trails and two T-bars, many believe it provides more skiing in a day than bigger, more crowded ski areas. Titcomb Mountain is an ideal training facility for high school or college teams, offering both cross-country and alpine trails in combination with state-of-the-art timing equipment.

Nordic Ski Centers

The Maine Nordic Ski Council offers a very detailed and useful Web site, including the ski centers, conditions, ski shops, and upcoming events relating to cross-country skiing in Maine. Visit www.mnsc.com.

Acadia Winter Trails Association/Friends of Acadia

43 Cottage Street, Bar Harbor
(207) 288-3340
For more information, visit
www.foacadia.org/

Acadia Winter Trails Association is a dedicated corps of local volunteers who groom 33 miles of the park's carriage roads for skiing and snowboarding.

Beech Ridge Farm XC Ski Center

193 Beech Ridge Road, Scarborough
(207) 839-4098

Beech Ridge Farm offers 21 kilometers of trails, skate lanes, novice and intermediate trails, open fields, lessons, snowshoe and pulk sled rentals, as well as a warming lodge, snack bar, and Friday night skiing on 5 kilometers of lantern-lit trails.

The Bethel Inn Touring Center

Broad Street, Bethel
(207) 824-6276
For more information, visit
www.bethelinn.com

The Bethel Inn offers 40 kilometers of trails for novice through advanced skiers, a warming hut on the trail, ski rentals, lessons, snowshoe rentals, a recreation center with a sauna, fitness machines, swimming pool, ice skating, sleigh rides, kick sleds, and pulk sleds.

Bill Koch Youth Ski League

15 Holly Street, Auburn
(207) 786-2297

The Bill Koch Youth Ski League is a family-oriented junior ski program for boys and girls ages 5 to 13. Races and events are held every Saturday during January and February.

Black Mountain

Glover Road, Rumford
(207) 364-8977

Black Mountain offers 35 kilometers of wide-tracked trails for all abilities, many of them hilly and challenging. You will also find ski rentals, lessons, a snack bar, alpine skiing, tubing, and ice skating.

The Birches Ski Touring Center

Off Route 6/15, Moosehead Lake,
Rockwood
(800) 825-WILD
For more information, visit www.birches.com

The Birches Ski Touring Center is an 11,000-acre private reserve with a lake trail to Mt. Kineo, Brassua Lake, and Baker Pond. There are 40 kilometers of groomed trails and unlimited backcountry. Also offered are cabins, a lodge, a restaurant, a sauna and hot tub, snowshoe rentals, and lessons.

Carter's XC Ski Centers

420 Main Street, Oxford
(207) 539-4848
For more information, visit
www.cartersxcski.com

Carter's offers 35 kilometers of trails for novice and intermediate, lessons, a full-service ski shop, a snack bar and lounge, as well as rentals for skis, snowshoes, kick sleds, and pulk sleds.

Harris Farm XC Ski Center

252 Buzzell Road, Dayton
(207) 499-2678

Operated by a second- and third-generation farming family, this 1,000 acres of open meadows and sheltered forest offers 40 kilometers of trails for novice, intermediate, and advanced, as well as skating lanes, rentals, lessons, snowshoes, pulk and kick sleds, and ice skating.

L.L. Bean Outdoor Discovery Program

Casco Street, Freeport
(888) 552-3261
For more information, visit www.llbean
.com/outdoorsOnline/odp/index.html

The L.L. Bean Outdoor Discovery Program offers ski instruction for all levels of cross-country skiers. It is held weekly in January and February in Freeport.

Lost Valley Touring Center

Young's Corner Road, Auburn
(207) 784-1561

Lost Valley Touring Center offers 10 kilometers of trails—2 kilometers novice, 7 kilometers intermediate, and 1 kilometer advanced. Ski rentals and lessons are available. There is also a lodge serving Alpine and Nordic skiers with a restaurant and snack bar.

Rangeley Lakes Cross-Country Ski Trails

Rangeley
Rangeley Cross-Country Ski Club
(207) 864-4309
For more information, visit
www.rangeleymaine.com

This nordic trail system totals 65 kilometers made up of several interconnecting loops. These loops wind through pristine forests, with intermittent fields and broad panoramic vistas. The result is a beautiful system of trails with terrain to accommodate skiers of all skill levels. Panoramic views can be seen from atop Burnham Hill, which boasts a warming hut. Season and day passes can be purchased at the lodge on Taylor Road or the Alpine Shop on Main Street.

Ski-A-Bit

Route 112, West Buxton
(207) 929-4824

Ski-A-Bit offers 40 kilometers of novice and intermediate trails with a few steep hills. Pulk sleds and skis can be rented, and there is a lodge with a snack bar. Free "mini" lessons are available for all first-time skiers.

Smiling Hill Farm

781 Country Road, Route 22, Westbrook
(207) 775-4818

Smiling Hill is a 300-year-old, 500-acre working dairy farm offering 35 kilometers of trails for novice, intermediate, and advanced skiers. There are also marked nature trails. Skis, snowshoes, ice skates, and pulk sleds can all be rented here. A full-service restaurant is available, and you'll find a gift shop and dairy store, too. Sleigh rides and animal exhibits are also offered.

Sugarloaf/USA Outdoor Center

5092 Sugarloaf Access Road,
Carrabassett Valley
(207) 237-6830
For more information, visit
www.sugarloaf.com

Sugarloaf offers 95 kilometers of groomed trails: 40 kilometers novice, 40 kilometers intermediate, and 15 kilometers advanced; plus 11 kilometers of snowshoe trails. There is a full-service café. Snowshoes, pulk sleds, and ice skates can all be rented here. You'll also find an Olympic-sized outdoor ice skating rink, state-of-the-art grooming machines, a chairlift on the trail system to Sugarloaf/USA Alpine Area base facilities, a PSIA-certified ski school, a ski shop, and repair services on the premises.

Sunday River Cross-Country Ski Center

Skiway Access Road, Bethel
(207) 824-2410

Sunday River offers 40 kilometers of trails for novice, intermediate, and advanced skiers. Skating lanes and lessons are also available, as are rentals for skis, pulk and kick sleds, and snowshoes. You may also enjoy sleigh rides and a lodge with a snack bar. An ice skating rink, ski shop, and repair services are all on the premises.

Titcomb Mountain Cross-Country Trails

Morrison Hill Road, West Farmington
(207) 778-9031

Titcomb Mountain offers 19 kilometers of trails for novice, intermediate, and advanced skiers. Upper-intermediate terrain is serviced by an alpine lift. A lodge with a snack bar and fireplace is on premises. Rentals are available.

Trains, Planes, and Things That GO!

Southern Maine ... 170

Balloon Rides, Portland ... 170

Beech Ridge Motor Speedway, Scarborough ... 170

The Maine Narrow-Gauge Railroad Company and Museum, Portland ... 170

Seashore Trolley Museum, Kennebunkport ... 170

Mid-Coast Maine ... 170

Belfast & Moosehead Lake Railroad Company, Unity and Belfast ... 170

Boothbay Railway Village, Boothbay ... 171

Brunswick Naval Air Station, Brunswick ... 171

Owls Head Transportation Museum, Owls Head ... 171

Down East Maine ... 171

Acadia Air, Trenton ... 171

Island Soaring Glider Rides, Trenton ... 171

Central Maine ... 171

Twin Cities Air Service, Inc., Auburn ... 171

Western Maine ... 172

Hi-Fly Parasailing, Naples ... 172

Sandy River Railroad Park, Phillips ... 172

T.A.D. Dog Sled Services, Sugarloaf/USA, Carrabassett Valley ... 172

Northern Maine ... 172

Crystal Snowmobile Tours, Caribou ... 172

Currier's Flying Service, Moosehead Lake, Greenville ... 172

The Cutting Edge Go-Cart Track at Blackbeard's USA, Bangor ... 172

Jack's Air Service, Moosehead Lake, Greenville ... 172

Red's Recreational Snowmobile Rentals and Service, Caribou ... 172

Trains, Planes, and Things That GO!

Southern Maine

Balloon Rides

293 State Street, Portland
(207) 761-8373 or (800) 952-2076
For more information, visit
www.hotairballoon.com

Take in the beauty of southern Maine, including Casco Bay and the White Mountains, as you float gently along in a hot-air balloon. Flights begin near sunrise or just before sunset, when the wind is lightest. Reservations and a deposit are required.

Beech Ridge Motor Speedway

70 Holmes Road, Scarborough
(207) 885-0111
Open seasonally April to September
For more information, visit
www.beechridge.com

Short-track car racing action is available to watch here, including the NASCAR Bush North Series, Go-Kart Racing, and many other special activities. Call for schedule of events.

The Maine Narrow-Gauge Railroad Company and Museum

58 Fore Street, Portland
(207) 828-0814
Open weekends year-round; daily in season; closed in January
For more information, visit www.mngrr.org

All aboard for a 3-mile train ride to see views of nineteenth-century forts, lighthouses, and the islands of Casco Bay. This collection of narrow-gauge train cars, which had been at the Edaville Railroad in Massachusetts, was moved back to Maine in 1993. The museum houses a 1901 parlor car, coaches, and many more exhibits. A special Christmas Lights Train is often featured during the holidays.

Seashore Trolley Museum

195 Log Cabin Road, Kennebunkport
(207) 967-2800
Open seasonally from May to October
For more information, visit
www.trolleymuseum.com

Take a trip on the old Atlantic Shore Line Railway and see how your ancestors traveled before the days of the automobile. Visit the restoration house and exhibit barns to see more than 250 restored trolleys. A snack bar and gift shop/bookstore are also on the premises.

Mid-Coast Maine

Belfast & Moosehead Lake Railroad Company

One Depot Square, Unity and Belfast
(800) 392-5500
Open seasonally from May to October
For more information, visit
www.belfastrailroad.com

Enjoy a narrated 90-minute scenic ride aboard a steam train from Unity or a diesel train from Belfast. Children of all ages will enjoy the "train robbery" staged by the notorious Waldo Station Gang! Then board the *Voyageur*, a former Mississippi riverboat, and cruise the waters of Maine's coast.

Boothbay Railway Village

Route 27, Boothbay
(207) 633-4727
Open seasonally from May to October
For more information, visit
www.railwayvillage.org

Here you can experience a 1.5-mile steam train ride, the ambience of a rural village with more than 28 exhibit buildings, and a collection of over 60 antique vehicles. Special events include the Annual Antique Auto Days during the third weekend in July, where you can enjoy a parade of more than 250 antique vehicles.

Brunswick Naval Air Station

Near Cooks Corner, Brunswick
(207) 921-2000
For more information, visit
www.nasb.navy.mil

While the air station is not regularly open to the public, it does host the famous Blue Angels precision flying team every other year, usually in July. The station opens its gates to the public for this event, often attracting upwards of 200,000 people.

Owls Head Transportation Museum

Route 73, Owls Head
(207) 594-4418
Open year-round
For more information, visit www.ohtm.org

Known for its landmark collection of pre-1930 aircraft, including the world's only operating Fokker C.IV, this museum also offers an excellent display of historic automobiles, carriages, bicycles, motorcycles, engines, and steam-powered vehicles. Most are maintained in operating condition and dem-onstrated at special events. Situated adjacent to the Knox County Airport, the museum offers a gallery and store, plus a 60-acre nature park with a children's area and picnic grounds and cross-country ski trails. From May to September, special weekend events are held twice monthly.

Down East Maine

Acadia Air

Hancock County–Bar Harbor Airport, Trenton
(207) 667-5534
For more information, visit
www.acadiaair.com

Scenic flights over Acadia National Park, Mount Desert Island, area lighthouses, and Baxter State Park are available for a modest cost. Offered on a first-come, first-served basis, except during the winter, when reservations are accepted.

Island Soaring Glider Rides

Hancock County–Bar Harbor Airport, Trenton
(207) 667-SOAR

Enjoy an adventure for two soaring over Acadia National Park on an exhilarating, motorless ride you'll never forget. Call for reservations.

Central Maine

Twin Cities Air Service, Inc.

81 Airport Drive, Auburn
(207) 782-3882 or (800) 564-3882
For more information, visit
www.flycharter.com

Enjoy a scenic air tour of the places you've wanted to see in Maine. Also available is the Introductory Flight, where they will show you how they take off, fly, and land the plane.

Western Maine

Hi-Fly Parasailing

Route 302, Naples
(207) 693-3888

Go for an exhilarating parasail ride over the Naples Causeway.

Sandy River Railroad Park

Mill Hill Road, off Route 4, Phillips
(207) 778-3621
Open seasonally June through October

Ride the original route of the Sandy River and Rangeley Lakes Railroad, which served the busy lumber and tourist businesses from 1879 to 1936. The train runs the first and third Sundays of each month. Railroad memorabilia are on display in the Phillips Historical Society Museum nearby.

T.A.D. Dog Sled Services

The Inn on Winter's Hill at
    Sugarloaf/USA, Carrabassett Valley
(207) 237-2514
For pictures, see www.samoyed.org/tad.html

Experience the thrill of racing over the snow pulled by a team of sled dogs. Tim Diehl is the owner and musher of this team of Samoyeds and has been racing sled dogs for 15 years. All of the sled dogs come from unwanted homes.

Northern Maine

Crystal Snowmobile Tours

P.O. Box 1448, Caribou
(207) 498-3220 or (207) 492-7471

Enjoy the North Maine Woods and easy access to Canada on the Interconnecting Trail System, which consists of more than 1,200 miles of groomed snowmobile trails.

Currier's Flying Service

Moosehead Lake, Route 15, Greenville
    Junction
(207) 695-2778
*For more information, visit
www.curriersflyingservice.com*

Scenic tours are available, as well as year-round wilderness charter services for camping and fishing trips.

The Cutting Edge Go-Cart Track at Blackbeard's USA

339 Odlin Road, Bangor
(207) 945-0233
*For more information, visit
www.blackbeardsusa.com*

Ride in an Indy-style two-seater go-cart over a high-banked, quarter-mile track with 3 major S-turns.

Jack's Air Service

Moosehead Lake, Greenville
(207) 695-3020

This seaplane operation on Moosehead Lake offers a unique experience for those interested in wilderness camping, hunting, or fishing. Local sightseeing tours are also available in their Cessna aircraft.

Red's Recreational Snowmobile Rentals and Service

559 Sweden Street, Caribou
(207) 492-5281 or (800) 451-5281

Located in the center of the Interconnecting Trail System, Red's offers snowmobile rentals and service.

chapter 20

Web Sites

Geography...174

History and Government...174

Organizations and Sports...175

Science and Nature...176

Summer Outdoor Activities...176

Winter Outdoor Activities...177

Web Sites

Geography

Cybermaps

http://maps.yahoo.com/py/ddResult.py

How long will it take to drive to Grandma's on Cape Elizabeth? Is there a quicker route than the one Dad has been taking for the past 10 years? Find directions to go almost anywhere in Maine on this site.

Gulf of Maine Weather Conditions

www.noaa.com/wx.html

How big are the waves 10 miles off the coast? What will the weather be like tomorrow? Here you will find detailed weather information from several sources, including data collected from buoys scattered around the Gulf of Maine.

Maine Lighthouses

www.cr.nps.gov/maritime/light/me.htm

Facts and figures, photos, and stories about almost all the lighthouses on the Maine coast are found at this site.

Maine Skycam

www.wgme.com/skycam.html

Views of Portland, Raymond, Augusta, Old Orchard Beach, and Sanford—updated every three minutes.

Mount Washington Observatory

www.mountwashington.org/

It is not in Maine, but you can see it from Maine! Check out the live view from the summit of New England's highest peak.

The Weather Channel

www.weather.com

www.accuweather.com

Enter your zip code and click "go" to check out the satellite photos, radar, and today's forecast.

History and Government

Center for Maine History

www.mainehistory.org

What is three stories high, made of brick, and has a fireplace in just about every room? It is the Wadsworth-Longfellow house in Portland, right next to the Maine Historical Society's Maine History Gallery.

Covered Bridges

www.state.me.us/mdot/maint_op/covered/coverbrg.htm

There used to be 120, but now only 9 wooden covered bridges are left in Maine. Each one has its own story.

Maine Databases

http://libraries.maine.edu/mainedatabases/

Periodicals, journals, encyclopedias—search sixteen databases for the facts you need. This site is for advanced users.

Maine History

www.waterboro.lib.me.us/mainehis.htm

This quality site by the Waterboro Public Library has lots of good links to Maine history sites. Check out their home page for other interesting links.

Maine History Internet Resources

www.state.me.us/sos/arc/historyday/mhd01.htm

Need to do research for a school paper on Maine history? This page has all of the links you'll need.

Maine Studies Sites

www.ockett-ms.sad72.k12.me.us/mesites.html

This site has great links to Maine history, Maine products, Maine science, and famous Mainers.

Maine Writers Index

www.waterboro.lib.me.us/maineaut/index.htm

This site contains information on many Maine authors, their lives, and their works, including Stephen King, Henry Wadsworth Longfellow, and Edna St. Vincent Millay.

State of Maine Kid's Page

www.state.me.us/sos/kids

Although the Maine Secretary of State does not get to negotiate treaties with other countries, his office does have a neat Web site. Learn about the branches of the state government, the state constitution, and interesting Maine facts and figures.

Organizations and Sports

Boy Scouts of America

www.scouting.org

www.boyscouts.com/

If you want information about the Boy Scouts, here are two sites to help you find out what it is all about.

Girl Scouts of the USA

www.girlscouts.org

This is the official site of the Girl Scouts. Check out the "Just for Girls" section.

Kids Radio

www.wmdr.org

Maine's only 24-hour radio station just for kids—check out the schedule.

Portland Pirates Hockey Team

www.portlandpirates.com

This site contains player profiles, schedule, and ticket information.

Portland Sea Dogs Baseball Team

www.portlandseadogs.com

The official site of the Sea Dogs Nation! Find schedule and ticket information. Check out the "Dog Bytes" section.

United Soccer Federation of Maine

www.soccermaine.com

Find out all about soccer in Maine, from tournaments and handbooks to soccer camps and clubs on-line.

Science and Nature

Gulf of Maine Aquarium

http://octopus.gma.org

More than just fish! This site has marine mammal, turtle, and lobster links.

The Lobster Institute

www.lobster.um.maine.edu/lobster

This site has lots of interesting lobster tidbits. Sign in to the Lobster Chat Room. Check out the live "Lobstah Cam."

The Lobsterman's Page

www.crewdog.net/lobsterpage/

Spend a day on the water with a lobsterman (complete with lots of photos). Check out the Lobster Links.

Maine Audubon Society

www.maineaudubon.org

What was that wacky-looking bird you saw? Check out the Weekly Bird Alert as well as information on conservation, field trips, and environmental centers.

Maine Maple Syrup

www.mainemapleproducers.com

What is a "Sap Cow"? It is a sugar maple with higher-than-average sugar content. Find out all you will ever want to know about maple syrup—and more—at this site.

Nature Watching

www.state.me.us/ifw/wildlife/ watchablewildlife.htm

It is not the flashiest site on the Web, but it is chock-full of information on Maine wildlife—where and when to look, and what you might see.

The Northern Lights

www.spacew.com/www/aurora.html

This site is a little technical (unless you're working on your Ph.D. in Astrophysics), but about halfway down the page is a graphic that estimates how visible "the lights" are going to be. If it is red over Maine, run outside—you are missing the show!

Satellite Viewing

http://liftoff.msfc.nasa.gov/ RealTime/Jpass/20/

Type in your zip code and see when the International Space Station, the Space Shuttle, and other satellites can be seen from your back yard. (If you get a message asking whether you want to install "J-Pass," click "Yes." It is a NASA program that will install in your "Temp" folder.)

Summer Outdoor Activities

Acadia National Park

www.nps.gov/acad/home.htm

Check out 120 miles of hiking trails and 57 miles of carriage roads great for biking and cross-country skiing at Maine's number-one attraction.

The Appalachian Trail

www.nps.gov/appa

Bored? Nothing to do? How about a 2,158-mile walk from Mt. Katahdin to northern Georgia? Find hiking information and links to other National Park sites.

Bicycle Trails

http://members.tripod.com/
~Kenyon_Karl/ME-home.htm

Some of the best bicycle trails in Maine are on old railroad beds. Many of the links include trail descriptions and maps.

Canoeing and Kayaking

www.maineoutdoors.com/canoeing/

Here are all of the links you'll need to plan your water adventure.

Children's Summer Camps

http://maine.maine.edu/~myca

This site has stuff for parents to help them pick the right camp, and stuff for kids so that they can make sure their parents pick the right camp! There is also an on-line directory of camps.

Maine Event Scheduler

http://maineevents.com

There is always something going on in Maine. Here it is broken down month by month.

Northern Maine Guide

www.mainerec.com

There is more to see in Maine than just the coast! Check out the section on the Allagash Wilderness Waterway.

Old Orchard Beach

www.oldorchardbeachmaine.com/
Famlyfun.htm

Here is a big directory of what to do at the beach with all the action!

Outdoor Stuff

www.maineoutdoors.com

From camping and canoeing to kayaking and hiking; at this site, you will find lots of information and some wonderful links.

Whitewater Rafting

http://maineoutdoors.com/
whitewater/rafting_sites.shtml

Here you will find links to all of the major rafting companies in Maine.

Winter Outdoor Activities

Ski Maine

www.skimaine.com

This is a well-designed site with maps, snow conditions, and race results. Check out the chat room and information about the Ski Maine Fifth Grade Passport program.

Snowmobiling

www.sledmaine.com

This site includes trail maps, snow conditions, and other snowmobiling information.

Winter Hiking and Backpacking

www.backpacking.net/winter.html

Find tips and techniques for winter hiking and snowshoeing.